Uncommon Uses for Common Household Products

By the Editors of FC&A

Publisher's Note

The editors of FC&A have taken careful measures to ensure the accuracy and usefulness of the information in this book. While every attempt has been made to assure accuracy, errors may occur. We advise readers to carefully review and understand the ideas and tips presented and to seek the advice of a qualified professional before attempting to use them. The publisher and editors disclaim all liability (including any injuries, damages or losses) resulting from the use of the information in this book.

The health information in this book is for information only and is not intended to be a medical guide for self-treatment. It does not constitute medical advice and should not be construed as such or used in place of your doctor's medical advice.

By love serve one another: For all the law is fulfilled in one word, even in this: Thou shalt love thy neighbor as thyself.

Galatians 5:13,14

FC&A
103 Clover Green
Peachtree City, GA 30269

Produced by the staff of FC&A
Cover Images: ©1997 PhotoDisc, Inc.

Fourth printing January 2001

ISBN 1-890957-39-9

Table of Contents

Uncommonly good uses for common household products

Table of Contents

Table of Contents

Uncommonly good ideas to make your life easier

Introduction

You don't have to look hard to find a ready-made product for any household need or chore. Anything you could possibly want is there for the asking across town at the superstore — garden gadgets, kitchen time-savers, and lotions and potions for you and your pet. And while many of the products on the market today are very effective and convenient, they all share one thing in common. They cost money.

But as of today, there's no need for you to waste your money on many of those expensive products. Unbeknownst to you, the right item for any job could very well be hiding in your cupboard. With *Uncommon Uses for Common Household Products*, you'll know just where to find these versatile helpers, how to use them, and how to re-use many of them again and again.

Native Americans of the Great Plains are often credited for having made use of every part of the buffalo they hunted — meat was eaten, bones used for tools, and hides made into shelter and clothing. This book will help you practice the same sort of resourcefulness that kept Native Americans fed and sheltered for thousands of years.

Maybe you brought home a new bottle of vinegar, only to find two you'd forgotten in your kitchen cupboard. Maybe the two-for-one bleach deal at the mega shopping club was just too good to resist. Or maybe that box of baking soda in your pantry is older than your youngest child. If situations like these were a problem in the past, they're not anymore.

Use a little of that extra vinegar to make your coffee taste better. A few sprinklings of bleach will keep curious critters from trashing your trash cans at night. And don't even think of ditching that old baking soda — it'll put a new shine on everything from your toilet to your windshield to your fine silver.

Uncommon Uses for Common Household Products shows you hundreds of new ways to put everyday items to work in the garden, the kitchen, the garage, and even in taking care of your kids or grandkids. In many cases, a common household item works better at an uncommon task than the commercial product designed to do the job.

To find an uncommon use for a particular item, simply turn to that chapter of the book. Or just browse through the expanded category section in the back. This helpful section has hundreds of tips uncovered by our experts, organized by use instead of by item. If you have any trouble finding what you're looking for, the detailed index at the end of the book should point you in the right direction. Try searching under the item you want to use or by the task you need to accomplish, or both.

Just about everything in your house can be used in more ways than one. Why buy a tiny bottle of expensive touch-up paint from the car dealer when a little dab of nail polish will do the trick? Why drive all the way to the gas station for a disposable funnel when you've got an empty two-liter soda bottle sitting in your kitchen? And why add to landfill problems when there are so many ways to reuse plastic bottles, Styrofoam, egg cartons, and glass bottles?

You hold in your hands a valuable reference that will help you get the most out of common household items — and your careful household budget. This book will show you how to use products you already have in your home to save time, money, and maybe even your planet.

The Editors of FC&A

Uncommonly Good Uses for Common Household Products

Aluminum foil

Make a cake plate. If you're worried about breaking or losing your good china when you take your homemade cakes to picnics, bake sales, or school functions, try this. Make a disposable cake plate by covering a sturdy piece of cardboard with aluminum foil.

> Aluminum foil was developed in 1947 by Richard S. Reynolds, nephew of the tobacco king, R.R. Reynolds. The paper-thin, lightweight metal was first used to protect cigarettes and hard candies from moisture.

Disguise worn spot in mirror. Do you have a beautiful old mirror that has developed a worn spot in the reflective coating? A quick and easy solution is to tape a piece of aluminum foil to the back.

Put a shine on your chrome. Rub rust off chrome with the shiny side of a piece of aluminum foil. Then buff with rubbing alcohol on a cloth.

Inexpensive scrubber for pots and pans. Aluminum foil can clean up a dirty dish, too. Scrunch up a few layers into a tight wad and scrape away.

Twice the heat for half the effort. Iron your clothes from both sides and cut your ironing time in half. Simply slip a piece of aluminum foil between your ironing board and your cover. The foil will absorb the heat from your iron and reflect it up into your clothes.

Create more light. If outdoor electrical lighting is a little dim in your yard or at your campsite, make the most of it by putting a piece of reflective aluminum foil behind the lamp.

Keep rolls warm longer. Those delicious yeast rolls you made for your dinner party will stay warmer longer if you put a piece of aluminum foil under the napkin in your breadbasket.

Watch out!

Foods like lemons and tomatoes that are naturally acidic shouldn't be wrapped in aluminum foil. The acids react with the metal, and it can affect the food's flavor.

Save cleanup time when painting. If you're tackling a big paint job, don't go to the trouble of cleaning your paintbrushes every night. Just wrap them in aluminum foil and put them in the freezer. The next day, defrost the brushes for about an hour, and you're ready to get back to work.

Add a patch without a hitch. An iron-on patch can give new life to a garment with a hole in it. To keep the patch from sticking to the ironing board — or another part of the garment, like the back of a pants leg — place a piece of foil under the hole. The patch won't stick to it. Just remember to wait until it's cool to remove it.

Foil an insect's plan for your garden. Use strips of aluminum foil as mulch in your garden around corn, cucumbers, and squash. The aluminum foil reflects light, which repels many insects.

Wrap up a "kiss." You can wrap a special gift to look like a giant chocolate kiss. Place the gift on a paper plate or circular piece of cardboard. Starting underneath the plate, wrap aluminum foil up around the item to form the "kiss" shape. Make the gift tag out of a long piece of white paper and stick it in the top.

Turn up your radiator's heat. If you have a radiator in your home, you can increase the amount of heat put out into a room very simply. Here's how. Cut a piece of rigid insulation or poster board the same size as the radiator. Cover it with aluminum foil and slip it between the radiator and the wall. You've just made your own insulated reflector.

Drench sun-loving plants with light. For houseplants that need a lot of light, like geraniums and cacti, line a windowsill with aluminum foil. The reflection will increase the amount of light available to the plant.

Give seedlings a head start. Aluminum foil and a small box are handy helpers when you start plants indoors from seeds. Line the box with foil, shiny side up, extending an inch or two above the sides. Punch drainage holes through both foil and the box bottom. Add potting soil up to a few inches from the top of the box and plant the seeds. Put it in a sunny window. The foil will reflect heat to the seedlings as they grow. Your plants should be big and healthy when it's time to transplant them.

Bake "shapely" cakes. You can fashion aluminum foil into Christmas trees, pumpkins, stars, hearts, and other interesting shapes to use as baking pans for special cakes.

> Guests at a modern wedding reception enjoy feasting on wedding cake. But there was a time when the cake wasn't eaten — it was thrown at the bride as a fertility symbol. Folks today prefer the neater practice of showering the bride and groom with rice or birdseed.

Correct a kitty. If a new kitten makes a mess, cover the spot with aluminum foil. This will keep him from doing the same thing again in the same spot. Over a few weeks, slowly shrink the size of the foil until it's gone.

Clear up VCR snow. If you see "snow" on your television screen whenever you play a videotape in your VCR, try putting a piece of aluminum foil between the VCR and your television. It may cut down on interference and clear up your picture.

Perfect pie crust. To keep the edges of your pie crust from browning too quickly and burning before the rest of the pie is done, put strips of aluminum foil over the edges. Your crust will be golden brown and perfect all over.

Keep paint where it belongs. Paint has a way of getting on everything in its path. Protect your faucets, door handles, and other fixtures from splatters by covering them with aluminum foil before starting your paint job. It's easy to scrunch around things, stays firmly in place, and is a snap to remove.

Make an emergency funnel. Don't worry if you're caught without a funnel, make one out of aluminum foil. It's easy and disposable — great for those real messes.

Line a paint tray. Use a layer of aluminum foil to line your paint tray. When you're through, just throw away the liner. Clean-up complete!

Root without tangles. Cuttings can take root quickly in water, but before you know it, they're all tangled. Make it easier from the start by covering the container of water with aluminum foil and poking a hole for each stem. This will keep them apart, and, as a bonus, the water won't evaporate as quickly.

Sharpen dull scissors. Layer several thicknesses of aluminum foil and cut through them a few times with your dull scissors. They'll come out nice and sharp.

Ammonia

Clean your oven racks. The easiest way to clean a blackened oven rack is to lay it gently on an old towel in your bathtub. Fill the tub with warm water and some ammonia, then let it sit. Much easier than scrubbing on your knees all day.

Watch out!

Never mix products containing ammonia with bleach or products containing chlorine. Ammonia and chlorine can form a deadly gas when combined. Read label directions and warnings carefully before mixing any cleaners.

Improve your view. A solution of three parts water to one part ammonia works wonders on windows and anything else a commercial spray cleaner is used for. Cheaper, too.

Quick way to clean your carpet. No time to shampoo the carpet, but you need it clean pronto? Simple. Mix one-half cup of clear ammonia with one pint of water, then mop very lightly across the surface of the carpet. You won't need to use much. Before you begin, test the solution on a concealed spot to be sure it won't damage the carpet. Never use ammonia on a wool carpet.

Remove stains from washable fabrics. Ammonia will help remove nonoily stains — like those from blood, milk, perspiration and urine — from most washable fabrics. Make a mixture of equal parts ammonia, dishwashing liquid, and water. Shake it together in a plastic squeeze bottle. Apply it directly to the stain, rub it in gently, let it stand for a few minutes, then rinse. This should not be used on acetate, acrylic, silk, spandex, or wool. For fragile fabrics, do not apply ammonia directly. Instead, hold the stain over the mouth of an open bottle of ammonia, and let the fumes permeate it. Then gently wash.

Disintegrate old cork. Have you ever gotten part of a wine cork stuck inside a wine bottle? After the wine is gone, pour a little ammonia inside the bottle, and let it sit outside for several days. The ammonia eats away the cork, and all you have to do is wash the bottle clean.

Get unsightly mildew out of wood. Your wooden patio furniture has seen better days, and now it's covered with mildew. Get rid of it quickly with this wonder wash. Mix one cup of ammonia with a half cup of vinegar, a quarter cup of baking soda, and one gallon of water.

> Ammonia was named after Ammon, the Egyptian sun god, because it was originally prepared from camel dung near the shrine of Jupiter Ammon.

Shoo, stray. Keep strays out of your trash by coating the bags with a little ammonia before putting them out for the night. You can even spray a bit on the outside of your garbage cans, and those scavengers will look elsewhere.

Don't lose your marbles. If a stain on a marble table top is driving you crazy, there's a sane solution. Mix a few drops of ammonia with hydrogen peroxide. Apply it to the stain and leave it for a few hours. Rub it with a clean, dry cloth, then wipe with a cold, wet cloth to remove any remaining solution.

See crystal shine. To clean a crystal lamp base, mix a few drops of ammonia in water. Apply with a soft cloth. Rinse with another cloth dampened with clear water. Dry it and watch it sparkle.

Apples

Clean aluminum cookware. Dull pots and pans will become bright again when you cook apples, rhubarb, or lemons in them.

Everyone has heard the saying "an apple a day keeps the doctor away." This reputation for healing goes back at least as far as the Arabian Nights. One of the stories featured a magical apple that could cure all diseases.

Roast a juicier chicken. Is your roasted chicken so dry it makes the Sahara look like a water park? Try this tip. Stuff a whole apple inside the chicken and roast as usual. Throw the apple away and serve your moist and tender chicken with pride.

Make a pretty centerpiece.
Decorate your table or mantle with apples. It's easy. Core several large apples and insert

candles of different heights. Add some greenery and you've got a terrific country look.

Ashes

Renew pewter's smoky shine. Cigarette ashes make a good cleaner for dull pewter. Apply the ashes with a moistened piece of cheesecloth. As you rub, it will turn darker. But a good rinsing will reveal the new shine.

> Think using ashes for cleaning purposes sounds a bit witless? Consider the words of Athelstan Spilhaus, "Waste is simply some useful substance we do not have the wit to use."

Cut the glare. If you don't mind looking like a football player, you can reduce glare while driving or working in your yard. Moisten a finger with oil, dip it in ash from your fireplace, and draw dark half-circles under your eyes.

Get bigger, brighter flowers. For bigger, longer-lasting blossoms, add wood ashes from your fireplace to the soil in your flower bed. The best time to do this is at the beginning of the growing season, but keep the ashes away from plants that like acidic soil, like azaleas and rhododendrons.

Baby powder

Remove grease stains from clothing. Did you splatter grease on your clothes while frying chicken for Sunday dinner? Next time, wear an apron, but for now, try putting some baby powder or cornstarch on a powder puff and applying it to the stain. Rub it in and brush off the excess powder when the stain disappears. For stubborn stains, repeat the process.

Shampoo without water. Baby powder can make a good dry shampoo for you or your pet. Just rub it in and brush it out. It will absorb excess oil and leave your hair or your pet's coat with a pleasant scent.

Smooth sliding for gloves. New rubber gloves have a powdery coating on the inside that makes them slide off and on easily. When that powder wears off, dust your fingers with baking soda or baby powder, or sprinkle a little inside the gloves. This works well for helping slide boots on more easily, too.

Brush away wet sand. You came to the beach for fun, not to clean up sand that gets tracked inside. You can leave the grains outside if you sprinkle baby powder over your wet, sandy skin. The powder will absorb the moisture, and the sand will brush off easily.

Protect your bulbs. Before planting bulbs, dust them with medicated baby powder to keep critters from munching on them.

Powder your playing cards. A light dusting of baby powder keeps cards from sticking together. Shuffling will go more smoothly, too.

Silence squeaky floors. If a certain spot on your hardwood floor sings to you every time you step on it, dust the area with a little talcum powder. Sweep back and forth until the powder has settled down into the cracks.

Polish scratches off glasses. If your eyeglasses have tiny scratches on them, don't toss them out. Make a paste of talcum powder and water. Rub this gently onto the lenses and wipe off. You'll be seeing the world in a whole new light.

Say goodbye to bathtub ring. Love to take baths but hate to clean up the ring? Try sprinkling a little talcum powder in your bath water. It will feel good on your skin, and your tub will stay clean.

Sleep tight. During hot weather, sprinkle some baby powder between your sheets for an extra cool sensation when you slide into bed.

Baby wipes

Clean keyboards. Baby wipes are for grownups, too. Keep them at your desk for an easy way to clean your calculator or computer keyboard.

Recycle as dust cloths. Some baby wipes can be laundered and reused. They come in handy for dusting and other cleaning chores.

Reuse the containers. When all the baby wipes are gone, those sturdy plastic containers make handy, stackable boxes for audio cassette tapes, pens and pencils, and small tools. They can also be used to store sewing supplies, first-aid gear, or makeup in your car. Use one to make a fishing tackle box, or cut a hole in the top and use it for a coin bank.

Make a quick getaway. After pumping your gas at a self-service station, no need to waste time washing your hands in the restroom. Just keep baby wipes handy for a quick cleaning, and you're on the road again.

Clean plastic playing cards. Leave the baby with the sitter, but take the baby wipes with you to your bridge game. If players eating chocolates or buttered popcorn get smudges on the cards, a quick swipe wipes them clean.

Baby bottoms are just the beginning. The next time baby spits up all over your blouse, use baby wipes to get rid of the stain and the smell. They are usually nearby when a baby is around, and they are gentle enough for most fabrics.

> Talk about someone who cleaned up in the baby business! In 1867, merchant, chemist, and inventor Henri Nestlé, founder of the Nestlé company, created a nutritious product for infants that could be used by mothers who were unable to breast-feed. He became famous when his new infant formula saved the life of a premature baby.

Remove mildew from books. To remove mildew from books, wipe the covers with baby wipes and apply powdered sulfur to the pages.

Bake ware

Simply super way to cut corn.
If you love fresh corn but can't bite it off the cob, or if you want to freeze summer corn for later, try this no-mess way to cut it off the cob. Take an angel food cake pan

and set the ear of corn upright into the center hole. As you cut, the kernels will fall into the pan, not all over your counter.

Make mini-meatloafs. Tired of the same old meatloaf? Try something new. Instead of using a loaf pan, fill cups of a large muffin pan with your meatloaf mixture. The mini-loaves will bake faster and more thoroughly. Freeze any leftovers. When you want a quick meal or snack, just pop them in the microwave.

And for dessert ... Make dessert time easy on yourself. Pour gelatin or pudding into foil cups in a muffin pan. You'll have quick, individual servings of dessert for everyone in the family with no mess and no cleanup.

Hold condiments. Cookout time can get messy, but you can keep all the condiments neat and organized. Put your favorites, like relish, pickles, chopped onions, and mustard, in the cups of a muffin pan. Cover with aluminum foil or plastic wrap, and you have a convenient travel container for your condiments.

Organize nuts and bolts. An old muffin pan makes a per-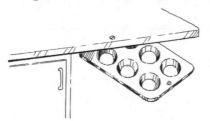fect organizer for odd-sized nuts, bolts, screws, and nails. You can even mount it under a shelf or bench top by securing it with a screw on one end. Use a washer as a spacer, and you'll be able to swing the muffin pan out to find that perfect fastener, then swing it back under when you're finished.

Store sanding discs. For an easy rack to store your abrasive sanding discs, cut an aluminum pie tin in half and secure it to the wall. Be sure to file or sand down the exposed edge because thin, cut metal can be very sharp.

Bake potatoes. Potatoes will bake more quickly and evenly if you stand them on end in muffin pans. Stuffed green peppers, apples, and tomatoes also bake better in muffin pans.

No more spills for Fido. Is your dog constantly tipping over his outside water dish? To remedy this problem, use an angel food cake pan. Hammer a stake through the center hole and fill.

Make mealtime fun and easy. If you dread mealtime with your toddler or if you have a sick child who's sick of being in bed, try serving snacks and meals in a muffin pan. It makes a nice diversion, and there's less mess, too.

Scare birds away. Keep the birds out of your garden with old tin cans and aluminum pie plates. If you hang them on copper wire stretched between two metal posts, you'll find your plants get greener after a storm. They'll attract more electricity, which helps turn oxygen into plant-enriching nitrogen.

Give the squirrels a scare, too. If the squirrels have been beating you to the punch in picking your fruit trees, it's time to strike back. Get yourself a dozen or so pie tins and string them up from the lower branches so the wind will catch them. The racket they make banging together should give your trees some relief from constant squirrel attacks.

A crowd-pleasing way to keep cool. Got a crowd-sized pitcher of lemonade or a punchbowl full of your favorite party beverage? Keep them cool in a big way with ice cubes made in muffin tins.

Make a clean sweep. Save time by keeping a dustpan handy in each bathroom and in your workshop. But there's no need to go to extra expense buying them. Recycle aluminum pie plates instead. Just cut one in half for two sturdy dustpans.

Stain removal is easy as pie. Place a clean absorbent cloth over an upside down glass pie plate to make an ideal working surface when removing stains from clothes.

Baking soda

Carpet freshener. You can make your own custom carpet freshener. Just combine three-fourths cup of baking soda with one-fourth cup of talcum powder, two tablespoons of cornstarch, and your favorite scent. Sprinkle mixture over your carpet, let stand for at least 15 minutes, vacuum, and enjoy the aroma.

> The Statue of Liberty received an All-American cleaning for the 1976 bicentennial celebration. She was cleaned with baking soda.

Drain cleaner. Here's a recipe for an all-natural drain opener. Mix together one cup of baking soda, one cup of salt, and a half cup of white vinegar. Pour this down the clogged drain, wait 15 to 20 minutes, then pour a big pot of boiling water down the drain. A word of caution — don't use this method if you've already tried a commercial drain opener that is still standing in the drain.

Cleaning grease from carpet. You don't need fancy carpet cleaners to remove greasy carpet stains, just reach for the baking soda. As quickly as possible, blot up as much of the grease as you can and sprinkle baking soda on what's left of the spot. Wait about an hour for the oil to be absorbed, and then vacuum it up.

> Baking soda is a great cleaner because dirt and grease stains usually contain fatty acids, which are neutralized by the baking soda. The neutralized acids break up and can be dissolved in water or just wiped away.

Deodorant. You realize you're out of deodorant, and there's no time to run to the store. Don't sweat it — you have a great stand-in right in your kitchen. Put a little baking soda on a powder puff, pat under your arms, and you'll be odor-free all day.

Mum, appearing in 1888, was the first successful antiperspirant. It was followed by Everdry and Hush in the early 1900s. But due to the modesty of people at that time, these products were purchased confidentially in drugstores. The first to bravely announce its intention to keep women "clean and dainty" was a product called Odo-Ro-No. In magazine advertisements, it went so far as to boldly declare that B.O. was socially offensive.

Ease insect stings. You never seem to have the right first-aid equipment around when someone gets hurt, but if you get stung or bitten by an insect, you probably have just the thing in your kitchen. Make a paste using baking soda and rubbing alcohol and apply to the sting or bite.

Find a lost shine. Here's a no-elbow-grease way to put the shine back on your silver. Line a baking pan with aluminum foil, shiny side up. Make sure it covers the pan completely. Add your silver pieces and cover with warm water and several tablespoons of baking soda. Wait 10 minutes and the tarnish will be gone without any work or expense.

People use a lot of baking soda but not as much as some cows. Dairy farmers often give their cows as much as 4 ounces of baking soda a day to help them digest their acidic diet.

De-bug your windshield. When a bug meets your windshield at 65 mph, he gets pretty attached to it. Here's an easy way to get rid of him and his friends. Put a half cup of baking soda in a quart of water. Wrap a mesh bag — the kind oranges, grapefruit, and onions are sold in — around a sponge. Dip it into the solution and scrub the glass clean.

Take the itch out of poison ivy. To relieve the burning and itching of poison ivy or oak, make a paste of baking soda and water. Gently spread the thick mixture over the affected area.

Give toilet stains the brush. Instead of using expensive toilet bowl cleaners, try baking soda or vinegar on the stains and scrub with your toilet brush.

Brighten your piano. Tired of the yellow keys on your old piano? Apply a baking soda and water solution with a damp cloth, one key at a time, being careful not to get any down between the keys. Wipe with a clean, damp cloth, then buff with a dry one.

Clean out the microwave. Your fridge isn't the only appliance a little baking soda can help. Think of the good it can do for the splattered-on walls of your microwave. Use a quart of warm water mixed with four tablespoons of baking soda to scrub and deodorize the inside.

Make your own bath salts. A soothing bath is hiding in your kitchen cupboard. Just dissolve baking soda into a warm tub, and you're on your way to a relaxing bath and softer skin.

> For baking purposes, baking soda won't last forever. To test its freshness, put one-quarter teaspoon in one tablespoon of vinegar. If the baking soda bubbles, go ahead and use it.

Tighten sagging chair bottoms. Cane chair bottoms can lose their charm when they sag. To make them taut again, soak two cloths in a solution of hot water and baking soda. Coat the entire surface from the top with one cloth, while pushing up from the underside with the other. Use a clean cloth to absorb excess moisture and put the chair in the sun to finish drying.

Clean iron cookware. Iron cookware isn't as easy to clean as the nonstick type but even cooked-on food will loosen up with this solution. Put two teaspoons of baking soda and a quart of water into the pot and bring it to a boil.

Presoak ovenproof glass cookware. To remove baked-on sugars and starches from glass cookware, soak it in warm water and dishwashing detergent with a little baking soda added.

Whiten your socks. To make those athletic socks look new again, hot foot it to your kitchen cabinet. Get out the baking soda and mix some with water to presoak your socks. It will loosen the soil, so when you throw them in the wash, they'll come out clean.

Take the stink out of shoes. So you've got smelly feet — no problem. Just coat the inside of your shoes with baking soda, and let them air out for a while. Repeat as necessary. If you don't want white smoke puffing out from your ankles, shake out the baking soda before wearing your shoes again.

Put out fires. If you have a tendency to overcook your food, a big box of baking soda might be just the thing to keep near your stove. Baking soda works well for extinguishing grease fires and electrical fires.

> Baking soda's fire-fighting ability is no secret. In fact, many commercial fire extinguishers use this common kitchen staple as one of their chief ingredients.

Ease acid indigestion. Baking soda helps neutralize stomach acid, which can cause indigestion and heartburn. For quick relief, drink a half glass of water mixed with a half teaspoon of baking soda.

No more start-up anxieties. Make a paste of one cup baking soda and one cup water. Paint this on your car battery posts to neutralize corrosion. Let it sit for about an hour, then clean it off.

Sweeten up sour sponges. When your kitchen sponge gets that yucky, stale smell, you know it's full of germs and bacteria. Soak it in a mixture of two tablespoons of baking soda and one pint of water.

Deodorize your dog. You aren't the only one who can use baking soda for deodorant. To keep your dog clean and odor-free, rub some baking soda into his coat and brush it out.

Watch out!

Don't add baking soda to vegetables. It will destroy some of the vitamins.

Help out your septic system. If you have a septic tank, help keep it fresh by flushing a cup of baking soda down the toilet every so often.

Scrub away melted plastic. If plastic wrap has melted on your toaster or toaster oven, you can get rid of the mess with a damp cloth and some baking soda.

Repel rain from windshield. For a slicker windshield, put a handful of baking soda on a dampened cloth and wipe your windows inside and out.

Cut grease with soft hands. Add a tablespoon of baking soda to your dishwater. It will cut grease and soften your hands at the same time.

Balloons

Raise a dust cloth. You're almost ready for the birthday party guests to arrive when you spot spider webs on the ceiling. It's too late to drag out the ladder, but if you bought a special balloon for the guest of honor, you're in luck. Just put a damp dust cloth on top of a helium-filled balloon, and you can bump away the web in a jiffy.

Hold on to the shape of your hat. To keep the shape of a cloth hat, dry it on an inflated balloon. Just be sure to tie down the balloon so your hat doesn't blow away.

Cool it. If you have a few uninflated balloons left over from a birthday celebration, no need to pack them away. Put them to good use. Fill them with water and freeze them to use as ice packs.

Send a creative invitation. For an unusual party invitation, blow up a balloon, but don't tie it. Hold the end closed while you write the details of who, what, when, and where with a marker. Release the air and put the balloon in an envelope. The person who gets it will have to blow it up to read it.

Practice clean and safe hunting. Nothing is more dangerous than a dirty gun. To keep debris and foreign matter from getting into your gun barrel, slip a balloon over the end.

Create novelty gifts for your next party. Don't settle for ordinary the next time you serve Chinese food. Surprise your dinner guests with unique "fortune balloons." Write out fortunes on slips of paper, slip one inside each balloon, then inflate. Everyone will have fun popping a balloon to read their fortune. This idea will work for other parties, too.

Get your cat off the furniture. A few balloons on the arms of your favorite chairs will send a loud and clear message — stay off — to misbehaving cats that land on them.

Keep your punch chilly. Need a novel way to ice up a punch bowl? Fill a balloon with colored water or juice and stick it in the freezer. When party time rolls around, slit the balloon with a sharp knife or razor blade and plop the ice into the punch bowl.

Put dinner guests in a festive mood. Whether you're entertaining business clients or kindergartners, everyone loves balloons. Write the names of your guests on balloons, tie them to chairs or small weighted items, and use them as place cards.

Protect your poor finger. You have a boo-boo on your finger so you put a bandage on it. But now you need to wash dishes and mop the floor, and you don't have any rubber gloves. You can keep the bandage dry by slipping a small balloon over your injured finger.

Clever way to carry flowers. A neat way to transport cut flowers is to stick them into a balloon with some water and fasten a rubber band around the neck of the balloon.

Bananas

Fertilize your plants. Banana peels are rich in potassium and phosphorus and can give your plants, especially roses, vegetables, and houseplants, an extra boost. Just follow these simple steps:

- air dry banana peels until crisp

- crumble and store in sealed envelopes at room temperature

- add to soil when planting

A fruity way to make silver shine. Don't toss out those banana peels. Blend them in your food processor until smooth and use as a paste to shine your silver.

Contrary to popular belief, you should store bananas in the refrigerator. Although the peels will turn dark, the fruit will stay fresh and firm longer.

Shine your shoes. Banana peels can make your shoes shiny. Just rub your leather shoes with the inside of the peeling, then buff with a soft cloth.

Basting syringe

Fill a small pet's water bowl. Here's an easy way to fill your pet's water bowl without taking it out of the cage — use a basting syringe. You can fill the bowl right through the bars of the cage.

Clean up spilled egg. If you drop an egg on your floor or counter, use a basting syringe to quickly suck up most of the slimy egg, and just wipe the rest away.

Fill a steam iron. Getting water into the tiny hole in your steam iron can be difficult. Make it easier by using a basting syringe. You can aim the water right where you want it.

Wake up to perfect pancakes. If you drip more pancake batter onto your counter than you wind up cooking, consider using a basting syringe. Fill it with batter and squeeze the perfect amount directly onto your griddle. No mess, no fuss, and each pancake will be the perfect size.

Bake no-drip muffins. A basting syringe can help you aim muffin batter, too. To fill your muffin tin without dripping the batter all over your cookware, fill a basting syringe with batter and squeeze the right amount into each muffin cup.

Get rid of gas. At the end of the summer grass-cutting season, it's a good idea to remove the gasoline from your lawn mower. A basting syringe is the perfect tool for getting out every last drop.

Clean out an aquarium. To give your fish tank a quick clean-up, use a basting syringe to "vacuum" the bottom. Keep this one separate from the one you use in the kitchen.

Change the water in your flower arrangement. If you don't want to completely take apart a flower arrangement just to change the water, use a basting syringe instead. You won't disturb a single petal.

No-mess plant watering. For small plants, tiny pots, or hard-to-reach containers, water with a basting syringe. It's especially handy for watering Christmas trees without spilling a drop.

Bedsheets

Don't throw that sheet away. Never throw out sheets, even if they've passed their prime for bed use. They're great for dropcloths during painting projects. And what easier way to pick up leaves than to rake them all into the middle of a big sheet? When you're done, just fold up the corners and drag them away to the compost pile.

Boost profits at your garage sale. Make it easy for shoppers to decide if that dress or pair of pants will fit. Tack up a bedsheet in the corner of your garage. Add a full-length mirror and you have a temporary dressing room.

Scare deer away from your garden. Want to keep deer out of your garden without hurting them? Run a string around the perimeter, about three or four feet off the ground. Cut strips from a white sheet and tie them along the string every few feet. A flash of a white tail is a warning signal to deer. The white strips, hung about tail height, should frighten them away from your peas and corn.

Wrap up Christmas. After the presents have been opened and the last cup of eggnog is gone, it's time to take down the Christmas tree. If you wrap a sheet around it before you drag it out of your house, you won't be picking up pine needles until spring.

Beer

Bake bread. Make a quick and easy bread for dinner tonight. The ingredients are simple — three cups of self-rising flour, one 12-ounce can of beer, and two tablespoons of sugar or honey. Put the flour in a bowl, make a well in the center, and pour in the beer. Add the sugar or honey, mix by hand, and bake in a greased pan at 350 degrees for about 45 minutes. Top with melted butter. Experiment with the recipe — use different types of beer to change the flavor.

> What's the difference between beer and ale? Not much. It's mostly a matter of the recipe. Beer, unlike ale, contains dried flowers of the hops plant.

Add new luster to gold. To put the shine back in your gold jewelry, pour a small amount of pale beer onto a soft cloth and buff gently.

Clean wood furniture. Warm beer makes an inexpensive cleanser for oak or mahogany furniture. Just wipe it on with a soft cloth.

> How much does a barrel hold? You may say it depends on the size of the barrel. But, in fact, a true barrel holds 36 gallons. Originally, each of the other sizes was given its own name. A firkin holds nine gallons, while a kilderkin holds 18. You can store 72 gallons of cider in a puncheon, but only 54 in a hogshead. And you can bet it takes a butt to hold 108 gallons.

Give your hair some bounce. What's the best solution for flat hair? Flat beer. Many commercial hair-care products can weigh your hair down, making it limp and lifeless. But a quick beer rinse can strip away soap film quickly. Just mix three tablespoons with a half cup of warm water, pour it on your hair, finish your shower, and rinse off. You'll love the results.

Make meat tender and tasty. You don't need expensive wine to marinate inexpensive cuts of meat. Beer does a fine job. Just marinate for about an hour before cooking.

Belts

Hold that ladder. You'll save space in your garage if you hang your ladder horizontally on nails in the wall. To keep it from slipping off if you bump into it, screw or nail an old belt into the wall, then buckle it around the ladder to hold it in place.

Make an organizer. Nail an old belt to the wall in your garage or workshop, putting several nails at even intervals, leaving loops for holding tools.

Make a pet collar. Don't pay a lot of money for an expensive leather collar for your dog or cat. You probably have an old leather belt you don't use anymore that would be perfect. Just cut it off to the appropriate length, poke new holes in it, and strap it on.

And a leash. To make an impromptu leash, run a belt underneath the collar and through the belt buckle — and hold on.

Make a temporary hinge. You can fix a broken hinge temporarily by nailing a short piece of a leather belt to the door and door frame.

Berry baskets

Put packets in their place. How do you store those little packets of dry soup, taco seasoning, and hot chocolate mix? Use plastic berry baskets. The packets fit in neatly and don't get scattered in your pantry.

Transport small pets. Tie or tape two berry baskets together to make a "kennel" for a small pet, like a mouse, hamster, or frog.

Use as a colander. Berry baskets make great colanders for draining small amounts of pasta or washing fruits and vegetables.

Protect your plants. You can protect your seedlings by putting an upside down berry basket over them. Water, oxygen, and sunlight can still get in but rabbits, squirrels, and birds can't. You can also protect bulbs from rodents by burying them inside a berry basket.

Hold flowers in place. If you're making a flower arrangement in a bowl or basket, put a berry basket in the bottom and stick stems through the holes.

Bleach

Clean stains from countertops. Bleach is a great stain remover, and white countertops and porcelain sinks are perfect candidates for its power. For particularly stubborn stains, soak paper towels in bleach, and put them over the stain. Be sure to wear rubber gloves to protect your hands. Cover with another paper towel soaked in water. Leave overnight and the stain should be gone in the morning.

Watch out!

Whenever you're cleaning with bleach, or any other cleaning solution with a strong smell, make sure you have plenty of ventilation. Open a window in your kitchen and one on the other side of your house. This will give you good cross-ventilation.

Clean the bowl with bleach. For a shine that puts to shame most commercial toilet cleaners, treat your bowl to a few minutes worth of soaking in undiluted chlorine bleach.

The stain tester. You're not sure how to attack that stain on your siding because you can't tell whether it's dirt or mildew. Let bleach help you out. Soak a rag in bleach and dab at the stain. If it starts to flake off, the stain is mildew.

Save your garbage from marauders. Are dogs constantly exploring your garbage and strewing it from one end of the neighborhood to the other? Sprinkle a bit of chlorine bleach inside the bag before you close it, and your canine friends will turn their discriminating noses up at the smell.

Kill germs from recycled items. If you're a bargain shopper and often pick up toys or kitchen items at garage sales or flea markets, you might be concerned about germs. If the items are waterproof, soak them for about five minutes in a solution of three-quarters cup bleach and one gallon of warm, soapy water. Rinse and allow to air dry in the sun, if possible. No more germs.

Clearly beautiful flowers. Don't draw attention away from your beautiful flower arrangement by letting the water in the glass vase get cloudy and murky. To keep it clear and sparkling, add a tablespoon of bleach for each quart of water in the vase. This will also help keep your flowers from drooping and fading so quickly.

Bobby pins

Protect your fingers from an angry hammer. Don't try to hold a small nail with your fingers because your fingers are what you'll end up hammering. Instead, grip the nail between the prongs of a bobby pin.

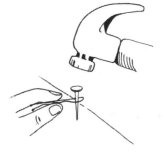

Wigs were at the height of fashion in the French court during the 17th century. To make them fit smoothly, people either cut their natural hair short or "bobbed" it with hairpins. Both the straight and U-shaped pins became known as "bobbing pins." In England, during the next century, they came to be known as "bobby pins." This is the name that held later when two-pronged pins were mass produced.

Hang ornaments. If you run out of ornament hangers at tree-trimming time, bobby pins are a good stand-in.

Mark your spot. Instead of folding the page down when reading, or relying on a bookmark that always falls out, use a bobby pin to mark your spot. Just clip it to the page, and it won't fall out or damage your book.

Bread

Wipe away dirt from walls. When making a sandwich for a toddler, take out an extra slice of white bread to wipe away the dirty hand prints or pencil marks he left on the wall.

Have you ever heard anyone say, "It's the greatest thing since sliced bread," and wondered exactly how long sliced bread has been around? In 1928, a bread slicer was used for the first time in a commercial bakery in Chillicothe, Mo. While we've been able to slice bread ourselves for centuries, we've only been able to buy a pre-sliced loaf since 1928.

Spot clean oils. Brighten a soiled oil painting by gently cleaning the canvas with a piece of white bread.

Wipe away lipstick stains. Use a slice of white bread to remove lipstick stains from fabric, or try a nongel toothpaste instead.

Safe way to clean up broken glass. Gently press a slice of bread over an area where you've broken glass, and you'll pick up the tiny slivers. Carefully throw the bread away.

Pre-clean your meat grinder. Send a slice of bread or two through your meat grinder before you put it in the wash. The bread will act like a sponge for larger bits and chunks.

Dishwashing hasn't always been a problem. There was a time when people just ate their plates when they were done. This wasn't as dangerous as it sounds. The first plates were made of bread. A round loaf was allowed to rise. Then it was turned over to flatten it. After it was baked, it was sliced into two edible plates.

Get a soft clean with soft bread. Use a few slices of crustless, fresh bread to clean nonwashable wallpaper and other delicate surfaces. The softer and doughier the bread, the less abrasive it will be on your delicate surfaces.

Freshen up marshmallows. When your marshmallows get hard and stale, put a couple of slices of fresh bread in the bag with them, close it, and leave for two or three days. Your marshmallows will become softer and fresher tasting.

Fix a salad boo-boo. If you went a little overboard with the mayonnaise in your tuna salad, egg salad, or other mayonnaise-based concoction, add some bread crumbs. They will absorb the excess mayo without affecting the flavor.

Cut down cooking odors. When you're cooking smelly vegetables, like cabbage, cauliflower, or broccoli, try putting a piece of bread on top to absorb most of the odor.

Keep cookies soft and fresh. Store cookies with a slice of white bread on top. This will keep them fresh-tasting longer.

Watch out!

Don't keep your bread in the refrigerator because the cold temperature breaks down the starches and makes it get stale quicker. Don't store it on top of your refrigerator, either, because the warmth will dry it out.

Better, safer broiling. Next time you're broiling meat, put a couple of slices of bread in the drip pan. The bread will soak up the grease, resulting in less smoking and less chance of the grease catching fire.

No more tears in the kitchen. Before you cut an onion, stab a small square of bread and push it down to the handle of your paring knife. When you start to cut, the bread will absorb those eye-watering fumes.

Clean suede. Is your suede coat dirty? To save on dry cleaning costs, try this clever tip. Rub a piece of stale bread over the stains. When the bread gets dirty, change to a new piece and repeat.

Butter

Remove ink from a baby doll face. A little person with an ink pen can give a doll a new smile as quick as a wink. To get the ink stain off the plastic face, try rubbing it with butter and leaving it in the sun for a few days.

Save your tablecloth from messy drips. If you are always getting drips on your table from your coffee creamer, dab a bit of soft butter or margarine just on the lip.

Swallow pills. If you have a difficult time swallowing pills, try rolling the pills in a little bit of butter or margarine. This will help the pills slide down your throat more easily.

> If the thought of a straight shot of butter makes you queasy, try a spoonful of applesauce instead. That should help the medicine go down, and four out of five dentists prefer it to Mary Poppins' cavity-causing "spoonful of sugar" method.

Keep your pasta in the pot. To prevent boiling pasta from boiling over, drop a lump of butter in the water before heating. The extra oil will help keep your pasta from sticking together, too.

Candles

Make a pin cushion. A wide candle makes a perfect pin cushion for your sewing table. The pins and needles will glide through fabric more easily when you pull them out of the wax.

Help drawers slide smoothly. If you have a desk or chest with drawers that stick, remove them and rub the runners with a candle. Slip the drawers back in place, and they should move smoothly in their tracks.

> Candles were originally made from tallow (solidified animal fat). They didn't burn very well, smelled bad, and could go rancid in storage, but had the advantage of being somewhat edible in an emergency. Candles made from beeswax were better, but when first developed, they were so expensive that only the very rich could afford them. For the sake of romance, we're lucky that pleasantly scented candles are so affordable today.

Weatherproof your labels. Rub a candle over a handwritten address label to keep the ink from smearing. The wax forms a weatherproof coating.

Plug it. Need to plug the holes in the bottom of a garden pot? Try a few old candle stubs.

Works well with wine, too. Can't find the cork to go back in the wine bottle after your party? Try warming up a candle stub until it's soft, wrap it in a paper towel, and push it into the bottle.

Tape it up. Before you use masking tape for protection when you paint, rub the edges of the roll of tape with a candle. The wax will make the tape easier to remove when you're finished, and it won't be as likely to pull off old paint with it.

Silence the squeak. One good way to quiet a squeaky door is to take it off its hinges, and rub a candle over the hinge surfaces that touch each other.

Cardboard tubes

Unclutter cords. Tired of all the cords from your beauty appliances taking up your bathroom counter space? Neaten up the area by sliding an empty toilet paper tube onto the cord of hot rollers, blow dryers, etc. Fold the excess cord inside, leaving just enough to plug in.

Hang pants neatly. Cut a paper towel tube down one side, and slip it over the bottom of a hanger to keep pants from wrinkling where they're draped over.

Protect seedlings. Push toilet paper tubes into the soil around seedlings that are susceptible to cutworms.

Dispense wrapping paper like a pro. Are you tired of trying to keep your wrapping paper stored neatly? Are the ends always unrolling? Then take an empty wrapping paper tube and slit it lengthwise. Slide it on top of a new roll, leaving the edge of paper hanging slightly through the slit. Not only will your paper stay neatly rolled, it will make wrapping your next gift a snap.

Save that artwork for posterity. If you have children, you know that each drawing they bring home is precious. But pretty soon you can be up to your neck in finger paintings. For easy, safe storage, save all your empty paper towel and wrapping paper tubes and roll the artwork up inside. Stick a label on the outside with the child's name and date. These tubes are much easier to toss into storage, and you don't have to worry about ruining those little treasures.

Keep extension cords under wraps. Put a paper towel or toilet paper tube around your looped-up extension cords, and they won't unravel in the drawer. This is also a great way to store cords to appliances you're not using. Just label the tube with a marker so you'll know which cord goes to which appliance.

Save your teapot spout. If you have a favorite china teapot, don't risk chipping the spout during storage or a move. Slip a toilet paper tube over it.

Carpet remnants

Protect your floor when moving furniture. Slide some carpet samples or remnants, soft side down, under the legs of a piece of furniture you want to move. This buffer will make a heavy piece much easier to move since you can slide it, and it also will protect your floor from the cruel ravages of moving.

Warm your toes this winter. If you live in a cold, snowy climate, you know that cold feet are the worst part of winter. Give Old Man Winter the boot by lining your boots with carpet remnants. Simply trace the outline of your shoe onto a piece of carpet, and cut it out slightly smaller. You'll have a nice layer of insulation between your toes and the cold ground.

> Hooked rugs were first created during Colonial times for beds, not floors. Since they were used only during cold weather, they were stored for long periods of time. Therefore, many early American rugs in good condition can still be found today.

Tool insurance. If your workshop has a concrete floor, it's a good idea to put down some carpet remnants, at least in the areas closest to your work bench. Your feet might not notice the difference, but tools and containers that get knocked off the bench will be much less likely to break.

Make mulch of it. Leftover carpet pieces, or old carpet you are removing from your home, will come in handy in your garden. Cut it in strips, and lay it between rows. It will kill weeds and serve as a mulch for your vegetables. It will also keep your shoes out of the mud as you walk through the garden.

Be prepared for winter emergencies. Stock your trunk with a few pieces of old carpet in case you get stuck in the ice or snow. They'll slip easily under your tires to provide extra traction.

Make a travel mat. A little carpet in your trunk can come in handy in other ways, too. Cut yourself a large piece, and stow it with your spare tire. That way, if you get a flat or have to look under the carriage, you won't have to kneel or lie on the dirty ground.

A scratching post for Mister Claws. Make a scratching post for your cat by covering anything tall and sturdy (a log, some boards, a wooden box, etc.) with carpet remnants. Not only will your cat love having a place to play, you'll be saving your furniture at the same time.

A litter box for a fickle kitty. If your cat won't use the litter box, it's time to get creative. Build a platform around the edge of the box with an inch-wide strip of rough carpet running along it. Perhaps this entertainment will make the box interesting enough to win kitty's favor.

Make a handy scrubber. Fit carpet remnants to blocks of wood, and use them to scrub metal screens clean. They can also be used to apply varnish or shellac to prevent the screens from rusting.

Outfit your car for less. Don't buy expensive floor mats for your car, van, or truck. Pick up carpet remnants from your local carpet store. Some samples are just the right size.

Keep it quiet. You can soften the clattering noise of such things as sewing machines and typewriters by slipping a small carpet remnant underneath as a pad.

Your portable home gym. If you have a larger remnant, you can make a workout mat. Just cut it to be several feet wide and about as long as you are. Stretch, do sit-ups, pushups, or aerobics in comfort. You can roll it up for quick storage or to take it on the road.

Paint under a door. To paint the bottom edge of a door, don't take it off its hinges. Instead, use a small piece of carpet. Put the paint on the carpet scrap, and hold it with one hand on either side of the door. Pull back and forth to coat the edge.

Cat litter

Get rid of driveway stains. An oil stain on your driveway or in your carport may seem like a permanent problem, but it doesn't have to be. Pour some paint thinner or mineral spirits on the stain, and sprinkle it with cat litter or sand. Let it sit for 12 hours, then just sweep it up.

Keep your garbage can fresh. Nothing smells as bad as garbage, right? Think again. A cat's litter box might be worse, and if not, it runs a close second. If commercial products can keep litter boxes from smelling bad, they should be able to keep your garbage positively fragrant. Just sprinkle some in the bottom of the can, and change it occasionally.

Watch out!

Be careful cleaning litter boxes, particularly if you're pregnant. Cat feces can contain parasites that cause a serious disease called toxoplasmosis.

Deodorize those stinky shoes. Shoes can get pretty smelly, especially athletic shoes. To remedy that, fill a couple of knee-high nylons with cat litter, and tie a knot in the top. Insert in sneakers and leave overnight.

Get rid of smoking odors. A bit of cat litter in the bottom of ashtrays will help control the smell of cigarettes and will put out the butts immediately.

Toss out paint the Earth-friendly way. If you need to dispose of leftover latex paint, mix some cat litter into the can and leave the lid off. When the paint dries up, you can just toss it with the rest of your trash.

Chalk

Reduce dampness in closets. To keep your closets dry and protect your clothes from mildew, tie several pieces of chalk together and hang them from a hook.

Prevent silver from tarnishing. You love using your grandmother's good silver when company comes but hate having to polish it after every use. Try putting a piece of chalk in the drawer with the silver. The chalk will absorb moisture and slow down the tarnish. Put some in your jewelry box, and your jewelry won't tarnish as quickly, either.

> The white cliffs of Dover are so-named because of their chalk deposits.

Keep a screwdriver from slipping. It seems like it takes you forever to fix anything because your screwdriver keeps slipping off. But if you rub a little chalk on the blade of the screwdriver, it will hold better to most surfaces.

Cover up water marks. You have a water mark on your white ceiling, but it's so hard to match the paint for a touchup, and you don't want to paint the entire ceiling. Try rubbing some white chalk on the spot instead. Blow off the excess, and repeat if necessary.

Lining up snaps is a snap. If you have trouble making sure both halves of a hook-and-eye or a snap are in the proper place, try this easy tip. Sew one part of the notion onto your fabric, then rub a piece of chalk over it. Close the fabric and the chalk will rub off onto the fabric at the proper spot for the other half.

Get rid of ring around the collar. This common stain on your shirts is caused by oils from your skin. If you rub the stain heavily with white chalk, the chalk will absorb that oil, and the stain should then wash out more easily.

Organize your tools. Pegboard is handy for hanging small tools neatly in your garage or workshop. Once you work out an ideal layout, trace around each tool with chalk. Then you can tell at a glance which tool goes where, and you'll always know just where to reach the next time you need it.

Charcoal briquettes

Make a dehumidifier. A humid closet can be disastrous for your clothes. Keep it dry with a homemade dehumidifier. Just put some charcoal briquettes in a coffee can, and punch a few holes in the lid.

Mold-free books. If your bookcase or storage unit has glass doors, put a piece of charcoal inside to absorb moisture that can cause mold on books.

Stamp out stumps. Save money when you have a large tree cut down. Instead of paying extra to have the stump ground out, you can get rid of it gradually yourself. Each time you cook out on the charcoal grill, when you finish the steaks and burgers, put the remaining live coals in the center of the stump surface. Each time it will burn a little deeper until finally the stump will disappear.

Keep stored appliances smelling fresh. Tie some charcoal in a pantyhose foot, and put it inside a refrigerator or freezer before a move. Even if the appliances are closed up for some time, they'll come out smelling sweet and fresh.

Reject rust in your toolshed. Drop a couple of charcoal briquettes in your toolbox to keep your metal tools from rusting.

Root for fresh water. When rooting plant cuttings, put a piece of charcoal in the water to keep it fresh.

Christmas trees

Put it to rest all over your home. With a couple quick chops, your used Christmas tree can find lots of little homes all around your house. Bushier branches can be snipped off and used to protect plants in your garden, the dried needles will be a welcome contribution to your compost pile, and the trunk can be easily transformed into a few logs for a warm January around the fireplace.

It's beginning to smell a lot like Christmas. With scraps cut from an old satin pillowcase and the needles from your Christmas tree, you can make small, aromatic pillows. Put them in drawers, closets, or trunks to spread that sweet evergreen smell to your clothes and musty places.

Do the feathered folks a favor. The easiest bird feeder you'll ever make is the shell of your Christmas tree, laid on its side in an out-of-the-way corner of your yard. For a nice touch (festive for you, delicious for your guests), don't take off the cranberry and popcorn strings before putting it out.

Stake your peas with Christmas trees. Make a trellis for your veggie garden in three easy steps:

- Prune a couple of trees down to their trunks. (Save the branches for winter mulch on your beds.)

- Plant them upright near your peas or pole beans.

- Run a few lines of string between the trees.

- Voila! An environmentally friendly trellis.

Serve slugs some prickly mulch. Those stiff branches and sharp needles can be as helpful to your garden as they are hurtful to your fingers. A few well-placed bushy branches can help defend your shrubs against winter freezes. And come springtime, those prickly needles make a great mulch that slugs will refuse to crawl over.

Brighten woeful winter windows. By the time fall rolls around, your window boxes can look pretty sad. Replace the dried up summer flowers with branches of evergreens. Fill the boxes with wet peat moss and sand and insert the branches. Keep them watered, and they should stay pretty throughout the winter.

Cloth scraps

Save your scraps for stuffing. By saving all your small sewing fabric scraps, you'll be able to use them to stuff pillows and cushions. Small, homemade pillows come in handy when traveling in the car, on camping trips, etc.

An American named Walter Hunt invented a sewing machine before either Elias Howe or Isaac Singer. But he never patented or publicized it. He feared it would put tailors out of business. He is better known for the safety pin, which took him three hours to create. He did get a patent for that invention, but he sold it for $400 to pay off a debt.

Keep the suds away. Tie an old rag or a wristband around your wrist when you're washing windows or walls by hand, especially if you're reaching above your head. It'll keep suds and water from running back down your arm and into your face.

Keep puppies content. When your dog has puppies, put one piece of old cloth for each puppy in her bed. Then, when the puppies go to new homes, send a piece of cloth with them. The new owners can put the cloth in the puppy's bed, and the familiar scent will help keep it from whining.

Pull off knobs that stick. If you need to get a stubborn push-on knob off an appliance, such as a stove, don't strain your hand. Simply slip the middle part of a rag under and around the lip of the knob, then pull the ends straight back. The knob should pop right off.

Protect your paint job. If you have to lean your ladder against the side of the house, a wall, or another painted surface, tie a couple of rags around the contact points of the ladder. Otherwise, you could find two more spots that need to be touched up.

A dog's doormat. Keep an old, clean rag by the back door for when you take your dog for a walk. When you come in from rainy or snowy weather, you can wipe your dog's feet before he gets into the house and tracks the day's weather all over your carpet.

Vacuum with care. Tie an old washcloth around your vacuum attachment when using it on the ceiling, woodwork, or anything else that could get scraped or marred by the hard plastic edges.

> The first vacuum cleaners had to be operated manually. Two people were needed — one to operate the bellows and the other to move the mouthpiece over the floor. The dust was blown into a box, but a lot of it missed and settled back on the carpet. It wasn't until the suction vacuum was invented in 1901 that the new cleaner proved its usefulness.

Break-proof your sink. When cleaning delicate dishware in the sink, first line the basin with a couple of old towels or a layer of rags. The occasional dropped wine glass will stand a much better chance of survival.

Quiet a drip. If that drip from your faucet is keeping you up at night, tie an old washcloth or hand towel around the spout. It won't fix the leak, but at least you'll get some sleep for a change.

Feed your plants from afar. Going away for a few days? Keep your houseplants watered with this handy trick. Line the bottom of your tub with several thick layers of old towels, then soak them well with water. Put your houseplants in on top of them, and they'll have water when they need it.

Clothespins

Clip for a quick pick. Keep a bag of clothespins in the laundry room. When you have an item that needs special attention before it's washed, clip a clothespin to it. That way, if you forget, you'll be reminded as you start to put it in the washer.

Keep fingers from getting burned. If you put a match into a spring-type clothespin to light charcoal, candles, fireplaces, etc. you'll have a little more safety distance between your fingers and the fire.

Ensure your privacy. Carry a few clothespins when traveling. If you get a hotel room with drapes that don't quite meet, just pull the edges together and clip them. You'll keep out any distracting outside light as well as unwanted peepers.

Make handy holders. Attach a row of clip clothespins to a closet wall with a glue gun. They make convenient holders for scarves and gloves.

Use all your toothpaste. It's frustrating to throw away a tube of toothpaste when you know there's more inside. A clothespin can help hold the back of the tube flat as you use up what's left in the front of the tube.

Keep snacks fresh. Clothespins are perfect for reclosing bags of potato chips, crackers, cookies, etc.

Don't cross your wires. If you change your own spark plugs, you might get confused about which wires go to which spark plug. You can fix that by writing numbers on wooden clothespins with a marker and clipping one to each wire.

Spread 'em. If you want to encourage the branches of your young fruit trees to spread out, clip a couple of spring-type clothespins together, and wedge them into the fork formed by the branch and the trunk.

Coffee

Hide small nicks in furniture. Instant coffee can make an instant cover-up for nicks in your wood furniture. Just make a paste with the coffee and water, and press it into the scratch with a soft cloth. For longer-lasting coverage, mix the coffee with beeswax or paste wax.

> Voltaire, a famous 18th-century French philosopher, supposedly drank 72 cups of coffee a day.

Restore faded cottons. If black lingerie and other black cottons are looking brownish and dull, add two cups of strong Maxwell House coffee to the rinse water when doing laundry. They'll turn dark again.

Keep down the dust from ashes. You can minimize the mess from cleaning out a fireplace. When you are ready to take the ashes out, sprinkle moist coffee grounds over them. They'll stay put while you remove them.

Fertilize your garden. Sprinkle coffee grounds around the plants in your garden to give them a little nutrient boost. But be sure and use grounds from a drip coffeemaker, not boiled grounds from a percolator. The drip grounds are richer in nitrogen.

Watch out!

Your garden plants may be delighted when you sprinkle coffee grounds around them. But indoors it's a different story. The acid may be too strong for potted plants.

Get rid of odors. The next time you have a bad odor in a small, enclosed space like a closet, freezer, or pantry, try setting out a bowl of fresh coffee grounds. Pretty soon things will smell country fresh.

No more musty smell. If you have major appliances that are bound for storage, whether it's for a couple of days or a couple of years, make sure they don't come home with a musty odor inside. Fill an old pantyhose leg or knee-high stocking with fresh-ground coffee (unused), knot it closed, and toss inside.

> Legend has it that in ancient Abyssinia, herders noticed their goats hopping around gaily after eating the berries from a small tree. They decided to give them a try, and soon they, too, were leaping and playing like kids. Eventually a beverage was made from the beans, and coffee drinking was born.

Plant caffeinated carrots. Before sowing your carrot seeds, mix them with coffee grounds. Not only does this add bulk, making planting easier, but you'll increase your harvest as well. That's because coffee grounds will keep root maggots from munching on the carrots. As an extra bonus, the grounds will help add nutrients to the soil around the plant as they decompose.

Highlight dark hair. Add some highlights to brown or red hair with black coffee. After shampooing, just douse your head with cold, black coffee, then rinse off with water.

> In the United States, almost 5,000 cups of coffee are consumed every second.

Banish bad breath. Garlic left you lonely? Chew on a coffee bean for fresher breath.

Odorless litter box. If your cat will accept the unusual, try mixing coffee grounds in with her litter. It will absorb odors and keep down that ammonia smell.

Handy beauty treatment. Don't just dump those used coffee grounds in the trash. Rub them gently all over your hands for smoother skin.

> Did you know that coffee is a fruit? Coffee beans are the seeds of a red berry found on a tall tropical shrub.

Coffee cans

Clean your paint brush. To soak a paint brush, put water or paint thinner in a clean coffee can, and cut an "X" in the plastic lid. Push the handle of the brush through the "X," place the brush in the can, and snap on the lid.

Make a seed sprinkler. If you need to scatter grass seed in small areas, you can make your own seed sprinkler from a coffee can. Poke holes in the lid large enough for the seeds to fall through, and sprinkle wherever you have a bald spot on your lawn. Keep an extra lid without holes on the bottom, and when you're through, just switch lids to make a handy storage container for your seed.

Keep toilet paper dry. When you're camping out there "in the rough," one luxury you don't want to be without is dry toilet paper. An empty coffee can makes a perfect waterproof travel container for this precious commodity.

Save charcoal. When you're finished grilling, don't just let the leftover charcoal briquettes burn into ash. Remove the pieces with tongs, and put them into a coffee can with holes punched in it. Run water over the charcoal to extinguish it, and let dry. The next time you're ready to grill, you can save money by mixing these pieces of charcoal in with the new ones.

> The first "tin cannisters" were used to hold rations for the British Royal Navy in the early 1800s. But it took another 50 years for someone to create a can opener. So how did hungry soldiers get at their grub? It's reported that the bayonet was created not as a weapon of war, but as a tool for opening cans.

Freeze up perfect hamburgers. Save the plastic lids from coffee cans, and layer them between raw hamburger patties. When you've got a good stack, put them in a container and freeze.

Create workspace storage. Empty coffee cans make great storage cubbies in the toolshed or garage. Nail them to shelves or the wall, either standing up or lying down. If they're on their side, label the plastic lid to make hardware easier to find.

Prevent paint drips. When painting overhead with a brush, you can use the lid from a coffee can to protect you from drips. Just cut a slit in the lid, and push it onto the handle of the brush, and the drips will hit the lid, not you.

Put the lid on your grapefruit. If a half of grapefruit is part of your breakfast routine, keep the other half fresh in the fridge by placing it upside down on a clean coffee can lid.

Make an emergency heater. Keep an empty coffee can, a candle, and some matches in the trunk of your car. If you're ever stranded during bad weather conditions, you've got a great little source of light and heat.

Keep your camera dry. Place your camera, keys, wallet or other valuables into a coffee can (with lid) while you're at the beach or on a boat. An empty coffee can will also keep your silverware and napkins dry and bug free on a picnic.

Lost and found in the laundry room. If you're forever finding odds and ends in pockets just before an item goes into the washer, keep a clean coffee can nearby. Drop the "lost" articles in the can, and wait for them to be "found."

A no-odor way to store leftovers. Although you shouldn't store food in open cans for long, a leftover that will get used up in a few hours can still make your fridge smell awful — especially that half-can of tuna, dog or cat food, or sauerkraut. Just drop the whole thing inside an empty coffee can and snap on the lid, and you'll have no odors and no problem.

> Just one pound of coffee contains more than 3,000 beans!

X marks the spot for plastic bags. Take a small plastic lid, cut an "X" in the center, and pull the ends of your bread bag through. A great way to seal plastic bags without hunting for a twist-tie.

De-stink your trunk. Can't get that musty odor out of a storage trunk? Fill a coffee can with cat litter deodorizer, and leave overnight.

Protect tender plants. Cut the bottoms out of coffee cans, and put them over newly planted seedlings in your spring garden. At night, put the plastic lids on for protection. Take them off during sunny days. Remove the cans when the threat of frost damage has passed.

Coffee filters

Sparkling clear windows. You want your windows to sparkle, but when you dry them with a cloth or paper towel, you always seem to leave lint on the glass. Try drying them with a paper coffee filter instead, and you may eliminate the lint.

The first coffee filter was invented by a German housewife, Melitta Benz. Tired of brewing coffee directly in the water, she took some blotting paper from her son's schoolbook, put it in a brass pot that she had poked holes in, and poured the boiling water over the coffee, through the filter, and into the pot. It was the first drip coffeemaker, and the Benz family began manufacturing Melitta coffeemakers.

A first-rate funnel. You can use the stiff, cone-type coffee filters as funnels by just cutting off the tip. One good use for this type of funnel is to separate eggs. Just place your funnel over a glass, and break the egg into it. The white will slide into the glass, but the yolk will stay put.

Catch drips from popsicles. Does the ding-ding of the ice cream truck bring back fond memories of icy cool treats on a stick? Do you remember how sticky your hands would be afterward? Keep that from happening to the young ones in your family. Just poke the stick of the frozen treat through a paper coffee filter, and it will catch those sticky drips.

Eleven-year-old Frank Epperson left his drink mixture of soda water powder and water out on his back porch one night in 1905. The temperature took a sudden turn, and the next morning he found his drink frozen with the stirring stick still in it. Eighteen years later, he began producing Epsicles in seven fruit flavors. Now there are more than 30 flavors of Popsicles to choose from.

Protect dishes. You can protect your good china in storage by putting a coffee filter between each dish to prevent scratching.

Keep the flavor, lose the fat. If you've got delicious beef or poultry broth to use for soups or gravies, don't worry about the fat. Simply strain it through a paper coffee filter, and you're left with flavorful, fat-free broth.

Save your potting soil. Before potting your next container plant, lay a paper coffee filter in the bottom of the pot. This will keep all the potting soil from washing out the drainage holes.

No-splatter microwaving. Cover your dish with a coffee filter before popping it in the microwave. Not only will it cook faster, but you'll never have to clean food splatters off the inside of your microwave again.

Keep cork out of your wine glass. If you're inept with a corkscrew and always seem to break the cork, you don't have to deal with bits of floating cork in your wine glass. Put a paper coffee filter over the mouth of the wine bottle, pour the wine through it, and leave the cork behind.

According to legend, rabies could be cured by drinking a glass of wine that contained some hair from a rabid dog. This is the origin of the expression "the hair of the dog that bit you" as a cure for a hangover.

No-mess taco night. Paper coffee filters are great for holding messy tacos, especially for kids. They'll help control spills from other foods, too, like chili dogs and sandwich wraps.

Rustproof your iron skillet. A cast-iron skillet is great old-fashioned cookware for even the most modern kitchen. Keep yours rust-free by storing it with a paper coffee filter inside.

Make colorful snowflakes. The little ones in your family can make "snowflakes" at Christmas time without using scissors. Just fold coffee filters into squares or triangles, and dip the corners into a solution of food coloring and water. Let dry, and then open up and marvel at the colorful designs.

Coins

A cheap warning system. You'll be away from home for a week or two — perhaps on vacation. When you get back, how will you know if there has been an electrical power failure? This is important because food in the freezer could thaw, spoil, and refreeze without your knowing it. Before you leave, place a penny on top of an ice cube in a tray. When you return, if the penny is still on top, you'll know the ice didn't melt, and all is well. If the penny is on the bottom, chances are the power was off long enough for food to spoil.

There are only two minting locations in the United States that produce coins for public circulation — Denver and Philadelphia. You can tell where your coin was made by the mint mark — the initial D or P. Mints in San Francisco and West Point, New York manufacture uncirculated bullion coins and commemorative coins.

Lift flattened carpet. If you move a chair or table, you may find that the legs have left indentations in your carpet. To fluff it up again, hold a coin on its edge, and scrape it against the flattened pile. It should quickly pop back up. If the carpet is densely matted, try holding a steam iron a few inches above the affected spot until the area is slightly damp before fluffing with the coin.

Test your tires. Having a flat beside a busy highway is dangerous and inconvenient, so make sure you replace your tires when needed. A quick way to see if you're ready for a new set of tires is to insert a penny into the tread. If you can't cover the top of Lincoln's head inside the tread, make tracks to the tire store.

Buy extra time for your posies. Keep cut flowers fresh longer by adding a copper penny and a cube of sugar to the vase of water.

Measure up. If you need to measure something but don't have a ruler handy, reach in your pocket and pull out a quarter. It measures one inch in diameter.

We all know how long a foot is, but not everyone knows that measurement was calculated from the length of Charlemagne's foot. An inch was the width of the knuckle on King Edgar's thumb, and a yard was the distance from King Henry I's nose to his fingertips.

Even out the wobble. If your ceiling fan insists on wobbling, try taping a coin to one of the blades. Experiment with each blade until you eliminate the annoying problem.

Cooking oil

Refresh wooden cookery. New wooden salad bowls and utensils look so pretty, but after a while they can dry out and crack. To restore that new glow, wipe them down with vegetable oil or shortening, let them sit overnight, and wipe off the excess the next morning. Keep wooden cutting boards in shape with the same technique.

Remove adhesive from glass. Dab a small amount of oil on the object with a paper towel or napkin, and rub firmly. If the adhesive is stubborn, use some toothpaste (as an abrasive) along with the oil. When all the adhesive is removed, wash the object with warm soapy water. Avoid using the abrasive on plastic as it can leave tiny scratches.

Nonstick lawn mower blades. Grass often will stick to your lawn mower blade, and the dampness can cause the blade to rust and become dull more quickly. If you spray a little cooking spray on the blade before cutting your lawn, the grass won't stick, and your blade should last longer.

Unsqueak door hinges. That squeaky door hinge is driving you crazy, but you don't have anything to oil it with. Check your cupboards before you drive to the hardware store. Cooking spray will eliminate that annoying squeak. Or try shaving cream — it should work just as well.

Pet food supplement. If you add a little Crisco oil to your pet's food every day, it will help his coat become shiny and lustrous. If you have a cat, it will also help prevent hair balls.

Crisco, the first solid vegetable shortening, was introduced in 1911. But women were so used to cooking with lard and butter that many of them turned down free one-and-a-half pound cans of it. Orthodox Jews eager for a kosher lard substitute bought some of it, and Crisco eventually found a broader market when World War I caused shortages of lard.

Snow shoveling made easy. Rub cooking oil onto your shovel, and watch the snow slide right off.

Protect your car from bugs. Washing bugs off your car's bumper and grill can be a grueling task. You can make that job easier by spraying on a little cooking spray when your car is clean. The bugs will wash off more easily, and it won't damage your car's finish.

Ease splinter removal. A painful splinter will slide out more easily if you swab the area with a little cooking oil first.

Shine your shoes. If you don't have any shoe polish handy, but you want your leather shoes to shine, rub them with some olive oil, and buff with a soft cloth.

Easier locking. Make your key work more smoothly by spraying it with cooking spray.

Keep your cake from a sticky situation. Spray your length of plastic wrap with vegetable cooking spray before covering an iced cake or batch of cupcakes. No more icing on the wrap.

Soften a stiff chamois. Soak a chamois cloth that has gotten hard and stiff in water and a spoonful of olive oil. It will come out soft and ready to use.

Keep the crows away. Fight crow's feet with olive oil. Just dab a couple of drops around your eyes each night before bed.

Ease an earache. Warm olive oil can ease a painful earache. Put a few drops in the affected ear, plug with cotton, and apply a hot water bottle or warm compress.

Deep condition hair. Hot oil treatments can be expensive at a salon, but you can do your own at home. Just warm up some olive oil, massage into your hair and scalp, and wrap your head in a warm towel. Wait about 20 minutes, then wash your hair as usual.

> Olive oil keeps longer than any other type of oil.

Save a "grate" amount of time. Tired of picking stuck-on food off that cheese grater? Rub it down with vegetable oil before the job, and clean-up will be a snap.

No-stick measurements. Before adding that cup of honey to your recipe, coat your measuring cup with cooking oil, then run it under hot water. The honey will slide out much more easily.

Ease the freeze. To keep your car's trunk from freezing shut in winter, wipe down the rubber gasket with vegetable oil.

Pick up stuck-on paper. Scraping stuck-on paper off a wood surface really puts your finish at risk. Show a little patience. Put a few drops of salad oil on the paper, let it soak in, then rub the paper away. Keep adding drops as necessary, and before long, the problem's gone with no scratches left behind.

Remove sticky tar. If you've gotten tar or pitch onto something by accident, it makes quite a mess. Rub a little olive oil onto the area and let it sit. The tar should soften up so you can scrape it off easily.

De-burr your furry friend. If Sparky picked up a few burrs chasing rabbits through the woods, work a little oil into his fur to help lift them out.

Cork

Protect your pictures and paneling. After you toast your purchase of that expensive new painting, put the cork from the wine bottle to good use. If you plan to hang the picture on wood paneling, cut a couple of slices off a cork

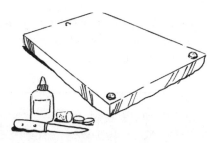

and glue them to the bottom corners of the frame to allow air to circulate. This will prevent a dark spot from developing behind the picture.

Store corn holders safely. If you've got corn holders floating around somewhere in your utensil drawer, you know finding them for your corn-on-the-cob dinner can be a time-consuming — and sometimes painful — job. Keep them handy by sticking them into a large cork.

Homemade depth stops. You want to drill holes to a certain depth, but how do you know when you've gone deep enough? If you're a clever craftsman, you use a depth stop, and if you're a really clever craftsman, you use a cheap depth stop made of cork. Simply drill a hole smaller than the bit you will be using through a regular cork, then screw

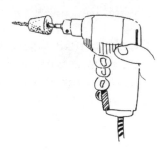

the cork onto the drill bit to the appropriate depth. The cork must be tight on the bit so it won't budge when it hits the wood.

Don't tip your rocker. If you love your wooden rocking chair and you're an enthusiastic rocker, or if you have small children who might rock back too far, glue a cork to the end of each rocker to keep the chair from tipping over.

Keep your keys afloat. Whenever you go boating or swimming, attach your keys to a cork. Then if they fall overboard, they'll float and you can retrieve them easily.

A quick fix for ceiling holes. If you've got a small hole in your ceiling, fill it with a matching size cork. Then cover it with spackle or just paint.

> People used corks for about 100 years before corkscrews were invented. Back then, corks were looser and had knobs on them so you could twist them off.

Store scissors safely. Stick the ends of your scissors into a large cork. This eliminates accidents, especially with sewing scissors in a sewing box.

Repair your floor. Got a hole in your linoleum? Chop up some cork and mix it with a bit of shellac. Fill the hole. When it's dry and hard, use a bit of touch-up paint to cover.

Don't crush your child's musical dreams. Little fingers can meet with big pain when a piano lid falls on them. To prevent such a musically-discouraging tragedy, fix a small piece of cork to each end of the keyboard. Now the lid can slam away with no risk to your little Beethoven.

> The word linoleum comes from the Latin words for flax (linum) and oil (oleum) because they were two of the original ingredients. The inventor, Frederick Walton, covered fabric with linseed oil (from flax), spread chopped cork and other fillers on it, pressed it onto burlap, and created a floor covering that was popular for many years.

Spare your tender fingers. A large cork is a natural holder of miscellaneous pins, tacks, or small nails so that you don't have little accidents waiting for you in the junk drawer. In the sewing kit, a cork can hold a good number of needles, and a cork has prevented who knows how many accidental hookings in the tackle box.

Make a trivet. You can make a handsome trivet out of a collection of leftover corks. Just cut them in half longwise and then connect them in a pattern with toothpicks, or arrange the corks side by side in a wooden frame.

Protect your furniture finish. Glue thin circles of cork to the bottom of unpadded lamps, vases, knick knacks or other items that sit on your wooden furniture to protect against scratches.

Don't flip your lid. If you have a pot that's missing the handle on its lid, just attach a wine cork with a screw. Now your pot is as good as new.

Cornstarch

Soothe sunburn. A paste made from cornstarch and water makes an inexpensive and effective sunburn reliever.

Handy dry shampoo. When you go camping, does it drive you crazy not to wash your hair for several days? Take along a box of cornstarch, and you can at least give yourself a dry shampoo. Just work it into your hair and brush out.

Get blood out of a carpet. It is almost as hard as getting blood out of a turnip, but if the stain hasn't set, you've got a chance. Make a paste of cornstarch and cold water. Rub it in gently and then let it set. It will get hard so you may have to soften it by hitting it with a hammer or mallet. Vacuum the powder. Repeat if necessary.

Quiet a squeaky floor. If your hardwood floor squeaks whenever you step in a certain spot, try sprinkling a little cornstarch or baby powder between the boards.

Keep fingerprints off furniture. When your furniture is freshly polished, it's particularly prone to smudgy fingerprints. You can prevent this by sprinkling your furniture with cornstarch after you polish, then buffing with a soft cloth. The cornstarch will absorb excess polish and get rid of fingerprints.

Earth-friendly spray starch. Mix two tablespoons of cornstarch with one pint of cold water, and put it in a clean spray bottle. The next time your clothes need a bit of stiffening, shake the bottle, spritz on, and iron as usual.

Make pasta pick-up easier. Dropped your spaghetti on the floor? Sprinkle the mess with cornstarch, and it won't slide around while you try to clean it up.

Get the gravy out. To pick up a gravy stain, cover the spill with cornstarch. The starch will absorb a good deal of the grease, making it much easier for you to wash. You can also use salt or talcum powder.

Scented body powder. Add about 10 drops of your favorite fragrance to two cups of cornstarch. Mix it well and let it sit for a day. Store in a glass or plastic container.

Correction fluid

Make scuff marks disappear. You are all dressed to go out when you notice a dark mark on your white shoe. With a dab of correction fluid, you can perform a neat emergency touch-up.

Correction fluid was invented by Bette Nesmith Graham, a typist who had the bright idea of covering up her mistakes with white paint. The company she founded, Liquid Paper, became a multi-million dollar corporation. At the time of her death, half her fortune went to her son, Michael Nesmith, of the 60s pop group, the Monkees.

Decorate with snowflakes. Paint winter snowflakes on your windows for the holidays. When it's time for them to go, make a quick swipe with a plastic windshield scraper, and you are all done.

Crayons

Color away carpet stains. Sometimes the inevitable happens, and you get a spot on your carpet. Whether it's a grease stain that won't come out or a bleach spot, fix it fast with a crayon. First look through the crayon box for just the right shade to blend with your carpet, then get down and actually color over the spot. Put a piece of wax paper over it, and iron on low heat. You can reapply as needed.

Make a sun catcher. Grate small pieces of different colored crayons onto a sheet of wax paper. Place another piece of wax paper on top, and press with a hot iron until the crayon shavings are melted together. Let cool, thread a string through the top, and hang in the window.

An average child will use up 730 crayons by the time he or she is 10 years old.

Cover scratches in your furniture. Select a crayon that matches the color of your wood, soften it with a hair dryer, then rub it gently over the scratch. Take a dry rag, and wipe away any extra.

Readjust your hemline. If your jeans got shorter in the wash, no need to put them in the give-away bag. Just take out the old hems. Then, to get rid of the faded hem lines, rub them with a crayon or magic marker of the same color as the jeans. Re-hem them to fit, then iron, using a press cloth.

> Only three Crayola brand crayon names have ever been changed — flesh, Prussian blue, and Indian red. Prussian blue became midnight blue in 1958 because Crayola decided kids no longer knew Prussian history. Flesh was changed to peach in 1962 as a result of the civil rights movement. And the company recently changed Indian red to chestnut because people thought the previous name referred to the skin color of Native Americans. Crayola says the color was based on a reddish-brown pigment found near India.

Cover bleach spots. You can recolor spots on fabric that got splashed with bleach. Choose a crayon that matches the color. Heat the area to be repaired by ironing it. Color in the spot while it's warm. Then cover with waxed paper, and iron again to set the color.

Quick fix for a fender bender. To cover a scratch in your car's paint, just get a matching-color crayon. Rub the crayon deep into the scratch to hide the flaw.

Cucumbers

Repel mosquitoes. For a natural mosquito repellent that will leave you feeling cool as a ... well, you know ... try this trick. Peel and puree a cucumber. Strain the liquid into an ice cube tray and freeze it. Before you go outside, rub your face and hands with the ice cubes. Mosquitoes will stay away.

> The cucumber (which was sometimes called the "cowcumber") was one of the first vegetables to be cultivated, although many early varieties of cucumber have disappeared.

Discourage ants the natural way. Lay cucumber peels along a well-traveled ant trail, and they'll take a hike.

Tell roaches to hit the road. Chopped-up cucumbers are a natural roach repellent.

Soothe tired eyes. For a little taste of spa life, cut slices of cold cucumber, and lay two over your tired, puffy eyes, then relax for 15 minutes.

Hold your dip. A large cucumber makes a unique container for your vegetable dip. Cut it, scoop out the insides, and leave a handle in the middle. A green pepper can do the job as well, if that's your veggie of choice.

Dental floss

Loosen cookies from a cookie sheet. The next time your home-baked cookies stick to the cookie sheet, try this. Take a long piece of dental floss and slide it underneath the entire pan of cookies, and they should slide right off the sheet.

Easy way to layer a cake. Want to make a fancy, multi-layer torte? Allow your cake to cool and remove it from the pan. Take a length of dental floss and gently saw your cake into the number of layers you need. You can use this technique to slice cakes and cheesecakes into perfect, no-mess slices, as well.

Stitch a strong hold. Heavy buttons won't come off coats as easily if you sew them on with dental floss. If you need a color to match the fabric, a colored marker should do the trick. The strength of dental floss is also a plus for repairing things made from heavy-duty fabrics, like tents, duffel bags, and convertible tops.

> How often is dental floss used for its intended purpose? Four out of five people claim they floss, and half of those say they floss daily. But dentists — who are looking into these mouths — believe only one person in 10 really flosses regularly.

Restring beads. When a string of beads breaks, whether glass or pearls, finding them all can be a challenge. Make sure that doesn't happen again by restringing them on dental floss.

Truss up that bird. Dental floss is a handy helper when trussing up turkey or other poultry for roasting.

Denture tablets

Clean jewelry. Here's an easy way to get your jewelry sparkling clean. Just put it in a container of water and drop in a denture tablet. Let it soak for a couple of hours, brush with a soft toothbrush, rinse well, and dry with a soft cloth.

Clean a thermos bottle. A thermos full of hot coffee can come in handy on a cold day, but coffee can stain the inside. To remove stains, fill it with water, drop in three denture tablets, and let them fizz your thermos clean.

> The King-Seely Thermos company lost the exclusive rights to the name "thermos" after a survey found that 68 percent of Americans considered thermos a generic term for any vacuum-insulated bottle.

Bubble away toilet stains. If you've got stubborn stains in your toilet bowl, try dropping in a few denture cleaning tablets. Let it soak for a while, scrub the bowl clean, and flush those stains away.

Detergent

Clean up your dusty leaves. To get the dust and dirt off the heavy, thick leaves of your favorite houseplants, simply mix a bit of dishwashing detergent with water. Moisten a soft cloth or paper towel and gently clean the leaves.

Get rid of stains on concrete. Need to lift a nasty grease stain off your patio? Dump a generous amount of dishwashing detergent over the spot and let it sit. After a while, rinse it away with boiling water, then repeat the process.

> If you think detergent and soap are the same thing, think again. While they may perform similar tasks, they are chemically different. Soap is made from fats or oils and alkali, but detergents contain surfactants and builders. Surfactants dissolve dirt, and builders soften water so the surfactants can do their job better. That's why detergents work better in hard water than soaps do.

Wash away crayon woes. A child's crayon drawing on a vinyl wallcovering is no match for a little detergent and a lot of determination.

Make a flea trap. An easy and inexpensive way to get rid of fleas in your home is to make your own flea trap. Put a tablespoon of detergent in a shallow pan filled with water. Try not to make bubbles in the water. Then put a lamp with at least a 60-watt bulb over the water. The fleas will be attracted to the light and jump in the water. In the morning, dump out the water and dead fleas, and repeat every night until the fleas are gone.

For whiter whitewalls. Scrub down your whitewall tires with a good stiff brush and undiluted laundry detergent. They'll shine like new.

You have lots of brands to choose from today, but it wasn't until 1946 that the first clothes-washing detergent became popular. The brand was Tide, and it's still around.

Protect electrical cords. Rub down your electrical and extension cords with liquid laundry detergent to keep curious pets from munching on the cords and shocking themselves.

Make camp cleanup a snap. Coat the outside of your pots and pans with a thin layer of dishwashing detergent before you put them on the campfire, and the black soot will wash right off — no scrubbing.

Wash away garden pests. To keep aphids, spider mites, and other pests away from your garden, spray your plants with a mixture of four tablespoons of liquid dishwashing detergent and one gallon of water.

Dishwasher

Clean your car wheel covers. When those spoked wheel covers get dirty, there's no need to hand scrub them. Just put them in your dishwasher and set it on the pots and pans cycle.

Keep your kitchen germ-free. Bacteria thrive in wet places and nothing gets wetter or germier than your kitchen sponges. Every time you wipe up a spill you may be spreading bacteria from one surface to another. Eliminate this problem by running your sponges through the dishwasher. To prevent the sponge from dropping to the bottom, use a clothespin to clip the sponge to the top rack. If they're small enough, you can put sponges in the silverware basket.

Super clean your dish drainer. Every week or so, run your dish drainer through the dishwasher. This will get the grunge off those hard-to-reach places.

Say goodbye to greasy filters. Run the fan filter above your stove through the dishwashing cycle a couple of times to get rid of greasy buildup.

Ditch dust. When your dustpan and brush need an occasional washing, do it the easy way. Just stick them in the dishwasher with a load of dirty dishes.

Egg cartons

Store Christmas decorations safely. When it's time to take the tree down, don't just toss your Christmas lights into any old box. Place the bulbs inside an old egg carton, and wind the cords around the outside. Next year, no breaks, no tangles.

Electric Christmas lights were invented in 1917 by 15-year-old Albert Saddaca. He was inspired by a fire in New York City that was caused by candles on a Christmas tree. The electric lights didn't sell well the first year, but after Albert thought of painting the bulbs different colors, they began selling like hot cakes.

Store small items in drawers. Separate paper clips, safety pins, thumb tacks, and marbles. Egg cartons make great organizers for a catchall drawer.

Light a fire. Put charcoal briquettes in each compartment of a couple of cardboard egg cartons. Then you can light the egg cartons, and when the briquettes start to burn, they'll already be evenly spaced out. This is also a great way to transport just the amount of charcoal you need for a cookout or short camping trip.

"Egg"cellent game storage. If your game boxes are falling apart, and it's hard to keep small pieces from getting lost in the bottom of the closet, store them in an egg carton. Label it, and close it securely with a rubber band.

Keep track of medicine. If you have many different pills to take throughout the day, use this handy memory tool to keep track of them all. Mark the cups of an egg carton with the hours of the day, then place the pills you need to take in the appropriate cup.

Store golf balls. Empty egg cartons make perfect storage containers for your golf balls.

> Golf balls originally were smooth, but golfers soon realized that old, beat-up balls with dents and dings in them went farther. Eventually, golf balls were made with dimples because it reduces the "drag" of air as the ball travels.

Look Mamacito, no hands. Flip an empty egg carton over, and rest taco shells in the grooves. You'll be able to fill several at a time and keep them upright for serving.

Fun time for little artists. Fill the little egg spaces inside an empty egg carton with different colors of paint, and let your kids go to town. Storage and cleanup are a snap, too — just close and toss.

Make a mini museum. An empty egg carton makes a neat display case for a child's rock or seashell collection.

Protect your tender tomatoes. Don't want to bruise your tender produce on the way to the picnic? Drop your cherry tomatoes, plums, apricots, and various other small items in an empty egg carton for a safe voyage.

Make cubes for the masses. Got more guests than ice? In a pinch, Styrofoam egg cartons can serve you up some respectable ice cubes, a dozen at a time.

What's more delicate than an egg? If an egg carton can safely guard a dozen fragile eggs, it can do the same for other small breakables. Use old cartons to store all kinds of delicate treasures, such as seashells, figurines, and Christmas decorations.

Eggshells

Feed your ferns. Some plants just love eggs. Indulge them. A few days in advance, crush some calcium-rich eggshells into the water you plan to give your ferns or blooming perennials. Let the solution stand for a couple of days, shake well, then water as usual and watch your garden grow.

"Egg"cellent way to start seedlings. Save your eggshells that are cracked in half, but still intact. When it's time to plant seedlings indoors, fill each half with soil and seeds. Set the egg halves back into an empty egg carton, and grow them as usual. When they're ready to transplant, simply make a few cracks in the egg, and plant the whole thing in your garden.

Clean stains off glassware. Do you have stains on your glassware or even your china? Try soaking them in a solution of vinegar and eggshells. They should come out squeaky clean.

Brew a better cup. Add some crushed eggshells to your coffee grounds. It takes away the bitterness.

Mineral-rich water. After hardboiling eggs, hang on to the water. It's rich in minerals. After it has cooled for a while, use it to feed and water your houseplants at the same time.

Make a disposable funnel. In a jam without a funnel? Grab an egg shell, poke a small hole in the bottom, and pour away. Best of all, it's disposable, so use it for those messy or chemical jobs.

The incredible, ornamental egg. For delicate Christmas ornaments or Easter eggs you can enjoy year after year, try egg-blowing. With a needle, prick a small hole in both ends of the egg, then gently blow the contents out into a bowl. After drying for a few days, the shells can be painted, dyed, or drawn upon to create personalized works of art.

Emery boards

Rough up slippery soles. If a new pair of hard-soled shoes has you slipping and sliding, give them a few scrapes along the bottom with an emery board or nail file.

Clean a pencil eraser. A dirty eraser can leave an oily smear on your paper. But after a few swipes with an emery board, your eraser will do its job neatly again.

Erasers

Clean out the grout. Wipe away a dingy bathroom with a common circular typewriter eraser. Simply roll it along the grouting to rub it clean. Many erasers like this even come with a fine-bristled brush on the handle end to help whisk the eraser crumbs out of the corners.

Get black heel marks off floors. Getting rid of ugly black heel marks on your clean floor is easy. Just erase them with an art gum eraser.

Pencils and erasers have been around for centuries, but they didn't "get together" until 1858. That's when H.L. Lipman, who was tired of searching for an eraser whenever he made a writing error, invented a pencil with an eraser attached to one end.

Make contact with your portable phone. If your portable phone is sounding kind of fuzzy, perhaps it isn't charging properly. Check the metal contact points on the phone and the base. If they are dirty, they can't do their job properly. Clean them regularly with an eraser to keep your calls coming in loud and clear.

Erase spots from delicate wall coverings. An art gum eraser is the perfect soft solution for dealing with spots on non-washable wallpaper. Just remember to rub gently with the grain, if there is one.

Give glass a glistening glimmer. Use a blackboard eraser to make all kinds of glass surfaces shine. You can clear a fogged-up mirror or wipe a car windshield clean as a whistle.

A gentle solution for strong fabrics. If a heavy fabric like canvas or sailcloth gets dirty marks on it, try removing them with a gum eraser.

Don't let dirt fall between the cracks. Cleaning the tracks of a sliding glass door is tough work for a broom, but no problem for something as small as an eraser. Just wrap a damp cloth around it, and you'll be in the groove.

Fabric softener

Tune out dust on your television screen. Have you noticed that your television screen attracts dust? That's because of static electricity. To eliminate annoying static and prevent dust from settling back onto your screen, wipe it with a fabric softener sheet once a week. You'll cut down your dusting time and clear up your view of your favorite program at the same time. If you really want to give dust the heave-ho, spray the sheet with window cleaner before wiping.

Keep luggage fresh. You don't do much traveling, so whenever you drag your luggage out of the closet to pack, it always smells musty. Put a fabric softener sheet in your luggage before you store it away, and the next time you're ready to hit the road, your luggage will smell fresh and ready to go.

Make your iron glide. To keep your iron gliding smoothly along, occasionally run it over a fabric softener sheet.

Tame flyaway hair. It's not fear. It's static making your hair stand on end. But there's no need for the scared look. You can smooth your tresses with a fabric softener sheet, and they'll stay calmly in place.

Bring springtime indoors all winter long. To get rid of musty winter odors throughout your house, place a fabric softener sheet in your heating vents. It will also help control the static electricity inside, too.

Shine floors. A simple way to keep your floors shining is to add one cup of liquid fabric softener to half a pail of water whenever you mop.

Would you cover your floors with something called "kamptulicon?" In the 1860's, the British House of Parliament used this hard but sticky floor covering in some of its rooms. It was a forerunner of linoleum, invented by a Briton, Frederick Walton. Linoleum became popular in America when Thomas Armstrong introduced "linoleum carpets" in cheerful colors and interesting patterns.

Camping never smelled so good. Place a fabric softener sheet inside your sleeping bags to keep them fresh-smelling between uses.

Get rid of cat hair. Use a fresh fabric softener sheet to get cat hair off furniture and drapes, wherever Fluffy likes to catch a catnap.

Remove baked-on foods. If you're left with a baked-on mess to clean up, don't despair. Put a fabric softener sheet in the offensive pan, fill it with water, and let it sit overnight. The next morning, cleanup should be a breeze.

Eliminate static cling from pantyhose. Fabric softener sheets eliminate static cling from the clothes you dry, but they can also work on the ones you don't dry. To prevent your skirt from clinging to your pantyhose all day, rub a fabric softener sheet over your pantyhose after you put them on.

When different fabrics rub against each other in the dryer, electrons are transferred back and forth, creating static electricity. When one fabric clings to another, it's because one of them has more electrons than the other. Fabric softener sheets act as conductors, and they also give all the fabrics in the dryer the same surface characteristics, which helps prevent electron transfer.

Dust off those video games. Use a fabric softener sheet to remove dust from video games.

Soften up your paintbrushes. Do your brushes get stiff and hard no matter how well you clean them? Try this tip after your next paint job. Wash them as usual, then rinse in water plus one capful of fabric softener. Blot out the excess and let dry.

Repel mosquitoes. Rub a fabric softener sheet on your skin to keep mosquitoes at bay.

Clean up Venetian blinds. Use a fabric softener sheet to wipe off your blinds. They'll come out clean and repel dust, too.

Shocking solution to static electricity. If winter time means you're constantly generating static electricity in your carpet, try this easy solution. Mix one part fabric softener with five parts of water into a spray bottle. Spritz your carpet and no more shocks. Your carpet should stay cleaner as well.

Keep laundry bags and hampers fresh. Tuck a fabric softener sheet into anything that's smelly for gentle, long-lasting deodorizing.

Clean up soap scum. Keep a supply of fabric softener sheets in your bathroom for quick in-between cleanups. Your tub, faucets, and fixtures will shine like new.

Cover drain holes in flowerpots. After you've used a fabric softener sheet in the laundry, give it a second life. Just fold it a few times and place it in the bottom of the pot. The soil won't escape but excess water will easily drain out.

Make shoes smell sweetly. No more stinky sneakers. Simply tuck a new fabric softener sheet into each shoe.

> It was an ancient Anglo-Saxon tradition for the father of the bride to transfer responsibility to his new son-in-law by handing him one of the bride's shoes. This led to the modern tradition of tying shoes to the newlyweds' car.

No more slips for area rugs. Recycle foam fabric softener sheets by sewing a few to the edges of an area rug. They'll help the rug grip the floor and keep it from sliding around.

Clear the air. You gave a party without enforcing your usual no-smoking-in-the-house policy. Now your living room smells awful, and it's too cold outside to open the windows to air it out. Place a few fabric softener sheets around the room and close the door. Chances are, in a day or two, the smell will be gone. This tip works well for your car, too.

So easy sewing. Thread your needle and run it through a fabric softener sheet to prevent snarls and tangles.

Film canisters

Store leftover seed. Plastic 35 mm film canisters make handy storage containers for leftover flower or vegetable seeds. They're airtight and block out light.

Keep your valuables safe. When you work out at the gym or in your garden, or when you travel, put small items, like rings and earrings, in a plastic film canister for safe keeping.

Make eyes in the cold. Your snowman won't lose his eyes when he first begins to melt if they are made from film canisters. Just push them deep into his frozen face, and he'll have 20/20 vision until spring.

No more scrounging for coins. Fumbling for change at a tollbooth is embarrassing and annoys people waiting behind you. Keep quarters handy for tollbooths, parking meters, and phone calls by storing them in an empty film canister in your car. No more digging through your pockets or purse for loose change.

Amuse your cat. Put a coin, pebble, or anything else that will rattle inside a film canister. Your cat will have hours of fun rattling and rolling it around.

Travel with a smile. To protect your toothbrush when traveling, cut an "X" in the middle of a film canister lid, large enough to slip the handle of your toothbrush through. Insert your toothbrush head into the film canister and snap the lid shut.

> The earliest toothbrushes were small twigs mashed at one end. Some tribes in Australia and Africa still use these primitive brushes to clean their teeth. Ancient Romans owned special slaves to clean their teeth, and in some cultures, the toothbrushing process was part of religious observances.

Make an emergency sewing kit. Keep a few needles, buttons, some thread, and a couple of safety pins in a film canister for an emergency repair kit to keep in your purse or car. The next time you pop a button on your way to work, you'll be glad you did.

Never be locked out again. Put a house key in a film canister and bury it in your garden. It's safer there than under the welcome mat.

Flour

Repel ants. Keep your house free from ants by making a line of flour wherever they might enter. That's one line they won't cross.

Ripen avocados. Avocados will ripen in a hurry if you bury them in a bowl of flour.

Mix up some papier-mâché. Stir together a cup of flour with two-thirds cup of water. Cut newspaper into one- to two-inch strips. Dip each strip into the mixture and run your fingers along it to remove excess paste. Apply the strips to your form or empty container. Keep adding strips until your masterpiece is complete. Then let it dry, paint it, and coat it with varnish.

> One ingredient in varnish makes quite a long journey before it finally reaches your workshop — raw shellac or lac. The story begins in India, where a certain insect feeds on fig, soapberry, and acacia trees. This bug secretes a resin that is melted and strained to form lac. When lac is mixed with alcohol, it forms varnish. The word, lac, comes from the Hindi word "lakh," meaning 100,000. The natives say these little insects are so numerous, they swarm in lakhs.

Polish brass in an instant. Make a paste of equal parts vinegar, salt, and flour and rub in well. It is especially good for brass pulls on wooden antique furniture, since commercial cleaners can leave white marks on the wood that may require professional restoration. They can also make the brass look unnaturally bright for antique pieces. Be sure to rinse the paste off carefully after you buff it to prevent corrosion.

Track your fertilizer. When fertilizing your lawn, if you mix a little flour in with the dry fertilizer, you'll be able to see exactly where you've spread it and identify any areas you missed. Use this tip when you're planting seeds, too, and you'll never overseed one particular area.

Keep nuts in their place. If you're making a cake that calls for nuts or dried fruits in the batter, try coating them with flour before you stir them in. This will help keep them from sinking to the bottom.

Food coloring

Test your toilet. You suspect a leak somewhere in your toilet, but you can't find it. To check if the leak is coming from the inside valves, dribble a few drops of food coloring into the tank. Now don't flush, just wait it out. If the coloring comes into the bowl without your flushing, you've found your leak.

Color cut flowers. If you're not satisfied with the shade of your bouquet, you can tint the flowers with food coloring. Just put a few drops of the desired color in the vase water, add your cut flowers, and eventually the petals will turn color.

No more egg mix-ups. Do you get your hard-boiled eggs mixed up with your raw ones? If you have ever whacked an egg that you thought was hard-boiled on the side of the counter and watched in dismay as raw egg oozed down your cabinet door and onto your clean floor, then you are ready for this tip. Drop a bit of food coloring into the water next time you boil eggs. It may look like Easter in your fridge, but you'll be able to tell your eggs apart.

Furniture polish

Help shower doors stay cleaner. Spraying your glass shower doors with furniture polish or lemon oil will help keep them clean longer.

Get dust off your dustpan. If you want to get dust and dirt into your dustpan without them permanently sticking there, try this. First, wash and dry your dustpan thoroughly, and then spray it with furniture polish and buff lightly. Next time you use it, the dirt should slide right out and into the trash.

Smooth sailing in the classroom. Rub a bit of furniture polish onto the metal rings in your notebook and your pages will turn smoothly.

Garden hose

Get help with your landscape design. Planning a new flower bed? Do like the pros and work with curved shapes instead of straight lines. Lay a garden hose out on your lawn and experiment with gentle curves and arcs. When you're happy with the design, secure the hose temporarily and use a spade to mark the edge of your new border. Remove the hose and get to work digging.

If you can't beat 'em, join 'em. Don't trash your garden hose just because it has a few holes. Instead, use an awl or screwdriver to punch a few extra, larger holes into it, then use the holey hose as a soaker for your flower beds or garden.

Frighten away pests. A beaten-up garden hose takes on new life with a little paint job. Many pesky animals are terrified of snakes, so make one. After you've finished creating your reptile, lay him out by the garden as a low-lying scarecrow.

Make a bark bumper. Ropes or wires tied around trees won't cut into the bark if you first cover them with a section of old garden hose.

Come to grips with a swing set. Pieces of an old hose can make it easier for little hands to grip the chains on a swing set. Just cut sections a few inches long, slit them lengthwise, and slip them over the chains.

> Can you guess the first practical item made from rubber? Was it rain boots or automobile tires? No, it was the water hose. The inventor, Dr. B.F. Goodrich, saw the need for it in the 1870s after a friend's home was destroyed by fire. The fireman's hose, made of leather, had burst.

Dental care for your saws. To protect the teeth of a hand-saw, and protect your hand from its teeth, cut a section of garden hose and make a slit down one side. Slip the edge of the blade into this sheath when not in use. For circular saw blades, use patches of old auto-tire inner tube. Just stretch the rubber all the way around the blade and store.

Make buckets easier on your hands. If you've ever had to carry a heavy bucket with a wire handle, you know it can really dig into your fingers. Next time, make it a little more comfortable with a piece of old garden hose. Just cut a short piece, slit it, and slip it over the handle of the bucket. You'll have a little cushion and a lot more comfortable grip.

Clean up the underworld. To keep your car's undercarriage clean and rust free, give it a good spring cleaning once a year. Put a sprinkler or a "lawn-soaker" hose under the car for a half hour or so and let it rinse away the salt and debris of the long winter.

Bumper guard your baby's walker. Baby walkers were a great invention except for the marks they can leave on walls. Solve this problem with a garden hose. Cut the desired length, split it down the middle, and slip it over the rim of the walker.

Organize workshop cords. If you've got power cords trailing all over your work area, you might like this tip for keeping them safely out of the way. Cut a short length of old garden hose and slit it lengthwise on a diagonal. Spread open the diagonal and tack the hose into the wall, ceiling, or other convenient location. Then push

your cord through the slit until it moves freely in your new cord hanger. You can attach several pieces of hose in this manner to "guide" power cords over a large distance.

Give your pliers a helping hand. Cut a length of garden hose and place it over the ends of your pliers to make gripping it more comfortable. Not only that — you'll be insulated from electrical shocks, and the hose will make it easier to hang your pliers on a wall hook.

Move furniture like a pro. When moving big items by yourself, line your securing ropes with small sections of garden hose at the points where they contact the corners. These rubber barriers will keep the rope from marring the finish and protect the item from other dings and collisions.

Squeegee your deck. Slit a piece of garden hose and slip it over the tines of a rake to make a king-size squeegee. You can then hose off your porch, deck, or patio and squeegee it dry.

Garlic

Keep dogs away from your plants. If your neighbor's pesky dog loves to "visit" all the beautiful plants in your yard, here's a harmless solution. Put a few cloves of garlic and some hot peppers, the hotter the better, in a blender and puree. Mix in a little water and pour this aromatic solution around the area you want to protect. The odor will offend the dog's delicate sense of smell, and he'll go looking for more attractive places to do his business.

Repel aphids. Are aphids destroying your tender new plants? Try this recipe for "terrible tea." Mince two cloves of garlic and put them in a pint of boiling water. After cooling, strain out the garlic bits and put the remaining liquid in a spray bottle. Spray new shoots and flower buds to protect them from aphid assaults.

Repair a cracked vase. If you've got a hairline crack in your favorite vase, take a clove of garlic and rub it along the inside. Let it dry. The crack should be sealed.

Tell plant pests to bug off. Tuck a clove of garlic into the dirt beside your houseplant and many common pests will run screaming.

For the strongest garlic taste, use the central, yellowish strip inside each clove. It's called the "lily."

Ward off fleas and ticks. Help keep your dogs or cats pest-free with a little garlic. If they'll tolerate it, place a few cloves in their bedding. And try mixing a touch of garlic juice in with their drinking water.

One more recipe to clear out bugs. Snails, caterpillars, and other rampaging pests don't like garlic. If you can't drive them out, try spraying this potent brew around the yard. Blend three garlic heads into six tablespoons of mineral oil and let the mixture sit, unrefrigerated, for two days. Add one pint of hot water and one tablespoon of oil-base soap and refrigerate. When you're ready to spray, combine just two tablespoons of this stinky mix with four pints of water, and watch those snails speed away.

Wage war on weevils. Place a few cloves of garlic in with your dried beans and grains, and you'll never see another weevil again.

Gelatin

Style your hair. Dissolve a teaspoon of gelatin in a cup of warm water, and you have an instant setting lotion for your hair.

Crisper curtains. When you wash sheer curtains, do they come out limp and wrinkled? Instead of starching and ironing them, dissolve a packet of plain gelatin in hot water and add to your final rinse. You'll have crisp, wrinkle-free curtains.

Whip up a better topping. Adding gelatin to whipping cream will give it extra holding power for prettier desserts. Simply mix one teaspoon of gelatin in two tablespoons of water. Heat until dissolved. Then add to one cup of heavy cream and whip.

Bring back the sheen to polished cotton. Polished cotton will look shiny again, and have more body, if you put a packet of plain gelatin in the final rinse cycle.

Stiffen delicate fabrics. One packet of unflavored gelatin dissolved in two quarts of hot water makes a good substitute for starch on delicate fabrics, like batiste and organdy.

Glass containers

Set a pretty table. Use a decorative, wide-mouth vase or glass jar as an unusual napkin holder on your breakfast or lunch table.

No-mess way to paint. If you've got drawer knobs or pulls to paint, you know how hard it is to keep the paint only where you want it. Try setting the knobs into the openings of bottles. You'll be able to turn the bottles as you paint, leave the knobs to dry, and never get a drop of paint on your fingers.

Resize a vase. You've chosen the vase that has the look you want, but it's too large for your bouquet. No need to look for another container. Just put a slender olive jar inside the vase. It won't be noticed, even in a clear vase. And the flowers inside it will stand up instead of flopping over the sides.

Store touch-up paint. When you finish painting, store a little of the leftover paint in an empty nail polish bottle. It's perfect for doing touch-ups later. Just make sure you label the bottle.

Coasters by the dozen. Glass containers, such as pickle jars, have flat, round lids that can quickly be turned into coasters. If you like your drink trays a little fancier, paint the tops and slip a circle of cork into the bottoms.

In 1810, Napoleon, believing "an army travels on its stomach," offered 12,000 francs to anyone who could find a way to preserve provisions for his soldiers. A French chef named Nicholas Appert won the reward with food boiled in glass jars and sealed with cork stoppers.

Make a potpourri pot. Fill a used jelly jar with some potpourri, punch a few holes in the lid, and you've got a sweet-smelling addition to an otherwise musty closet.

Turn pests into pets. Kids like bugs. But if they want them in the house, they'd better keep them locked up. Punch a few holes in an old pickle jar, and little Jimmy can watch his favorite spider or grasshopper sit on a twig for hours.

Hang a fishbowl. Goldfish don't care much whether you bought their bowl at a fancy pet store or ate pickles out of it last weekend. Transform that glass jar into an interesting conversation piece by adding a little gravel, a couple of swimmers, and suspending it from the ceiling in a macramé hanger.

Gloves

Clean mini-blinds the quick and easy way. Turn a fleece-lined glove inside out, put it on, and spray the fingers with your favorite cleaner. Then run your fingers between the slats of the blinds.

Or you can slip on cloth gloves over rubber gloves. Dip your fingers in a solution of one teaspoon ammonia and one quart water. Rub each slat between your fingers and thumb.

Give a hand to do-it-yourself rubber bands. Need extra heavy-duty rubber bands? Cut wide strips from an old rubber glove.

Watch out!

Don't wear rubber gloves when you polish your silverware or use rubber bands to hold pieces of it together because rubber will darken silver.

A second career for secondhand gloves. Thin or worn gloves can still provide comfort. Use them as liners for thicker gloves in winter, or wear them under rubber gloves to cut down on that sticky, rubbery feel.

Entertain with finger puppets. Story time is more fun when finger puppets tell the tale. A permanent marker and a few fingers from an old cotton glove can quickly give you a whole cast of characters. To be even more creative, add features with buttons and yarn.

The Vietnamese have performed water puppetry, called mua roi nuoc, for over 1,000 years. The puppeteers stand waist deep in water and control their puppets with bamboo rods. The characters seem to magically leap out of the water onto their floating stage.

Splish-splash baby's takin' a bath. Babies can get pretty slippery and squirmy when you're trying to give them a bath. To increase your gripping power and keep that wet infant from slipping out of your protective grasp, wear a pair of cotton gloves.

Make a fun ice pack. Fill a transparent rubber glove with water and freeze for an inexpensive ice pack. If you need to use it for an injured child, add food coloring or slip a small toy inside to distract him from his injury.

Give pet hair the brushoff. Pet hair on the furniture can be a mess and an embarrassment. An easy way to get rid of it is to put on a rubber glove and rub your hand over the upholstery. You'll find the pet hair rolled up into an easily removable ball.

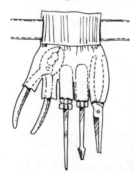

A second life for gloves in the toolshed. If your work gloves are split at the fingers, don't toss them out. Instead, cut off the fingers, make a couple of slits along the cuff, and thread it onto your belt. It makes a handy place to store your screwdrivers or pliers while working.

Cap broom handles. Cut a finger off an old rubber glove and slip it over the end of your broom. Then when you have to prop it against a wall, the rubber will keep it from sliding, and you'll be protecting your wall from scratches at the same time. This tip also works well on outdoor utensils, like hoes and shovels.

Glue

Seal ends of newly pruned plants. When you prune your plants, seal the ends of stems and branches with Elmers glue to prevent the plants from drying out too quickly. This also keeps insects from feasting on the tender, newly exposed part of the plant.

Stop traveling rugs. If an area rug doesn't want to stay in place, use your glue gun to make a zigzag or other pattern on the bottom. Let it cool and turn it over. It should stay put. Out of glue? Sew a rubber jar ring to the bottom.

Tighten a screw hole. Holes sometimes get too large to hold in a screw. Here's the solution. Soak a cotton ball in ordinary white glue, stuff it into the hole, and let it dry for 24 hours. Then try your screw.

Subdue a stubborn squeak. A little glue placed in just the right crack can silence a creaky floorboard forever.

Keep buttons on clothing. Some manufacturers give you extra buttons with a new garment. But you can save yourself the hassle of sewing on replacements if you don't lose them in the first place. Before you wear a new item of clothing, squeeze a dot of super glue in the center over the threads. Your button should stay in place, and you can use those extra buttons in a more creative project.

Modern super glues stick better than the old-fashioned kind because they are synthetically made from petroleum chemicals. Older types of glues were made from natural sources, like gums from plants. The molecules in super glue undergo a chemical change when exposed to the slightest moisture, which is why they stick to your skin so well.

Remove a splinter without pain. Got a splinter? Don't drag out the instruments of torture. Dab the area with a little white glue. Let it dry, then peel off the glue and the splinter. This works for cactus needles, too.

Plaster in a jiff. A few small cracks in the ceiling don't have to mean a whole new plaster job. Just mix a little white glue with baking soda, and use the paste to cover the small cracks. If the ceiling isn't white, use food coloring to match the color of the plaster.

Stick to a good starch substitute. Old-fashioned powdered starch really works well to stiffen doilies, but it may be hard to find. Plain white glue makes a good — and fast — substitute. Just brush some on your doily.

Glycerin

Wash away oily fabric stains. Glycerin is a grease cutter that can usually be found with laundry products at the supermarket. It works well to remove oily stains on most washable fabrics except acetate, triacetate, and rayon. Make a solution of one tablespoon each of glycerin and liquid dishwashing detergent and eight tablespoons of water. Shake these together in a squeeze bottle, then apply directly to the stain. Let it work for several minutes before rinsing.

Make defrosting the refrigerator easier. If you don't have a frost-free refrigerator, you probably find defrosting a big hassle. Fortunately, you can speed things up next time by using this tip. After defrosting, wipe the sides of the freezer compartment with glycerin. When it's time to defrost again, the ice will come off much easier.

It took many years and many less-than-successful attempts before the modern refrigerator was invented. An early system, designed by Raoul Pictet of Switzerland in 1874, did not end up helping housewives but was eventually used to create the world's first artificial skating rink in London.

Remove alcohol stains. If you spill alcohol on your clothing or a table linen, treat the stain immediately. Even though it starts out clear and fairly harmless looking, it can turn brown quickly. The longer this kind of stain sits, the more difficult it is to get out. Put a few tablespoons of glycerin — which you can buy at the drugstore — in a sink of cold water. Soak the garment in this solution, then rinse with a mixture of cold water and half a cup of white vinegar.

Defog mirrors. Before you get in the shower, moisten a cloth with glycerin and spread it across your bathroom mirror. When you're ready to dry off, your mirror will be steam-free.

The superstition that breaking a mirror brings seven years of bad luck has been around since ancient times. A real reason for fear was introduced in the 15th century when the first glass mirrors with silver backings were made. They were very expensive, so only the wealthy could afford them. A servant who broke one was in big trouble — perhaps for longer than seven years.

Soften plastic. The easiest way to clean your plastic shower curtain is to toss it in the washer. Help keep it soft and pliable by adding a few ounces of glycerin to the rinse water.

Hair dryer

Remove crayon marks from wallpaper. You treasure your children's artwork but not on your new wallpaper. To easily remove crayon marks, heat the wax with a blow dryer then wipe it off with a paper towel. The same process works to remove candle wax from furniture and countertops.

Defog mirrors. You climb out of a hot shower, and your mirror is fogged up. Instead of wiping it with a towel and streaking it, use your hair dryer to blow the fog away. You'll get a clear view quickly, with no streaks.

Clean silk flowers. Your feather duster doesn't seem to make a dent in the dust accumulating on your favorite floral arrangement. Try using your hair dryer on the lowest setting to blow the dust off silk or dried flowers.

What do the vacuum cleaner and the electric blender have in common? They both contributed to the invention of the modern hair dryer. Early advertisements for the Pneumatic Cleaner suggested drying hair with the exhaust of the vacuum cleaner. Efforts to make an electric blender resulted in the development of a small motor. Together they made a lightweight, handheld dryer possible.

Quick dry that water spot. You're dressed and ready for work when you discover water spots on your clothes. Luckily, your hair dryer is still handy for a quick blow dry, and you're on your way.

Thaw frozen pipes. When your pipes freeze, your hair dryer may be the best tool to thaw them out. A hair dryer set on high will thaw frozen pipes slowly. If you use a propane torch, you could heat the water too quickly, causing steam to form and bursting your pipes.

Travel light with a portable clothes dryer. No need to pack a lot of undergarments. Just wash those unmentionables in the bathroom sink and quick dry them with your hair dryer.

Lift off shelf paper the easy way. You're ready to change the shelf paper in your cabinets, but you dread the hassle of removing the old paper. Just warm it up with a blow dryer. That should loosen the adhesive enough so the paper will peel off easily.

Blow away wrinkles. Your plastic shower curtain or tablecloth has been packed away and now it's wrinkled. You can't iron plastic, so what do you do? Just blow away those wrinkles with your hair dryer. As the plastic gets warm, the wrinkles fall out.

Ouch-less first aid. Removing adhesive bandages can be painful. Usually, you just grit your teeth, rip, and hope it's over quickly. Here's a better way. Use your hair dryer to warm and soften the adhesive. This will make changing bandages virtually painless.

Soothe itching under a cast. Got a cast? Can't scratch? Don't despair — just shake some baby powder inside the opening of your cast and blow it in with a hair dryer. Just be sure to use the cool setting.

Make some modern-day bellows. Use your hair dryer on a low setting to get the fire going in your fireplace or wood stove. Beats having to blow and blow and blow.

Tell dust to blast-off. Picture frames with lots of carvings can be difficult to clean. Instead of trying to dust them the usual way, set your hair dryer on cool and give them a quick pass. You can use this tip for other hard-to-clean items around the house, just be aware that you're not actually picking up any dust, you're blowing it somewhere else.

Remove sticky decals. Ever try getting bathtub decals off? It can be a back-breaking, fingernail-bending process. Instead, set your hair dryer on the hottest setting, and let it blow on the decals. The heat should loosen the adhesive enough so they peel right off.

Find relief from chickenpox. If someone you love is suffering from chickenpox, you're probably suffering right along with him. Help make the unbearable itching bearable by turning on the hair dryer. Use the cool or warm settings — never hot. A little warm or cool air on the skin can be welcome relief.

Get rid of melted plastic. You forgot about the plastic bread wrapper that melted on the hot stove top burner while you were fixing dinner. Should you turn the heat back on to scrape it off? There's a better way that gives you more control over the temperature. Use hot air from your hair dryer to soften the plastic. Then just scrape it off with a putty knife.

Give your engine a warm boost. Car won't start in cold weather? Try a few minutes' worth of hot air from your hair dryer aimed at the carburetor.

Hair spray

Give bugs the spray. If you don't have bug spray handy when a pest starts buzzing around your head, use hair spray. It will make the bug's wings stiff and sticky. He'll drop like a stone and then you can swat him.

Preserve flower arrangements. Spritzing hair spray on greenery or baby's breath will help it stay fresh-looking longer.

Remove ink stains from clothing. You've had a bad day. Your favorite ink pen leaked all over your favorite skirt. You may have to buy a new pen, but the skirt can be saved with an old remedy for ink spots. Just spray hair spray on the stained area, blot until the stain comes up, and wash as usual.

> Around 2697 B.C., a Chinese philosopher perfected a mixture of soot from pine smoke, lamp oil, gelatin of donkey skin, and musk. He called it India Ink.

Stiffen ruffled curtains. If you want the ruffles on your curtains to stand out, rather than drooping unattractively, try spraying them with hair spray.

Turn your child's artwork into a family heirloom. Give artwork a quick layer of hair spray, and the colors will stay brighter longer.

Thread a needle with ease. Spritz a bit of hair spray on your fingers and rub it onto the end of your thread. Let it dry and you'll have a sharp point to slip through a needle.

Keep that zipper up. Got a zipper that's always sneaking down? Spray it. That's right. Cover the rest of the garment so it doesn't get ruined and spray hair spray onto your zipper. Let it dry and no more worries. For this to work, make sure your hair spray contains lacquer.

Most inventions go through many changes and many names before becoming the product we know today, and the zipper is no exception. Back in 1851, the first device to hold pieces of fabric together was called the Automatic Continuous Clothing Closure. Over the next 50 years, the design and the name were modified several times. It became the Clasp Locker, the Judson C-curity Fastener, the Separable Fastener, and then, finally, the zipper.

Give plant lice a new "do." African violets are often attacked by little critters called plant lice. To get rid of them, gather up your spray and a plastic bag. Coat the inside of the bag with hair spray then pop it over your plant and tie it shut. Leave it on for only a day.

Emergency pantyhose repair. You've got a run in your pantyhose and no nail polish in sight. Spritz a small amount of hair spray onto the run and let it dry completely. You should make it through the day worry-free.

Keep that shine. You worked hard to shine up your sparkling white shoes. After the polish has dried, take just a little more time to give them a quick coat of hair spray. It will seal the polish and make your shine last longer.

Hangers

Remove static cling from clothing or hair. Static can make your hair stand on end and make your skirt embarrassingly clingy. One simple solution is to run a wire coat hanger over your hair or skirt, or between your skirt and slip. The static electricity will transfer from you to the wire, and you should be static free.

Make marshmallow roasters. If you're roasting hot dogs or marshmallows over a campfire, straighten out a few wire coat hangers to use as skewers.

> The hot dog got its name from a 1906 cartoon that showed a dachshund inside a frankfurter bun.

Blow gigantic bubbles. Small children delight in chasing bubbles. Keep them happy and occupied by making Goliath-size bubbles with a wire hanger. Simply bend the wire into a circle with a handle. Pour the bubble solution onto a cookie sheet, dip the hanger, and pull slowly through the air.

Pack a handy camping tool. Toss in a few coat hangers,  the kind with cardboard tubes on the bottom, the next time you go camping. When you get settled, unhook the tube from the wire, slip a roll of paper towels over the tube, and hook the wire back in. Hang it up on a convenient tree branch, and you've got towels at your fingertips. This idea works for toilet paper, too.

Skim your pool. Keeping a pool clean involves a lot of hard work and expense, but at least you can make your own pool skimmer. Just bend a coat hanger into a circle and straighten the hook. Cut the legs off a pair of pantyhose and attach the panty part to the wire circle, and sew up the opening.

Put the power back in your flush. If your toilet doesn't seem to be flushing as forcefully as it used to, perhaps the small holes just under the rim of the bowl have become clogged with lime or mineral deposits. Bend the end of a wire coat hanger into the proper angle and gently poke the holes clean.

Believe it or not, the water closet began quite nobly. In 1596, Sir John Harrington, a very talented inventor and godson to Queen Elizabeth, set about making a "necessary" for his godmother and himself. Although the queen used the device he fashioned, Harrington was so ridiculed for his invention that he never built another one.

Make a bookend. If your books keep falling over on your desk, make a bookend out of a hanger. Just snip off the hook with wire cutters and bend it into a 90-degree angle. Slide one end under your books, and the other end will hold them up.

Keep vents blowing strong. The outdoor vent from your clothes dryer can easily become clogged with hair, lint, and other debris. The best way to keep it clear and blowing free is to reach in there every now and then with a straightened coat hanger and pull it all out.

Store hardware the easy way. For an easily accessible, highly visible way to store the nuts and washers in your workshop, untwist the ends of a few wire coat hangers and run the hardware through. When you need one, just slide it off.

Kick rust out the door. Your car doors probably have drainage holes along their bottom edges that are designed to drain moisture and keep rust from forming. If they get clogged, they can't do their job. Keep the holes in good working order by cleaning them with a wire hanger once a year.

Stake your flowers. Certain flowers, like gladiolas, tend to grow tall and spindly. To keep them from falling over, use a straightened coat hanger as a stake. If you form a loop at one end, the flower can grow right up through it.

Clear clogs from vacuum hoses. Has your vacuum lost its pulling power? Unwind a hanger and bend one end into a hook. Insert it into the vacuum cleaner hose to pull out whatever has it stopped up.

> The first motorized cleaning devices simply blew dirt around — not a perfect solution. Hubert Booth, a British engineer, wanted to prove his idea of a new design that sucked up dirt instead. He put a handkerchief over his mouth, knelt down on a dirty floor, and sucked in air. The handkerchief caught the dirt, and he went on to build one of the first filtered vacuum cleaners.

Make a hose highway. If your garden hose must run over a flower bed to get where it needs to go, give it an alternate route with a few coat hangers. Cut the hooks off the hangers and bend what's left into the shape of an "M." Stick them in the ground making a raised path across your flowers, then guide your hose into the bend of the hanger. Voilá — a garden monorail.

Hang a birdhouse. Wire coat hangers make good, sturdy lines for hanging birdhouses outside. Attach them with any sort of wire, just don't use string. String and rope are no match for a squirrel's sharp teeth.

Plug up caulking tubes. Cut the hook end off a wire coat hanger and use it to stop up the opening of a tube of caulking or other such material.

Become a topiary master. Wire hangers become garden art when you recycle them into beautiful topiary frames. Just bend the hanger into whatever shape you like, then unbend the hook and drive it into the ground. Plant dwarf ivy around the base and keep an eye on its vines, making sure they attach themselves to the wire.

Before long, the ivy will have transformed your old hanger into a little green man or animal, or your favorite letter of the alphabet.

> The word topiary comes from the Latin "topia" meaning ornamental gardening. It dates back to 1592 and means the art of training, cutting, and trimming trees or shrubs into odd or ornamental shapes.

Easy cleanup after a painting party. You were lucky enough to have friends help you paint your walls, but now you have several messy paintbrushes. No problem. You can clean them all at once. Just suspend them in a can of solvent by running a wire coat hanger through the holes in the paintbrush handles and bending the wire down over the sides of the can.

Dry those wet sneakers. You can hang up freshly washed sneakers and other washable shoes to dry by bending both sides of a hanger up. Hang the hanger on a rod and slip a shoe over each upturned edge.

Make a miniature greenhouse. You can start your seedlings in the garden early if you have the proper protection. Cut the hooks off of wire coat hangers. Straighten the wires, then bend them into U-shapes. Press them into the soil over the rows, spaced about 12 inches apart. Drape clear plastic over them and anchor with rocks or bricks. Leave the ends open so air can circulate. On sunny days remove the plastic. You can quickly replace it when temperatures drop. When frost is no longer a threat, pull up your greenhouse and store it until next year.

Ice cube trays

Handy frozen veggies. If you've got extra onions, celery, peppers, or other seasoning vegetables, go ahead and chop them up. Place a couple of tablespoons into each compartment of an ice cube tray. Fill with water and freeze. Put the frozen cubes into labeled freezer bags. Next time your favorite hot recipe calls for chopped veggies, you're ready to go.

Organize your jewelry. Tired of digging through your jewelry box for a matching pair of earrings? Separate them by using ice cube trays — one pair in each "cube." You can also put rings, pins, and necklaces in the compartments, and the trays will stack neatly in a drawer.

Save that soup. Whenever you have just a little leftover soup or stew, you can pour it into an ice cube tray and freeze. It will keep longer than it would in the refrigerator, and the next time you make soup, you can just add the extra cubes to the pot.

Ice cubes

Remove gum from clothing. Every time this happens you swear your children will never get chewing gum again. But right now, you need to get the stuck-on gum out of your daughter's Sunday dress. Rub an ice cube over the gum to harden it. Then you can scrape it off with a spoon or other utensil, and wash as usual.

> Chewing gum has been around for over 900 years. The ancient Greeks chewed mastic gum, a resin from the bark of the mastic tree. They used it to clean their teeth and freshen their breath. Today, the average American chews 300 sticks of gum a year.

Fluff up your carpet. If you've got areas of carpet mashed down from heavy furniture, fluff them back up by placing an ice cube in each "dent." Let it melt, then come back with an old toothbrush, toothpick, coin, or just your fingers to perk up the nap.

Remove fat from soup. You're on a diet, and you're trying hard to eat low-fat. Try sliding a few ice cubes into your soups and stews to remove excess fat. The fat will congeal around the cubes as they melt, and you can fish it all out with a spoon. Reheat, and you have an ultra-low-fat dish to enjoy.

Easy indoor gardening. If your houseplants overflow every time you water them, try dropping a few ice cubes on the soil instead. They will melt slowly with no mess. This is also a great tip for plants that are too high to reach easily with the watering can or for no-spill watering of Christmas trees.

> The largest recorded iceberg, 208 miles long and 60 miles wide, was sighted in 1956 in the South Pacific Ocean by the U.S.S. Glacier.

Keep pet's water fresh. On really hot days, make sure your pet has fresh, cool water to drink all day long. Drop a few ice cubes into his water bowl in the morning.

A cool way to take medicine. If the taste of cough syrup or other medicine makes it hard to swallow, try sucking an ice cube first. Your taste buds will temporarily deaden from the cold, and that icky medicine will slide right down. Great tip for young children.

Remove a splinter painlessly. Just numb your finger with ice before you dig a sticker out, and it won't hurt.

No more stamp-licking. If you've got lots of envelopes to send out, don't lick all those stamps. Place a couple of ice cubes in a small bowl, and simply rub the stamp over a cube. Your tongue will thank you.

> Can you beat this? In 1995, Dean Gould of England licked and affixed 450 stamps in four minutes to set a world record.

Take the heat out before freezing. Don't send your freezables right from the oven to the icebox. Cool them off first. Put hot pans in a sink full of ice water until they've cooled. This will help your food freeze more quickly, and your freezer won't have to work as hard, which means you'll save money.

Fresh-tasting rice the second time around. Reheat leftover rice in the microwave with an ice cube on top. The added moisture will really perk up the taste.

> To get more flavor from a meal, alternate bites of one food with bites of another. The first second or so of taste stimulation is the most powerful, so the following bite of the same food may have only half the flavor of the first. To really savor each morsel, switch stimulants by changing foods.

Degrease the disposal. Fatty foods can do a number on garbage disposals. If yours is clogged with a greasy mess, throw a few ice cubes in, and run it. The cold will help the fat congeal to a point where the machine can deal with it.

Inner tubes

Big bands are back. Use the inner tubing from a bicycle tire or a very old car tire to make oversized rubber bands. Such strong rubber can serve as a powerful clamp when gluing large things together or to keep cargo on the roof rack of your car.

> The earliest two-wheeled, foot-propelled vehicle was built in the 1600s and was a wooden beam attached to wheels but with no handlebar — the rider had to steer with his feet. Soon, the design improved to include handlebars, pedals, and iron tires. But it wasn't until the late 1800s that a machine similar to the modern bicycle was produced.

Cut and paste. If you've got inflatables, you're going to need patches. Pieces of inner tubing can be cut and used as patches when holes or leaks spring up. Just rough up the edge of the hole with sandpaper, then use rubber cement to keep the patch in place.

Make a totally tubular toy. Want a slingshot that really launches 'em? Tie a length of rubber inner tube between the prongs of a forked stick. Tom Sawyer would be green with envy.

The longest slingshot distance was 1,565 feet, 4 inches.

Let slipping rugs lie. Does your area rug slide around on your hardwood floor? Put the brakes on it by stitching a few patches of old inner tubing to the underside.

Tie off a leaky pipe. A sudden plumbing crisis can be quickly, if temporarily, brought under control if you wrap the leak tightly with an inner tube, and tie it off.

Iron

Lift out grease spots. To get grease stains out of wallpaper, first blot the spot with a paper towel to soak up what you can. Next, hold a piece of absorbent paper or a paper sack over the spot, and press down on it with a warm iron — not too hot and no steam. The stain should lift onto the sack. Repeat as necessary using a fresh sack.

Hot tip for repairing furniture. If you've got a dent in your wood furniture, don't despair. As long as no wood fibers have been broken — you'll have to look at the damage carefully to determine this — you can literally iron the dent out. Grab a damp cloth, and place it over the dent. Set your iron on medium, and hold it on the cloth. When the cloth has dried, re-dampen it, and apply the iron again. Repeat this until the dent is lifted.

Smooth down peeling tiles. Nothing's uglier than peeling floor tile. If your vinyl is coming up at the corners, don't try to glue it down. Instead, hold a warm iron to the surface to soften the adhesive underneath. That will let you pull the tile up completely. Then you can coat the back more thoroughly with a new layer of adhesive.

No more carpet dents. When you move a big piece of furniture, it often leaves four little calling cards embedded in the carpet. Get rid of them quickly by laying a damp towel across the indentations and pressing lightly with an iron.

Remove water marks from wood. Someone left a glass of water on your coffee table, and now you have a white ring to deal with. Cover the spot with a few blotters or tissues, and press it with your electric iron. Use a warm setting. If it doesn't disappear, rub it in the direction of the grain with a little camphorated oil on a soft cloth. Be sure to remove all the oil since it can damage the wood.

Ladder

Organize an herb garden. An old wooden ladder makes an ideal herb garden organizer. Just lay it on the ground, fill the spaces with soil, and plant different herbs in each section.

Set up a temporary buffet. When planning a party, you may discover you need more space for the food and drinks. A quick solution is to use two ladders with a board between them to create a serving area.

> Everyone knows it's supposed to be bad luck to walk under a ladder. This superstition probably originated when criminals had to walk under a ladder on their way to the hangman's noose, while the hangman himself stepped around the ladder.

Create a rustic trellis. A rickety old ladder isn't safe for climbing, but it can make an interesting trellis for climbing roses or other vines. Old rakes and other long-handled garden tools can also serve as unique trellises.

Hang pots and pans. Suspend a ladder from your kitchen ceiling with rope or wire, and you have an unusual hanger for your pots, pans, and utensils.

Lemons

Clean yellowed ivory. If you have ivory-handled silverware or other old ivory items, you know they can turn yellow with age. A natural way to restore the original color is to rub the ivory with a piece of lemon dipped in salt.

Give wood an extra coat of protection. When wiping down your wooden furniture, give it an extra boost of protection from the elements with a lemon solution. Start with one quart of mineral oil and add 10 drops of lemon extract. Don't use too much, and be sure to wipe the furniture down afterward with a soft cloth.

Lighten up. If life gives you dark, dull hair, don't make lemonade. Use that tangy juice to lighten it up. To make a lemon rinse, mix one tablespoon of lemon juice into a gallon of water.

Clean out your microwave. If you've got hardened food on the inside of your microwave, don't scratch the finish with harsh cleaners. Instead, mix three tablespoons of lemon juice into one and a half cups of water in a microwave-safe bowl. Microwave on high for 10 minutes at the most. Then just wipe off the softened food with a dish rag.

> The first microwave oven weighed 750 pounds and stood 5 feet, 6 inches tall. It was used only in places where large quantities of food had to be cooked quickly, like restaurants, railroad cars, and cruise ships.

Freshen your garbage disposal. Your garbage disposal can develop some interesting smells. Eliminate those odors by putting some ice cubes and lemon rinds into the disposal and turning it on. It will come out smelling lemon fresh.

Superclean your fingertips. Fingertips and nails in need of a quick cleaning? Churn them through a halved lemon. They'll come out remarkably clean, inside and out.

Put a gleam on your fireplace. After washing and drying your slate hearth, coat it with lemon oil for a killer shine.

Remove mineral deposits. Half a lemon makes a handy way to apply lemon juice to mineral deposits on a faucet. Let it soak in for a while, wipe off, and rinse. Repeat if needed.

According to the 1998 Guinness Book of World Records, the largest lemon ever grown weighed 8 pounds, 8 ounces.

Shine stainless steel. Make those pots and pans brighter, both inside and out. Just rub them with lemon juice on a cloth. Out of lemon juice? Vinegar works just as well.

Dry up blemishes. Instead of spending money on astringents or acne medications, try dabbing blemishes several times a day with lemon juice.

Repel fleas. For a natural flea repellent, chop up two lemons in a quart of water. Boil for an hour, and then let it sit overnight. Strain the liquid and spray on your pet.

Fleas were responsible for transmitting the plague from infected rats to people. Because of this, these tiny insects have been responsible for more deaths than all the wars in history combined.

Out of bleach? No worries. Do you have stains? Clean them naturally with lemon juice. Cut a lemon in half, and rub it on a fruit juice stain. And get rid of rust or tea stains on fabric by applying lemon juice, then salt. Let the item dry in the sun, then wash normally.

Freshen stale air. If you're going to leave your home empty while on vacation, you don't want to return to a house that smells musty. Before you go, cut a lemon in half. Put each half in a saucer, and place them in rooms at opposite sides of the house. When you return, it will be to the smell of fresh air.

Keep fruit from turning brown. You want your fruit salad to look perfect for the party, but it would save your schedule if you could chop up the fruit ahead of time. Go ahead. Just toss it all in some lemon juice, and it won't turn brown. The fruit will stay fresh-looking, and the flavor will remain fruity.

Clean up Spot's spots. If your dog or cat has an indoor accident, you need to get rid of every trace or else the animal will probably repeat the mistake. First, wipe and scoop up as much as you can, then put down lemon juice or vinegar to help with the odor. Scrub the area with warm soapy water until the stain is gone. Finally, rub it down with an old rag dipped in ammonia.

Are you tired of cleaning up after Fluffy and Fido? Perhaps you need this little invention — a pet toilet. It was actually patented in 1980 and consists of an attachment that sits on top of your conventional toilet. A ramp leads up to the device and after your pet does his duty, a sensor automatically opens the trap door and flushes.

Bleach thyself. If your fingernails or toenails are looking a little yellow, or the skin on your feet is a funny color, go for the produce. Cut up a lemon, and rub the juices into the areas that are discolored.

Clean odors from your cutting board. That cutting board can get pretty rank after a few rounds of onions or garlic. To help lift the stink such foods leave behind, rub the surface with a fresh slice of lemon. Afterwards, just rinse and wipe dry, and voila, no lingering odor.

Keep cats at bay. If you've got cats that love to lie in your flower beds, scatter lemon peels around their favorite plants. They don't like the smell of citrus.

Make fluffy rice every time. Add a teaspoon of fresh lemon juice to the water first thing, and your rice will never be sticky again.

> Rice is actually the common name for a species of annual herbs in the grass family. It has been cultivated for more than 7,000 years and is the principal food for almost half the world's population.

Soften paintbrushes. Sometimes, no matter what you do, your paintbrushes end up hard and stiff. Give them new life with a bit of lemon juice. First, bring the juice to a boil and dip in your brush. Remove the pan from the heat, and let your brush soak for about 15 minutes. Wash with soap, and your brushes should come out soft and ready to use.

End cold sores on a sour note. If you're troubled by a fever blister or cold sore, dab a little lemon juice on. You'll be smiling again in no time.

Magnets

Remove steel wool particles from wood. When you're refinishing wood furniture, you may use steel wool to give it a final light sanding before staining or painting. But you don't want any tiny particles left to mar your smooth finish. The answer is to go over the surface of the furniture with a magnet to pick up any steel dust left behind. Then use a sticky "tack cloth" for a final dusting.

Retrieve pins and needles. Can't find a needle you just know you dropped on your carpet? Go over the floor with a magnet before you find that needle with your bare feet.

Hook that lost silverware. Got silverware or other metal objects lost down the kitchen drain? "Bait" a piece of heavy string with a small magnet, and go fishing.

Handy storage for your broom. Attach a magnet to your broom with a screw, about halfway down the handle. Then you can store it attached to the side of your refrigerator, between the refrigerator and the wall.

Smart and safe tool organization. Attach a strong magnetic strip to an area above your workbench for light hand tools like scissors, screwdrivers, files, etc. They'll be out of reach from little hands and always where you can find them.

Marshmallows

Stop ice cream drips. Are you always rushing to eat your ice cream cone before it melts and drips? Now you can enjoy your cool treat at your leisure. Place a large marshmallow in the ice cream cone before you fill it.

The ice cream cone was invented in 1904 at an exposition in St. Louis. One particularly hot day, an ice cream vendor named Charles Menches was selling ice cream so fast he ran out of dishes. Another vendor nearby was selling a Middle Eastern wafer-like pastry called Zalabia. Menches took some Zalabia, rolled it up, plopped ice cream in it, and the ice cream cone was born.

Happy birthday without the wax. Are you tired of eating candle wax along with your birthday cake? Push each candle into a marshmallow, then set it on the frosting. Any drips are on the marshmallow, which you can simply toss out, and your cake will look festive, too.

According to Jet Puffed Marshmallows, which are the best-selling brand of marshmallows, Americans buy more than 95 million pounds of the fluffy white confections every year.

Frosting that's easy as ... cake. Out of frosting for your cupcakes? Don't worry. Plop a marshmallow on top of each one a minute or so before they're due to come out of the oven. Instant gooey frosting.

Top your pumpkin pie. Pumpkin pie with whipped cream on top is pretty yummy, but for a slightly different treat, put a layer of miniature marshmallows in your pie shell before you fill it with pumpkin. As the pie bakes, the marshmallows will rise to the surface for a deliciously different topping.

Marshmallows are one of the world's oldest confections, dating back to ancient Egypt (2000 BC). According to some accounts, the pharaohs discovered that when you squeeze the mallow plant, which grew wild in marshes, it produced a sweet, sticky substance that could be made into a confection. They liked it so much, they decided that only royalty could eat it.

Matches

Unfreeze a lock. When you're dealing with a frozen lock, why not try a burning key? Heat your trunk or car door key with a match, then quickly put it in the lock and turn.

In the 10th century, the Chinese made fireworks by stuffing explosives into the stems of bamboo. They called them "arrows of flying fire." They watched the yellow and reddish amber colors shoot into the air at celebrations of all kinds. Eight centuries would pass before the chemical combinations to produce other colors would appear.

Say goodbye to worms. Worms in your ferns? Drive them out by driving in a few matches. Matches stuck headfirst into the soil around your plant will light the way for the worms' retreat. Use between four and six matches depending on the size of your fern.

Note to self — buy more matches. Make yourself a little reminder book with an ordinary book of matches. Just remove the matches by unstapling the base. Next, replace them with small slips of paper, cut to the size of the book. Restaple them in place, and you'll never be without scratch paper again.

Mayonnaise

Facial mask for dry skin. If you have dry skin, don't spend a lot of money on expensive facial creams and masks until you try a mayo-mask. Use whole-egg mayonnaise, and apply to your face. Leave it on for 20 minutes, wipe off the excess, and rinse with cool water.

> By some accounts, mayonnaise was created by the duc de Richelieu of France. He supposedly named it after the British fort of Mahon, which his forces conquered in 1756. Other sources say the word mayonnaise was derived from a French word for egg yolk, "moyeu."

Remove water stains. To get water marks off your wood furniture, rub in mayonnaise. Let it sit all night, then wipe off.

Make a hair conditioner in the kitchen. Even if you hate mayonnaise on your sandwiches, you might like what it can do for your hair. For deep conditioning, massage mayonnaise in, let it sit for about five minutes, and wash as usual. Or you can blend together one-fourth cup of mayonnaise and half of an avocado. Use the mixture just as you would a commercial conditioner, leaving it on your hair for five to 10 minutes. Rinse out, and enjoy your shiny hair.

> The first safe commercial hair dye was created by the French Harmless Hair Dye Company. Its success may have been helped when the company changed its name to L'Oreal.

Forget the flannel. If you used a flannel-backed cloth on your dining room table, and now you have fuzzy flannel stuck to the finish, don't despair. Try putting a generous amount of mayonnaise on the area, let it sit for about an hour, and then wipe off.

Milk

Restore body to permanent press clothes. If permanent press items have gotten limp, add a cup of powdered milk to the final wash and wear rinse cycle.

Mend china with milk. You found a crack in one of your grandmother's china plates. Miraculously, you can mend that crack with milk. Just place the plate in a pan, cover it with milk (a powdered milk and water solution will work just as well), and bring to a boil. Reduce the heat, and simmer for about 45 minutes. The protein in the milk should meld the crack together.

> Dried milk has been around a long time. Mongol soldiers in Genghis Khan's army dried mare's milk in the sun and then mixed it with water in a bottle hung from their saddles. By the end of the day, the horse's motion turned the mixture into a thin porridge.

Buttermilk cleans bronze and copper. If your bronze or copper piece is an antique, be sure you really want to remove any corrosion on it — sometimes that lowers its value. If you do want to clean the item, first carefully lift off any loose flakes of corroded metal. Then wash or soak it in buttermilk (use hot buttermilk on unlacquered bronze). Rinse and dry well.

Protect tomato plants. If you're a smoker and a gardener, beware of tobacco mosaic virus. It can be transferred from your hands to your tomato plants. However, a common household item can retard the growth of this virus. Before touching tomato plants, rub your hands with milk.

Thaw fish with added freshness. If you thaw frozen fish in milk, it will taste fresher. And maybe you can convince your family that you just pulled it out of the lake instead of your freezer.

Mothballs

Repel pests. Scatter mothballs around your garden and flower beds to keep rodents and even cats away.

No more rusty tools. Place a few mothballs in your toolbox to prevent rust.

Clean riddance to fleas. You love Fluffy but hate fleas. Kill fleas every time you vacuum by adding a couple of mothballs to your vacuum cleaner bag.

> A flea can jump 150 times its own length, which is the equivalent of you jumping almost 1,000 feet in the air.

Keep more than moths away. Tucked away in drawers and closets, mothballs will absorb moisture and keep things dry, preventing mildew as well as moths.

Make those moths sing out of tune. Don't think that moths are only attracted to sweaters. They'll also make a beeline for the felt hammers on your piano. Give them the brush-off with a few mothballs or moth crystals sprinkled inside.

Nail polish

Emergency car repair. The road is a hazardous place for your car. Your windshield can get hit with flying debris, and your car's body can suffer numerous dents and dings. However, you may have an emergency repair kit right in your cosmetic bag. Clear nail polish can fill small holes in your windshield and in your paint job. If you catch the damage early, you can prevent rust from forming — at least until you can get a more professional repair job.

Who says nail polish is for sissies? Early Egyptian, Babylonian, and Roman military leaders could be found before a battle having their nails painted to match their lips. And if that wasn't enough, they also had their hair lacquered and curled before they faced the enemy.

Tighten drawer knobs. Do the knobs on your drawers always work themselves loose? Put an end to that problem by coating the screws with clear nail polish and then screwing them back in.

Help thread a needle. You love to sew but getting the thread through the eye of the needle can be exasperating. If you dip the end of your thread in nail polish and let it dry, you'll be threading with ease.

Nix the nicks. Clear nail polish can fill in small nicks and scratches on varnished wood floors and glass or Plexiglas surfaces — and no one will ever know.

Repair damaged lacquer. Don't attempt to restore antique or valuable lacquered pieces this way, but if you have chipped places on modern, mass-produced items, nail polish may do the trick. By mixing colors, the chances are good you'll be able to get just the shade you need to hide those tiny scrapes.

Keep jewelry from tarnishing. Costume jewelry can be inexpensive and attractive, but it may also discolor your skin. To prevent this, paint clear nail polish on the jewelry wherever it comes into contact with your skin.

Make water-safe marks on fabric. Sending your curtains to the cleaners? Before you yank them down, use a bit of nail polish to mark the spots where each hook will need to be reinserted. The nail polish won't wash away during dry cleaning and will make rehanging the curtains a much easier task. Don't forget to make your marks on the back side of the curtain.

Keep your buttons on. To help keep your buttons from falling off, whenever you buy a new garment, take the time to dab a little clear nail polish on each button. It will help keep the thread from unraveling.

Lace your shoes with ease. When the ends of your shoelaces get a little frayed and difficult to lace, try dipping the ends in clear nail polish and letting them dry.

> According to folklore, if you make a wish while lacing someone else's shoes, that wish is more likely to come true.

"X" marks the spot. Paint a large red "X" with nail polish on the side of a container that has anything poisonous in it. Teach your children that a red "X" means danger.

Repair lace. If you've got a tear in your lace curtain or table-cloth, make a fast and easy repair by placing a piece of wax paper under the cut and brushing a little clear nail polish across the damage.

The quickest way to kill chiggers. Paint a chigger bite with clear nail polish and get fast relief.

Practice burn prevention. Use red nail polish to mark the hot water knobs on sinks your small children use. This will help them learn and remember the difference between hot and cold.

For your eyes only. Dab a bit of nail polish on the flap of an envelope and seal. It dries fast and is very secure since it will resist steaming.

Make measuring easier. Reading the measurements on a set of white plastic measuring cups can be difficult. To make it easier, paint over the numbers with red nail polish. When it dries, scrape the nail polish off the raised measurements. The background will be red and the numbers white. Now you'll be able to tell at a glance if you have two-thirds or three-quarters of a cup.

Fill in nicks in your washer. Sometimes your washing machine develops small nicks in the tub that can rust and stain your clothes or snag them. To prevent this, cover up those nicks with clear nail polish.

Catch that run. If you snag or tear your pantyhose, don't run to the store to buy a new pair. A drop of clear nail polish at the bottom of the run will stop it in its tracks.

Fight rust rings. Paint the bottoms of any metal cans that stay in your bathroom or kitchen — like shaving cream and air freshener — with a coat of clear nail polish, and you won't have to worry about getting ugly rust rings on your countertops.

Newspaper

Fit candles snugly into holders. Don't light that loose candle — not when there's a chance it will fall over. For a tighter fit, put small circles of newspaper in the candleholder.

Iron on the go. When traveling, it's easy to pack a travel iron but not an ironing board. Make one no matter where you are by sliding a stack of magazines or newspapers inside a pillowcase. Lay it on the floor or a bed and press those wrinkles away.

> Women who tried the earliest electric irons had two complaints — they were too heavy, and they were causing them to lose sleep. That's because electricity was first used to light up a dark house. So the power companies turned on the generators only at night. Women, therefore, had to wait until dark to do the ironing. A survey by a sympathetic meter reader from Ontario, Calif., led to electricity being made available around the clock one day a week. That day was Tuesday, the day most women reserved for ironing.

Give moths the bad news. Keep moths away from your woolen sweaters and blankets by wrapping them in newspaper before storing. Make sure you tape all the edges closed.

Clear away canister odors. If you have an unpleasant smell in a wooden canister, stuff it with newspaper. Leave it for a couple of days. If the odor isn't completely gone, repeat with fresh paper.

Pick up broken glass. You dropped a glass, and it shattered into a million pieces. Sweeping can leave behind tiny bits that can cut bare feet. An easy way to clean up the glass is to moisten a piece of newspaper and press it on the floor where the glass shards fell. The bits of glass will cling to the wet paper, and you can just toss them away.

A better way to clean windows. What's cheaper than paper towels for cleaning windows? Newspaper — and it's not only cheaper, it's better. Just crumple up a few sheets of yesterday's news and go to work.

Make Easter basket "grass." Instead of buying grass for Easter baskets, just shred up the slick, colorful advertisements that come with your newspaper. The paper makes pretty, multicolored "grass" to nestle those Easter eggs in.

> Which came first — the chicken or the birth certificate? In Germany, during the early 1880s, people gave colored Easter eggs etched with the name and birth date of the recipient. They were acceptable in a court of law as evidence of age and identity.

Clean your grill. After you've finished cooking, an easy way to clean your grill is to dampen newspaper and place it on top of your warm grill rack. Close the lid and leave the newspaper for 20 to 45 minutes. The wet newspaper will steam clean your grill and all you have to do is wipe it off — just don't let the paper stay too long and get dried on. Then you'll have an even bigger mess to clean up.

Get the funk out of your trash compactor. Line the bottom of your trash compactor with several layers of newspaper to fight nasty odors. The newspaper will suck up much of the smell of decomposing food and protect the bottom of the compactor from sharp, damaging objects.

Extra! Extra! Gardener finds cheap mulch! A few layers of newspaper in your garden helps keep the soil moist and breaks down into mulch. Don't use the funnies or other colored sections because the inks might contain lead.

> The most massive single issue of a newspaper was the Sept. 14, 1987, edition of the Sunday New York Times. It weighed 12 pounds and had 1,612 pages.

Eliminate earwigs. If earwigs have launched an assault on your young plants, it's time to strike back. Roll a damp newspaper into a tight roll and tie it so it doesn't come apart. Deliver this special edition to the doorstep of your damaged plants and leave it overnight. In the morning, the paper will have become an earwig hotel. Burn the newspaper and prepare another. Keep doing this until you don't find any earwigs in your trap.

Beat your fruit trees. If those apple and pear trees aren't providing you with much fruit, maybe they've gotten lazy. They may need a good "whupping." Take a rolled up newspaper and

whack them up and down the trunk. You may have a hard time explaining this to your neighbors. Just tell them that the vessels carrying sap to the leaves and buds sometimes shrink. This lashing will help loosen them up. You'll be surprised how much your harvest will improve. By the way, some old-timers believed the best results came from whipping fruit trees by moonlight in early spring.

Put down a puppy place mat. Spread some newspaper beneath your dog's food dishes to soak up the water that he will inevitably slosh. A word of caution — don't do this if you used newspaper to housebreak your dog. The results could be quite unappetizing.

Shoo, bird. Birds' nests are usually a welcome addition to your garage or yard, but not when the little family moves in right above your front door. Look out below! To get rid of unwanted nests and keep them from returning, stuff balled-up newspaper into the nesting space.

Safely remove a broken bulb. Getting a broken light bulb out of a socket is tricky business, but newspaper can help. First, put on a pair of thick gloves. Then, take a wad of newspaper and press it down into the glass, turning counterclockwise. A few turns should loosen the bulb, and you can wrap it in the newspaper and throw it away.

Most people think Thomas Edison invented the light bulb, but it was actually patented first in England by an inventor named Joseph Swan and in the United States by William Sawyer. Although Edison lost a lawsuit over the patent rights when he began making money on the design, he still gets a good deal of credit for the invention. That's because he owned the power company that made light bulb use possible. You may have heard of it — General Electric.

Keep your fire blazing all winter long. Make emergency logs for your fireplace with newspapers. Roll them tightly, tie them up, and soak them in soapy water. Let them drain dry by standing on end. (Check with the manufacturer before using these in a wood stove.)

Stuff 'n dry wet shoes. If you got caught in the rain, you've probably got wet shoes. Here's a simple tip to prevent damage to your shoes. Stuff them with crumpled newspaper to absorb the moisture, then put them somewhere that's not too hot so they can dry slowly. If your shoes are really sopping wet, you may need to change the paper a few times.

Custom wrap your exotic gift. To give a gift an extra exotic flair, wrap it in foreign newspaper. You can buy them at some newsstands or pick up a copy at an authentic ethnic restaurant.

Nylon net

Remove cobwebs. Wrap net around the end of a yardstick and secure it with a rubber band. Spray it lightly with a dusting spray. Use it to get to those spider webs in hard-to-reach corners.

Help for a messy birdcage. To keep your bird from tossing seeds all over your floor, wrap a length of nylon net around the cage. Don't cover the cage entirely — just a few inches near the food dish.

Give artwork the look of the masters. It's easy to take an inexpensive glossy picture and make it look like an oil painting worth hundreds of dollars. Simply cut a piece of nylon net slightly larger than the picture and tape it down tightly over it. Brush on a light coat of shellac. After just a few seconds, remove the net carefully and allow the picture to dry. You'll have a piece of art that will leave your friends guessing.

> According to the 1998 Guinness Book of World Records, the most valuable painting in the world is the "Mona Lisa," appraised at $100 million dollars.

Save your seeds. Stop the birds from gobbling up your newly planted seeds by spreading your bed with a piece of nylon net.

Go lint-free in the dryer. Add a few large pieces of nylon net to your next dryer load and say goodbye to lint.

Onions

Give bee stings the buzz. Hold a slice of onion to a bee sting for a few minutes to soothe away your pain.

Watch out!

Don't store onions and potatoes together because moisture from the potatoes will cause the onions to sprout.

No more new-paint smell. A freshly painted room is very satisfying — except for that lingering smell. One way to counteract those fumes is to chop up a large onion and put it in a bowl of water. Set it in the room for a few hours. Amazingly, it works.

Emergency smelling salts. A guest suddenly feels faint. You don't have any smelling salts handy. The strong odor of an onion may be a good thing for once. You can wave a cut onion under his nose and perhaps revive him.

Onions loom large in the medicine cabinet of American folk remedies. To fight a cough, all you needed to do was wear one sock filled with split onions and another filled with black pepper. For a really tough cough, you'd have to complete the outfit with cabbage leaves tied to your chest and a necklace of either salted herring or pork strips. Talk about feeding a cold!

Spray away bugs. To keep away yard bugs, purée onions and water, and simply spray. Better yet, add some finely blended onion to one of the garlic or pepper bug recipes listed in other sections of this book. When it comes to harsh-smelling additives in the garden, more is better.

Orange peels

Keep cats out of your yard. If you want to keep the neighborhood cats from using your yard as a litter box, just gather a couple of items that you would normally toss in the trash. Sprinkle a mixture of orange peels and coffee grounds around the border of your yard or garden, and send those kitties elsewhere.

Make your own potpourri. After you've eaten the deliciously juicy insides of an orange, don't throw that peel away. Cut it into chunks, and simmer it on the stove for a fresh fragrance all through your house. Just be sure and add water as needed.

> Catherine of Avalon, married to Henry VIII, missed the delicious oranges from her sunny homeland of Spain. Although she sent for some, by the time they made the journey to England they were inedible. Thus, marmalade was created to preserve the flavor and satisfy the queen's craving for oranges.

Scent your closet. Take a whole orange and cover it completely with cloves. Hang it in your closet for a fresh scent and to repel moths. It will dry and last for years.

> Pomander: a clove-studded orange, lemon, or apple.

Orange smoothie ant repellent. Blend up a mixture of orange peels and water until smooth, and pour it onto an anthill. It's best to do this first thing in the morning before they leave the nest.

Paintbrushes

Brush away sand. No need to get sand in your car when you go to the beach. Keep a paintbrush handy to brush off your feet before you get in.

Dust difficult areas. You probably don't paint very often, so make those paintbrushes do double duty as dusters. A small brush with soft bristles is ideal for dusting decorative molding, knick-knacks, china, and other fragile items. Use a small, slightly damp brush to pick up dust from keyboards and sensitive surfaces with intricate corners and crevices. Try a soft brush on lampshades and mini blinds. Use one with stiffer bristles for carved or wicker furniture, windowsills, screens, and baskets.

Baste and barbecue. Buy a paintbrush to keep near your grill or stove. Paintbrushes are great for brushing on barbecue and other sauces, and they clean up easier than pastry brushes.

Paint soil over seeds. A large paintbrush comes in handy when planting a garden row. You can brush just the right amount of soil over the seeds.

Pantyhose

Smooth sanding ahead. It's not always easy to tell just by feeling when you've completed your sanding job, especially if you have rough hands. To make sure you've gotten it smooth as silk stockings, pull an old pair of pantyhose over your hand and rub. The nylon will catch on any spots that need more sanding.

Pack tight and pack right. The next time you pack for a business trip or vacation, remember the newest packing buzzword — roll. Roll up your garments and slide the bulky items into pantyhose tubes (cut the foot and panty off a leg). This keeps everything from unrolling and results in a neater suitcase.

Make contact with a lost lens. To find a lost contact lens, cover the nozzle of your vacuum cleaner with a piece of pantyhose. Secure it with a rubber band, and vacuum the area where you lost the contact. The suction will be strong enough to attract the contact, but the pantyhose will keep it from being sucked inside. When you have to dust lots of small items, stretch the pantyhose over your vacuum's brush attachment.

Necessity is the mother of invention, which is probably why the Hoover vacuum cleaner was invented by a janitor with a severe allergy to dust. The janitor, James Murray Spangler, made his contraption from a tin can, a broomstick, a flour sack, and an electric motor. He sold his invention to a businessman named William Hoover, who made Spangler his superintendent of production and Hoover a household name.

Recycle even when you're recycling. Cut old pantyhose legs into long strips and use them to tie up bundles of newspapers or magazines and double your recycling efforts.

Get a leg-up on gardening. Use long strips of pantyhose to tie plants or young trees onto stakes or trellises. Since they're stretchy, your tender stalks won't be damaged as they grow.

Stuff it. Recycle old, clean pantyhose as stuffing for toys or other craft projects.

Keep garbage bags secure. To keep your garbage bags from slipping down inside the can, cut the elastic waistband from a pair of pantyhose. It makes a giant rubber band that you can put over the rim of the garbage can to hold the bag in place.

Mothball holder. One leg of an old pair of pantyhose makes a handy holder for mothballs. Just stuff a few mothballs in the toe and tie the top to your closet rod.

Keep dirt in its place. Your potted plants need drainage, but you don't want the soil to drain away, too. Line the bottom of your planter with pantyhose. It will allow the water to drain but keep the soil in place.

Make outdoor cleanup a snap. After a hard day in the garden or garage, you may not be allowed back in the house without washing up at the outdoor faucet. You won't have to go hunting for soap if you slip a bar into the toe of an old stocking. Tie the end around the faucet and lather up right through the stocking.

Hold pleats in place. There's no need to iron the pleats of your favorite skirt every time you wear it if you store it inside a stocking leg. Remove the leg from the rest of the pantyhose and cut off the foot. Pull the stocking over the skirt. Store it flat, and when you are ready to wear it again, your pleats will fall neatly into place.

Stow away wrapping paper. To keep partially used rolls of wrapping paper from getting torn, put them inside the leg of an old pair of pantyhose. If you have several rolls, you can put a roll in each leg and drape it over a hanger, one leg on each side, and hang it in your closet. Store several pair on one hanger.

Make a thrifty scrubber. Wrap a piece of pantyhose around a sponge to make an inexpensive scrubber.

Mix up manure tea for your plants. Manure makes a great organic fertilizer. If you'd like to use it in liquid form, put a few scoops into a pantyhose leg, tie the top, and place in a bucket of water. (To make it easier to remove the pantyhose when it's done, tie the top to the bucket handle.) Let it brew for a few days. When you are ready to use it, dilute with plain water. For tender young plants, which can burn easily if it's too strong, mix three parts water to one part tea. It should look like weak iced tea.

Fall storage for bulbs. Place bulbs inside the legs of pantyhose, label, close off the end, and hang for storage until next season.

Inspect a suspect washing machine. If you've noticed an unusual amount of tears or snags in your clothing, the culprit could be in your washing machine. A rough spot inside can really do a lot of damage. To check your machine, wrap an old pair of pantyhose around your hand and rub along the inside surfaces of the washer. The pantyhose will snag on any sharp edges or problem areas. You can then sand these down with some fine sandpaper.

Distill your own water. If your iron or humidifier calls for distilled water, but you hate to pay for it, distill your own by running rainwater through a few layers of old, clean pantyhose.

Protect produce from pests. Floating row covers can protect your crops from insects, but with a little more effort, you can get the same effect for a lot less money. When fruits and vegetables are small, cover them individually with lengths of old pantyhose and tie the ends. They stretch as the fruit grows and dry quickly after a rain, but bugs can't get in them.

Flour baking pans with ease. Fill the foot of an old, clean pantyhose leg with flour and keep it in your canister. The next time you have to flour a baking pan, just shake the foot lightly. This also works well if you need a floured surface to roll out bread or pastry.

Make Fido a tug toy. Do you have lots of ruined pantyhose lying around? Here's a way to put them to good use and make your dog happy at the same time. You'll need nine single legs, so cut and separate what you need. Tie all of them together at the top, then separate them into three groups of three. Braid each group and knot at the bottom. You've got a great tug-of-war toy. Just be careful your best friend doesn't chew off and swallow any pieces.

Take the "hairy" out of cleaning your hairbrush. If cleaning your hairbrush is a chore, try making the job easier with pantyhose. Cut a small piece off an old pair and press it firmly down over the bristles. Use a comb if you need help getting it all the way down. When it's time for a cleanup, simply pull the pantyhose off. The loose hair will come with it.

Manicures without the mess. Cut lengths of old pantyhose into small squares and use them instead of cotton balls or tissue to remove old nail polish. You can store the squares in an empty tissue box or other recycled container for easier handling.

Stash onions. Keep onions handy and dry by storing them in the leg of an old pair of pantyhose. Just drop the onions in one at a time and tie a knot between each one. Hang in a cool, dry place. Whenever you need an onion, just snip one off with scissors.

Great for vacation souvenirs. Fill an old, clean pantyhose leg with your collection of seashells from the beach or rocks from a wilderness trail. Knot the end and you've got a great way to transport your treasures home.

Make a punching bag. If you need to work out your frustrations, or you just need to work out, you can make a punching bag with an old pair of pantyhose and a soccer or volleyball. Just put the ball in the panty part, tie the waist shut, and suspend it from the ceiling by tying the legs to a hook.

Create disposable underwear. Here's a way to actually make your suitcase lighter the longer you travel. Cut the legs off pantyhose that have runs or tears. Pack the brief in your suitcase, and you've got disposable panties. Wear them once and toss away.

A fishy solution. A small section of pantyhose stitched to the rounded end of a wire hanger makes an excellent net for retrieving dead friends from the fishbowl.

The hair up there. If you've got long hair, you know that working in the garden on a windy day or traveling in a convertible can be a hair-raising experience. One quick solution is to cut the end off a pair of pantyhose. *Voilà* — instant hair net.

Paper bags

Overwinter your geraniums. If you don't have a sunny  window for your geraniums, you can still keep them alive through the winter. In the fall, take them out of their pots and shake off most of the soil. Put each plant in a paper bag. Then, make a cover by opening another paper bag and pulling it over the top of the first one. Store them in the basement or other cool and relatively dry place. In the spring, cut the top off, leaving just a stub, and repot it.

Cheap wrapping paper for mailed gifts. Don't waste money on expensive wrapping paper for mailing boxes. Simply cut open a paper bag along the seams until it's a large rectangle. Turn it so any printing is on the inside and tape it securely.

With a flip of the wrist, the bag-boy opens a brown paper bag, and it stays open by itself while he fills it with your groceries. Although this clever invention is taken for granted, the machine-produced "Self-opening Sack" was a welcome improvement over the earlier hand-pasted, V-shaped bags. Invented in 1883, its use boomed with the appearance of supermarkets in the early 1930s.

Make durable covers for school books. Don't buy thin, expensive book covers that will rip within the first week of school. Use paper bags and let the kids decorate them with stickers or markers.

Crush "dem" dry bones. What do you do with leftover chicken bones? They smell bad in the garbage, and you can't put them down the disposal. Instead, dry them in your microwave, put them in a strong paper bag, and crush them with a hammer. When you're finished, take them out to your garden and sprinkle them around the base of your plants. They'll thrive on the extra nutrients.

The paper shopping bag was invented by an enterprising grocer. He wanted to encourage his shoppers to purchase more than they could conveniently carry in their arms. It took over four years to design and originally sold for five cents.

Ripen fruit. To help fruit ripen more quickly, put it in a paper bag and store the bag in a dark place.

Light up your drive. For holidays or parties, line your drive with paper lanterns. Just fill paper bags halfway with sand, put a small votive candle in the center, and light.

Paper clips

Keep the iron hot. If your iron seems to be "losing steam," check the underside. Your steam holes could be clogged with mineral deposits. If this is the case, simply unbend a paper clip and use the little tool to break up and remove the guilty parties, then it's back to the ironing board.

Pit your cherries. Open up a paper clip so it forms a little hook, then use it to pit cherries. Just stick the hook under the pit, twist, and give the cherry a little pinch with your other hand. The pit should pop right out.

Paper cups

Protect your oven light. When cleaning your oven, cover the light bulb with a paper cup. You'll still have some illumination while protecting the bulb from oven cleaner.

In 1908, entrepreneur Hugh Moore produced a machine to dispense cold drinking water in a disposable paper cup for the price of one cent. Spending a penny to quench thirst, however, never caught on. But the passing of sanitation laws banning the public sipper saved the day. Moore found success selling his Health Kups, later known as Dixie Cups, without the water.

Give baby plants a fighting chance. Cutworms and other hungry bugs are out there just waiting to munch on your newly transplanted seedlings. Encourage them to go elsewhere using this handy tip. Cut the bottom out of a plastic foam cup and plant the seedling with the cup around it. Half of the cup should be submerged, half showing above ground.

Keep shavings out of your eyes. If you ever have to drill a hole in the ceiling, put a paper cup over the drill bit to catch most of the shavings as they fall.

Paper plates

Save gift wrapping. Here's a great way to recycle bows using a paper plate. Poke a hole in the center of the plate. As each gift is unwrapped, thread the attached ribbon down through the hole so the bow is left on top. At the end of the party, you'll have a whole bouquet of ribbons and bows that can be used again.

Homemade drip guard. Don't dribble paint all over the place — put in a drip guard. Just tape or glue a paper plate to the bottom of your paint can for an extra wide lip of drip protection.

Store fine china safely. Layer your china plates and bowls with paper plates or bowls to keep them from scratching each other.

> In case you've wondered where the saucer got its name, there's a good explanation. These little dishes didn't always hold cups. Originally they were used to hold — you guessed it — sauces.

Emergency cleanup solution. For a quick and easy solution to messy floors, make a substitute dustpan out of half a paper plate.

Protect your floor — and your face. Drips are a fact of life when painting the ceiling, but if you give your brush a paper plate collar, you won't have to clean those drips off your floor. Just cut a hole in the middle of the plate, and push the brush handle through.

Paper towels

Make a coffee filter. You simply must have your coffee in the morning, but you're out of coffee filters. There's no need to panic — as long as you have some paper towels in the house. Use one to make an emergency coffee filter.

> Paper towels were the result of an error. A supply of toilet paper came from the mill to the Scotts brothers' paper company where it was to be cut down into smaller rolls. One roll, however, was too heavy and wrinkled for bathroom use. Instead of returning it to the mill, someone suggested perforating it and selling it as tear-off paper towels. Thus, Sani-Towel, later to be known as ScotTowels, was born.

Save your pots from rust. Stack your cast-iron pots with a paper towel placed between each one. Store the lids separately. This will cut back on mustiness and help keep away rust.

Remove silk from corn. To make sure you get all the silk from an ear of corn after you husk it, rub it down with a damp paper towel.

Cook healthier bacon. If you love bacon, but not the fat, cook it in your microwave. Lay a few strips side by side on a paper towel, then place the paper towel on a plate. Cover with another paper towel and cook. The paper towels will absorb the fat, leaving you with crispier, leaner bacon.

Keep bread dry. If you freeze bread for later use, put a paper towel into the bag or container. The towel will absorb moisture that can make bread soggy when it thaws.

Line vegetable bins. Those cucumbers looked nice and fresh going into your refrigerator, but now, three weeks later, they don't look so hot. Next time, make that messy cleanup job easier. Line the bottoms of your vegetable bins with paper towels.

Prevent paint lids from sticking. The next time you pour paint out of a can into a tray or other container, twist some paper towels and stuff them into the rim of the paint can. The paint will pour over the paper towel. When you're finished, just remove it and toss away. The rim will be paint-free, and the lid won't stick the next time you try to take it off.

Do a sprout test. Don't throw away leftover seeds. Some seeds can stay fertile for several years. Test those packaged for an earlier year by placing a few between two sheets of paper towel. Wet them and keep them moist. Check from time to time to see if they are sprouting. If 80 percent sprout, you can feel confident about using the rest of the seeds in the packet.

A cleaner opener. After a while, your can opener can get a bit grungy around the blades. Scrub it with an old toothbrush, then "open" a few layers of paper towels with it to clean the blades thoroughly.

Peanut butter

Get gum out of hair. Work some peanut butter into the hair with your fingers, and you should be able to comb the gum right out. To get the peanut butter out, just shampoo.

Other things, too. Remove gum from leather by placing a small amount of peanut butter on the gum. Wait a few minutes, then peel it off. If removing gum from fabric has left a stain behind, rub some peanut butter into the stain, wipe off, then rinse before washing the fabric as usual.

> Ever wonder why peanut butter sticks to the roof of your mouth? It's because the high protein content draws moisture from your mouth.

Plug up drippy cones. That little hole in the bottom of an ice cream cone can drip melting ice cream all over your hands. Plug it up in a tasty way by dropping a small amount of peanut butter into the cone before scooping your ice cream. You'll have less mess, and your last bite of cone will hold a surprise.

> Peanuts were first ground into butter in the 1890s. But it was another 30 years before it became popular with jelly in the classic sandwich.

No more fish odor. Do you love fried fish but hate the lingering smell in your house? Next time you're ready to fry up a batch, drop a small amount of peanut butter into the pan with the fish.

To catch a mouse. Forget the stereotype of the cheese-loving mouse. What mice really love is the same thing most kids really love — peanut butter. Use some to bait your traps and the mice will come running.

Did you know that each ounce of Cracker Jack contains exactly nine peanuts? That's fewer than the number of peanuts found in the boxes sold at the 1893 Chicago World's Fair — but there was no prize back then. Trinkets first appeared in Cracker Jack in 1913.

Petroleum jelly

Kissably soft lips for less. Don't spend a lot of money on those fancy flavored lip balms. You always leave them in your pocket and ruin them in the wash anyway. Petroleum jelly will keep your lips soft and smooth for a fraction of the cost. You can even add a few drops of red food coloring for an inexpensive lip gloss.

Help for your plumber's helper. For greater stability and a better seal on the drain, rub a little petroleum jelly around the ring of your plunger before putting it to work.

Keep your car battery corrosion-free. Corrosion on your battery terminals can keep you at a standstill. Although you can clean the terminals once they're corroded, taking a few minutes to cover your clean battery terminals with petroleum jelly can prevent corrosion from forming in the first place.

The first automobile to be produced in quantity was the Curved Dash Oldsmobile, built in 1901 by Ransom E. Olds.

Wipe away water marks. Here's an easy way to remove water marks and other imperfections from wood furniture. Smear the area with petroleum jelly, let it sit for 24 hours, rub it in, wipe off the excess, and polish your furniture as usual.

Detour annoying ants. Whenever you feed your animals outdoors, you have to deal with annoying, persistent ants. To keep them from taking over your pet's food bowl, spread a circle of petroleum jelly around the bowl. The ants won't cross that line. To keep them out of your hummingbird feeder, smear petroleum jelly on the pole or hanging string.

Smooth sliding shower curtain. To keep your shower curtain sliding smoothly, rub petroleum jelly on the curtain rod.

Make melted-on plastic disappear. If you have plastic melted to the side of your toaster, don't get steamed. Just massage a little petroleum jelly onto the plastic, make some toast to heat up the toaster, and wipe off the sticky mess with a paper towel.

Stop birdseed-stealing squirrels. Try petroleum jelly to stop squirrels from eating your birdseed and chasing off the birds. Coat the pole of your bird feeder with petroleum jelly, and the squirrels will slide right down whenever they try to climb.

Slip off a ring. A tight ring can be painful and annoying. Try smearing petroleum jelly around your finger to help the ring slide off.

Put the shine back into dull china. Your good dishes can glow like new again. Rub them with Vaseline, let them sit for an hour, then polish with a soft cloth.

Cheap and easy makeup removal. Don't spend money for fancy makeup remover. Petroleum jelly is a safe and inexpensive way to remove mascara, eyeliner, lipstick, and other makeup.

The first glittery eye shadow was worn by both men and women in ancient Egypt. They made it by crushing the iridescent shells of insects and mixing it with malachite, a green mineral they crushed into a powder.

Try this super hand softener. Before bed, rub petroleum jelly on your hands, then slip on cotton gloves or mittens. In the morning, you'll wake up to softer, younger-looking hands.

Make changing outdoor light bulbs a snap. Weather, dirt, pollen, and dust can all make outdoor light bulbs seem welded into the fixture. Here's a bright idea. Smear a thin layer of petroleum jelly on the base of the bulb before you screw it in. When it's time to change the bulb, you'll be done in a flash.

Keep baby's eyes shampoo-free. Before giving baby a bath, rub a little petroleum jelly above and around her eyes. The shampoo-laden rinse water will be diverted away from her eyes, and you'll avoid a potentially tearful situation.

Protect yourself from fiberglass. When installing fiberglass insulation, always cover as much skin as possible with clothing. Any skin that remains exposed should be coated with petroleum jelly. This layer of protection will make it harder for slivers of fiberglass to get into your skin.

Shine patent leather shoes. Petroleum jelly can put a quick and easy shine on patent leather shoes.

The inventor of Vaseline petroleum jelly ate a spoonful of his creation every day. He gave it credit for his long life. He died at age 96.

Stop squeaking doors. If a squeaky door is driving you crazy, take it off its hinges, coat the hinges with petroleum jelly, and rehang the door.

Protect your dog's feet. Exposure or dry skin can cause your dog's soft footpads to crack or peel. A little petroleum jelly will help soothe the discomfort and encourage healing.

No more sticky lids. Spread petroleum jelly on the inside of your glue lid, and it will never get stuck again.

Soften up your face. After washing your face, gently rub a small amount of petroleum jelly into your wet skin. Keep rubbing and adding water until your skin no longer feels greasy.

Pillowcases

Take lettuce for a spin. If you need to make salad for a crowd, here's a time-saving strategy. Wash greens and place them inside a double layer of cotton pillowcases. Close securely with a rubber band or twist tie, and toss inside your washing machine with a large, clean towel. Run the spin cycle for a few minutes, take the lettuce out, and store in your fridge until you're ready to toss and serve.

Storing off-season clothes? Create your own dust covers for free. Instead of throwing out old pillowcases, make a small slit in the center of the seam opposite the opening and slip it over a hanger. No more dust on your winter suits. If you close up the opening by adding a fabric fastener, like Velcro, or a zipper, you can use it to store out-of-season blankets.

Wash delicates. You don't have to buy a special bag for washing your delicate lingerie. Just put them in a large pillowcase, tie the top shut, and wash on the delicate cycle.

Say goodnight to cobwebs. Get rid of cobwebs in those hard-to-reach corners with this handy, homemade tool. Take a long-handled broom and slip a flannel pillowcase over the bristles. Secure it around the handle with string or a rubber band. The cobwebs will cling to the flannel. You can turn it inside out when it gets dirty, clean up some more, then throw it in the wash.

Give beloved stuffed animals new life. Favorite toys never look the same after they've been through the washer, but Teddy has to have an occasional bath. To get your stuffed friends nice and clean, put them inside a clean pillowcase, close the top using some string, and wash and dry as usual. You and your child will be pleased with the results.

Double linen duty. When you have a new baby in the house, you suddenly have a lot of unexpected expenses. Instead of paying high prices for specialty sheets for a baby's bassinet, use a standard-size pillowcase instead.

Make an inexpensive travel bag. Whether you're going to Grandma's or camping with the guys, a "squishable" suitcase makes loading the car easier. Take a pillowcase — king-size if you're a big packer — and install a zipper, drawstring, or Velcro to close the end. Pack your stuff and toss it in the trunk. Kids will love having a personalized bag made from their favorite character linens.

Layer for smarter traveling. When packing a pillow for the car, slip on several pillowcases. Your pillow will be more comfortable, and you can peel off the top pillowcase when it gets dirty and use it as a laundry bag. This will keep stains and odors from getting onto your clean clothes in your suitcase.

Pipe cleaners

Clean pressure cooker vents. A pipe cleaner is just the right size and shape to get inside the holes on the cover of your pressure cooker. The rough fibers will loosen any clogs when you insert it and jiggle it up and down a few times.

Safe haven for safety pins. Don't let runaway safety pins make your sewing kit a disaster area. Thread them neatly onto a pipe cleaner and twist the ends together.

Keep your shoes on. If you break a shoelace, a pipe cleaner makes a strong emergency replacement.

Get a perm with no commitment. You want the funky curls but not the commitment. Try this hair trick. Bend a pipe cleaner in half, forming a narrow U-shape. Starting at the closed end, begin weaving wet hair in thin strands back and forth through the pipe cleaner. Twist each one together at the end to hold them in place. When your hair dries, just take them out.

Better burning stove. If the holes in your gas burner get clogged or caked with spilled food, use a pipe cleaner to get rid of those troublesome clogs. It's just the right size.

Plastic bags

Protect chandeliers from paint. Cleaning paint off glass isn't fun, but cleaning it off a crystal chandelier is downright drudgery. To protect your chandelier from spatters when painting your ceiling, wrap a plastic garbage bag around it.

Keep your feet warm and dry. Even the best-made snow boots and galoshes can leak. Keep your feet dry by slipping a plastic grocery bag over your socks before putting on your foul-weather gear. You can tuck the ends into your pants or tighten the bag around your ankle with an old shoelace. Either way — no more wet feet. This will also make sliding your foot into tight boots a little easier.

Banish snow and frost.

If scraping snow and ice off your windshield in the morning isn't your favorite way to start the day, try covering your windshield at night with a plastic garbage bag or sheet of plastic. Hold it in place by closing the doors on the edges. In the morning, lift off the garbage bag, and you'll have a perfectly clear windshield.

Super-duper pooper scooper.

Keep a plastic bag with your dog's leash so you'll remember to take one with you on every walk. When you need to clean up after Fido, put the bag over your hand, scoop it up, turn the bag inside out, knot it, and take it home.

Make shampooing your carpet a snap.

Don't worry about moving your furniture into the garage when you shampoo your carpet. Simply pull a plastic grocery bag up over each furniture leg, using a rubber band or tape to secure it firmly in place. Move each piece only as much as necessary, then move it back into place.

Toss-away paint tray liners.

Instead of expensive roller tray liners, slip two plastic grocery bags — one going in each direction — over your roller tray. Reverse the bags as you take them off and toss away.

Protect your faucets.

Cover your sink faucets with plastic grocery bags whenever you're planning a messy job. Whether it's painting or heavy-duty cooking, your handles will stay nice and clean.

Pull up poison ivy.

Don't take chances when removing poison ivy or other rash-inducing plants from your yard. Cover your hand and arm with a plastic garbage bag. Pull the plants up by the roots. With your other hand, carefully pull the bag off your arm and over the plants. The offending plants are bagged and ready to be disposed of.

Environmentally friendly mailing. Recycle plastic grocery bags in a new way — use them as packing material instead of plastic foam peanuts. Just scrunch them up and put them around the item you're mailing. The person on the other end can use the bags in hundreds of ways, too.

Make garment bags. Plastic trash bags make great, inexpensive garment bags. Just cut a slit in the bottom of the bags for the hanger to slip through.

Shake out your dust mop. To get the dust off your dust mop without redistributing it in the air, tie a plastic grocery bag over the head of the mop and shake. The dirt and dust will come off in the bag, and you can just take it off and throw it away.

Worry-free holiday storage. Storing hanging decorations can sometimes be tricky — they often end up creased or broken. Next time, try clipping them to a hanger and slipping a large trash bag, with a small slit cut in the bottom, upside down over the whole thing. Tie the bottom of the bag to keep dust out. Hang it in your attic, shed, or garage.

Emergency storage on the go. Save an empty tissue box and stuff it with small, plastic grocery bags. Keep it in your car for garbage, wet shoes, or other messy emergencies.

Line bathroom trash cans. Does your bathroom trash can almost run over before you get around to emptying it? Here's an easy way to tackle that chore. Keep a few plastic grocery bags in the bottom of the trash can. Line the trash can with one of the bags, letting the top drape neatly over the sides. When it's almost full, pull it up by the handles and tie them in a neat bundle. Pull another bag into place, and your chore is practically done.

New life for old vases. If you've got an old vase that has cracks or chips and no longer holds water, line it with a plastic grocery bag — but check the bag for holes first. Pour in some water, add flowers, and you can get many more years of enjoyment from an old treasure.

Make a waterproof apron. When you have to do chores that might get your clothes damp and dirty, make a disposable apron out of a plastic trash bag. Just cut holes for your head and arms and slip it on. When you're finished, toss it away or, better yet, save it for next time.

Heat up your tomatoes. Cover the ground around your young tomato plants with black plastic trash bags to give them an extra boost. The extra heat collected by the black plastic will make the plants grow stronger and fuller.

Make a clean sweep of things. Cover your dustpan with a plastic grocery bag before you tackle a big mess. Then when you're done, turn it inside out, tie a knot, and drop it in the trash can.

Quarantine your plants. If one of your plants gets infested with bugs, move it if you can, but if you can't, treat the problem and cover the plant with a plastic bag. This will keep the bugs from spreading to healthy plants.

Make better use of bits of time. Create a "waiting time bag" with a plastic grocery bag. Fill it with material for little projects — like postcards and pen so you can quickly write a note when stuck in traffic. Or put clothes that need mending and a film canister containing a threaded needle and buttons in your bag. Whip it out in the doctor's office while you wait for your checkup. Or carry a photo album and loose pictures. This could be a big project if done all at once. But done in bits and pieces, it's completed before you know it.

Keep birds out of your garden. Are birds stealing things from your garden? If so, cut long strips from a plastic garbage bag and staple them to the rim of a paper cup. Glue the cup to the top of a five-foot bamboo stake or other pole. Stand it in your garden where the breezes will cause the plastic to flutter, and the birds will stay away.

Plastic bottles

Create some cool summer fun. Do your kids love to run through sprinklers and have water fights? Don't waste money on plastic squirt guns. Instead, recycle plastic squeeze bottles from your kitchen. Clean them thoroughly, fill with water, and let the fun begin.

Decorate your cakes like an expert. Fill a clean mustard or ketchup squeeze bottle with icing. Now it's a snap to frost your cookies, cupcakes, and cakes with professional-looking designs and lettering.

Roll on the glue. For crafts projects, make a handy glue dispenser from an empty roll-on deodorant bottle. Just pop off the ball top and wash the parts thoroughly. Fill the bottle with glue. Put the ball back in place and you're ready to roll.

Dispense plastic bags. You can make a dispenser for your plastic grocery bags from an empty soda bottle. Just cut off the top and bottom of a two-liter plastic bottle and discard. Attach the bottle to the inside of your cabinet door with small nails or screws. Stuff the bags into the top, and pull them out of the bottom — one at a time.

Save on your water bill. If the toilets in your house are the older models that use over three gallons of water for every flush, you may want to try this water-saving tip. Fill a plastic soda bottle with water and set it in your toilet tank. This will cut the amount of water used.

Keep string at your fingertips. For handy string storage, take a clean two- or three-liter plastic bottle and cut off the bottom. Nail the bottle upside down into the wall and place a roll of string inside. Feed the end of the string through the bottle's neck. For even more convenience, attach a pair of scissors to the bottle with a separate length of string.

Space seeds in your garden. Here's a quick way to get the right amount of space between seedlings in your garden. Use a plastic bottle with the same diameter as the distance the seeds should be sowed. Just follow the directions on the seed packet. Beginning at the end of the row, press the bottle into the soil firmly enough to leave an impression. Place one or two seeds in the center of that circle. Make the next circle by placing the edge of the bottle beside the first circle. Continue this process to the end of the row. Your plants will be neatly spaced without tedious measuring.

A great way to store crunchy veggies. It's easier to choose healthy snacks if they're readily available. Keep carrot and celery sticks fresh and crunchy in your fridge by using this handy tip. Take a clean two-liter bottle and cut off the top to the desired height. Partially fill the bottom with cold water and a few ice cubes. Stand your veggies up in the water, and you'll always have healthy munchies on hand.

Make a disposable funnel. Cut off the pouring end of a clean two-liter bottle, and you have a great funnel for messy jobs in your kitchen or garage. When you're through, just toss it away.

Transport flowers without crushing. The next time you take cut flowers somewhere, don't lay them on your car seat without water. Instead, cut the top off a two-liter bottle, making sure it's tall enough for your flowers to completely fit inside. Add a few inches of water, stand your flowers inside, and cover the opening with plastic wrap and a rubber band.

> The first plastic was called celluloid. But it wasn't used first, as you might assume, for photographic film. When ivory was in short supply, a billiard ball manufacturer paid a $10,000 award to the inventor of the first celluloid product — the celluloid billiard ball.

Spare the rag. Dust knickknacks and small items with air, and save yourself the trouble of moving them. An empty bottle of dishwashing liquid can squeeze just enough pressure to do the job with ease.

Dispense cooking oil. A well-rinsed dishwashing liquid bottle makes a handy dispenser for cooking oil. You can control how much you add, and you don't have to deal with messy drips.

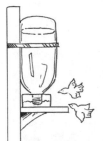

Invite the finches for dinner. House finches love sugar water just like hummingbirds, but they need a different kind of feeder. Just fill a tuna can and a plastic soda or water bottle with sugar water, then turn the bottle over into the can so the spout is submerged. Secure the bottle to a nearby wall or post, and you're all set.

Apply sunscreen without the mess. If you have kids, you know getting them to sit still while you squeeze on sunscreen is quite a job. Make it fun and neat with an old roll-on deodorant bottle. Wash all the parts thoroughly, then fill it with your favorite suntan lotion. You'll be able to apply it without messy drips or blobs.

Foolproof arts and crafts. Wash and dry several empty roll-on deodorant bottles and fill with different colors of paint. Give your kids big pieces of paper and let them go to town — all the fun and creativity without messy jars and brushes. Afterward, put the lids on and save for the next project.

Inexpensive chew toys. In a pinch for something to amuse the puppy? Give him a clean plastic bottle. Gnawing on that will keep him away from more valuable things that he could be chewing. Be careful what you give your young dog, though. The more his toys resemble things he's not supposed to chew, the more confused he'll be.

Write your name in the snow. An empty bottle of dishwashing liquid is magically transformed into a giant magic marker for your child when filled with colored water.

Make the watering rounds a little easier. Ever try to pour a cup of water into a hanging plant? Make it easier on yourself by watering hard-to-reach plants with a dishwashing liquid bottle.

Plastic food containers

Make stepping stones for your garden. You can make attractive, inexpensive stepping stones for your yard or garden using plastic food containers, like margarine tubs. Choose different sizes and shapes for variety. Coat the inside of the container with petroleum jelly, mix up a bag of concrete following the directions on the bag, and put about two inches of the mixture in each plastic container. Stir gently to get rid of any air bubbles and smooth the top. After about an hour, add decorative touches, like trinkets, pebbles, writing, or leaf imprints if you desire. Let your stepping stones sit for a couple of days before removing them from the containers.

Build a picnic moat. Are ants crawling up the legs of your picnic table trying to join the feast? Stop them cold with mini moats. Pour an inch of water into four empty margarine tubs, cottage cheese containers, or tuna cans, and stand each leg of the table in one of the pools.

> Bakelite, developed as a substitute for rubber, earned its inventor, Leo Hendrik Baekeland, the title "the father of plastics." Because it was hard and heat resistant, and an electrical current couldn't flow through it, many uses were quickly found for this modern, synthetic material.

Prepare tender seedlings for transplant. Some vegetables don't transplant as well as others. Squash and cucumbers, for example, have long roots that are easily damaged, but you can improve their chances of success. Start them in a plastic berry basket. Just line the basket with newspaper, add some soil, and plant four or five seeds. Put them in a sunny spot until it's time to plant them in your garden. Snip off the tops of several seedlings to give the others more room to grow. Cut the bottom out of the basket and plant it, container and all, into the ground. The roots can continue growing without being disturbed.

Lure away wasps. If wasps are making your outdoor activities miserable, lure them away with a little sugar water in a plastic food container. Cut a small hole in the lid and snap it on over the sugar water. The wasps will be drawn in and trapped inside.

Make a hoop for needlework. A plastic tub that once held margarine can be recycled as an embroidery hoop. Wash the top and bottom and remove the center of the top, leaving only the rim. Cut off most of the bottom, leaving an amount equal to the depth of the rim. Stretch cloth over the bottom part and secure it by snapping the rim over it.

A nifty way to knit. Poke a hole in the lid of a clean, plastic ice cream bucket and store your knitting yarn inside. Feed the end through the hole, and you'll never have a tangled mess on the floor again.

Make a cozy toad house. Every garden needs hop toads. They eat thousands of caterpillars, cutworms, slugs, and grubs every year. To make them feel welcome in your neighborhood, you need to provide an attractive place for them to live. Take a large plastic food container; turn it upside down; cut out an arched doorway; place it in a moist, shady place; and anchor it down with dirt around the sides.

A tricky way to store Halloween treats. If your little ghosts and goblins like to go trick-or-treating, they'll probably enjoy making their own candy containers. Use a clean, plastic ice cream bucket, and let them decorate it with stickers or markers.

Safe packing for fragile flowers. If you need to box up artificial flowers for storage or mailing, use this tip to keep them from getting crushed. Take clean, plastic food containers and poke holes in the lids. Thread the flower stems through the holes and snap the lids, with the flowers inside, onto the plastic containers.

Foil pests in your pantry. Use clean, plastic ice cream buckets to store flour, sugar, and grains in your pantry. They'll keep everything fresh and bug free. Stick a label on the outside and finding the right ingredient will be a snap.

Learn to love leftovers. You can save money if you never throw away plastic margarine tubs. They're great for storing leftovers in the fridge or the freezer.

> Those flexible, pastel-colored plastic housewares called Tupperware were invented by Earl S. Tupper in 1948. They quickly became popular with women who bought them at home parties. But what made Tupperware most unique were the flexible lids that made it possible to "burp" the bowls and other containers. This removed excess air, creating a vacuum. Leftovers sealed with this new technique could be expected to stay fresh longer.

Travel doggie dish. An old margarine tub makes a great food dish for Fido when you take him on the road.

Button up your sewing table. Plastic containers of all sizes can bring order to your sewing area. Margarine tubs are good for larger items, like spools of thread, while old pill bottles can help you keep track of little buttons and snaps.

Plastic milk jugs

Pour some sugar. When you store sugar in a canister, you have to fill a sugar bowl or dip your spoon into the canister. Instead, store it in a clean, dry, plastic milk jug. The sugar will pour out easily into your spoon or measuring cup.

A cooler way to store perishables. For a perfect addition to your cooler — whether you're returning from the grocery store or going on an extended trip — fill a clean, plastic milk jug with water and freeze. Your perishables will stay cold, and you'll have cold drinking water, too.

Smart and slow garden watering. It's always better to give your garden plants a slow, thorough watering. To make this job

 easier, take an empty gallon plastic milk jug or two-liter soda bottle and punch several small holes in the bottom. Bury it near your plants with the mouth above the soil line. Fill it with water and some slow-release fertilizer, and watch your garden grow.

Recycle automotive oil. If you change your own oil, you're saving money, but make sure you save the environment, too. Catch that motor oil in a clean, plastic milk jug and take it to a local service station or recycling center.

Share the paint, not the mess. The bottom halves of a few gallon milk jugs come in quite handy when two or more hands are trying to paint out of the same can.

Conserve energy in your deep freeze. Experts agree, a full freezer uses less energy. If you have trouble keeping yours stocked with food, try this handy tip. Fill clean, plastic milk jugs with water and set them in the bottom of your freezer. You'll keep your food colder using less energy, and you'll have plenty of fresh drinking water in case of an emergency.

Make a handy scooper. Clean, plastic milk jugs can be turned into great scoopers. Here's how. Hold the jug so the handle is on top. Use a marker to draw a wedge on the diagonal and cut out this section. You now have a great way to dispense things like cat litter, birdseed, and sand. You can take the cap off for filling small spaces, like bird feeders. It will also do double duty as a funnel.

Make mini greenhouses. If you want to start the planting season early, or if you have small plants or seedlings that need protection from the weather, grab a plastic milk jug or soda bottle. Cut the bottom off and place it over your plant. Leave the top off for air and water.

Handy paint storage. If your garage is full of old paint cans that are rusty and dented, start storing leftover paint in clean, dry, plastic milk jugs. Use a funnel to pour in the paint and add a few marbles. All you have to do is shake the jug vigorously to mix the paint before using. Don't forget to copy down all the brand and color information from the can onto a label or piece of masking tape. You might also add notes about where you used the paint.

Practice winter safety. Fill plastic milk jugs with sand or kitty litter and store them in the trunk of your car. They'll come in handy the next time you're stuck in ice or snow, and the extra weight in your trunk will increase traction in bad weather.

Feed the birds. A plastic milk jug makes a good bird feeder. Just cut a large hole in one side and hang the jug in your yard. You can add a perch by poking a chopstick through the bottle under the feeding hole.

Pour a better batter. Next time you're in the mood for waffles or pancakes, transfer your batter into an empty milk jug before hitting the griddle. You'll pour just enough batter each time, and if you have leftovers, just put the jug in the fridge.

Popsicle sticks

Name that vegetable. A lot of plants look the same when they're small. To keep up with what you've planted, use a permanent marker to write the names on popsicle sticks. Place them in the proper rows as you plant. They will last a full season, and at harvest time, you can pull them up and toss them on the compost heap. They'll rot and become part of the soil for next year's garden.

> A century plant gets its name from the belief that it only blooms every hundred years, but the name is inaccurate. Although the plant does take a relatively long time to flower, most bloom and die by their 10th year.

The right tool for the job. An old popsicle stick comes in very handy when mixing up small batches of paint. It can also serve you well for many small jobs, like spreading glue or digging holes in flower pots.

Build a popsicle box. With a little glue and imagination, popsicle sticks make great construction beams for miniature houses, trinket boxes, pencil holders, and just about anything else a child can dream up.

Color guide for painting. Whenever you paint the interior of your home, dip one end of a popsicle stick in the paint and let it dry. Using a permanent marker, write the name of the paint color and the room in which you used it on the other end of the stick. Save these sticks, and you'll never forget the name of the paint if you need to buy it again. You can also take the sticks with you when you shop for window treatments, wallpaper borders, or decorating accessories to help you coordinate colors.

Potatoes

Remove excess salt from soup. If you were a little too generous with the salt shaker, and now your soup makes you pucker, cut up a peeled, raw potato into a few medium-size pieces and add them to the pot for about 10 minutes. Just as the potatoes are starting to get soft, fish them out. They will have absorbed the excess salt.

> Vichyssoise was invented because King Louis XV of France was paranoid about being poisoned. He had so many servants taste his soup that by the time it reached him, it was cold. He soon decided he liked it that way, and the cold potato soup soon became popular.

A new way to start your cuttings. Give your geranium cuttings a better start in life with a potato. All you have to do is bore a hole in the potato, slip the geranium stem inside, and plant the potato.

Make a scouring pad. A raw potato cut in half makes a good tool for removing rust from cookie sheets or other bake ware. Just dip the potato in baking soda or scouring powder and scrub away. The moisture from the potato holds the powder on, and the starch from the potato helps remove the rust.

The first potato chip sprouted from the exasperation of a Native American chef, George Crum, at a fancy resort in Saratoga Springs, N.Y. A dinner guest complained that the french fries were not thin enough. So Crum sliced and cooked a thinner batch. When these, too, were rejected, Crum decided to slice them so thin and fry them so crisp the complaining guest would not be able to eat them with his fork. The guest, however, was thrilled with the paper thin, crispy chips, and so were other guests. Crum eventually opened his own restaurant, and the chips became the featured item.

Slice up some worm bait. Earthworms are good for the soil in your garden. Worms in your houseplants are another story. If you think your houseplant is suffering a worm attack, place a slice of potato on the soil. The worms will crawl out for a snack, and you can grab them.

Rub food stains away. After you've cut up brightly colored vegetables, like carrots or pumpkin, you may have stained fingers. A slice of raw potato, rubbed across your skin, will lift off those stains.

Remove a broken light bulb. A raw potato makes a handy tool for removing the end of a broken light bulb from its socket. Make sure the switch is turned off, push the potato into the socket, and turn.

Rubber bands

No more messy spoons. Is your mixing spoon forever sliding down into the bowl as soon as you let go of it? Wrap a rubber band around the handle, and it will stay on the edge.

Keep track of your liquids. If you have liquid containers in your workshop, it may be hard to keep track of how much you have left in each of them. Make it easier on yourself by wrapping a rubber band around each bottle or can at the approximate level of the contents. You can adjust the rubber band as the level goes down and have a good idea of when it's time for a trip to the store.

Don't flip your lids. Does your church or social group have a lot of covered-dish dinners? To keep the lid on your covered dish while transporting it, stretch a large rubber band over the top, from one handle to the other.

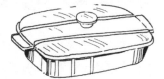

Temporary childproofing. If you have small children in your home, your cabinets probably have childproof latches. But what if you just have small children coming to visit? For a quick way to childproof your kitchen, secure cabinet handles to each other with extra-large rubber bands.

Tidy up your sewing box. If you wrap a rubber band around each spool of thread, it will keep the thread from unraveling.

Improve a child's grip. Children sometimes have a difficult time holding onto a water glass. A wide rubber band, slipped around the glass, can improve their grip and lessen the chance of spills.

Organize your car. Wrap a couple of rubber bands around the sun visors, and you'll have a handy place to slip maps, pencils, directions, tickets, etc.

Dripless painting. This tip will keep the rim of your paint can from overflowing with paint. Instead of wiping your paintbrush on the side of the can to remove the excess, stretch a large rubber band around the can so part of it is across the opening. Wipe your brush against the band, and the excess will drip right back into the can. No mess, no waste.

Keep cutting boards in place. Does your cutting board slide around whenever you chop something vigorously? Wrap a couple of rubber bands diagonally across each corner, and it will stay put so you can hack away at those veggies with as much gusto as you like.

Rubbing Alcohol

Rub hair spray away. Use rubbing alcohol to remove hair spray from bathroom mirrors and curling irons.

No-streak window wiping. Need clean, streak-free windows and need them fast? Wipe them down with rubbing alcohol.

Free windshields from frost. Don't spend time on cold winter mornings scraping frost off your windshield. Keep a spray bottle of alcohol in your car. Just spray it on the windshield, and you'll be able to wipe the frost off easily.

Keep a clear view in winter. When you wash your windows during cold weather, add a half cup of rubbing alcohol to every quart of wash water. After washing them down, polish the windows with newspaper. This will keep them free of frost all winter. If you don't have alcohol handy, try the same recipe with antifreeze.

Loosen tight shoes. If your new shoes are pinching your feet, try swabbing the tight spot with a cotton ball soaked in alcohol. Walk around in the shoes for a few minutes to see if they've loosened up enough to be comfortable. If not, put on a different pair of shoes.

Quick-clean chrome fixtures. Polish those chrome bathroom fixtures with rubbing alcohol. It will leave them spotless, and since it evaporates, you won't have to rinse.

Remove ticks from your dog. If a tick has a hold on your dog, dab a little alcohol on its back, then pull it out with tweezers. Make sure you pull it out straight and clean. Anything you leave behind can become infected.

No more ring around the collar. If your shirt collars are constantly stained, wipe your neck with rubbing alcohol each morning before you get dressed.

Clean that dirty Venetian. Wrap an old rag around a spatula to make a neat tool for cleaning the delicate slats in Venetian blinds. Dampen the rag with rubbing alcohol, secure it with a rubber band, and you're on your way to cleaner blinds.

Two cleans in one. Alcohol can be used to clean your phone, too. For the small areas, use a cotton swab. For the larger areas, use a paper towel or cloth. The alcohol will tidy up the phone and kill germs at the same time.

Make an emergency ice pack. To make a slushy ice pack that will mold around an injury, mix one part rubbing alcohol with three parts water in a zip-lock bag. The alcohol will keep it from freezing completely, resulting in frozen "slush." When you need to use it, simply take it out, pop it into another bag or wrap in a cloth, and apply to the injury. It also works great for soothing headaches.

Salt

Spiff up silk flowers. Getting silk flowers really clean is a challenge, and salt can help. Just put the flowers into a large paper bag, pour in one cup of salt, shake vigorously, and remove. Give them a couple of shakes over the bag to get rid of any lingering salt, and your flowers will be clean and bright.

Kiss lipstick stains goodbye. Lipstick stains on your glassware can be embarrassing at a dinner party. To avoid that situation, quickly rub a little salt on the rim of your glasses before washing them.

> Roman soldiers were paid a "salarium" or "salt money," which is how we got the word "salary." And a good soldier was considered "worth his salt."

Clean up spilled eggs. Crying over spilt milk is nothing compared to the crying you'll do over spilled eggs. They're so slimy and hard to clean up. Try pouring salt on top of the spill to cover the eggs, and then just wipe up with a paper towel, and you won't have to wipe away any tears.

Relieve a sore throat. Your mother probably told you to gargle with salt water whenever you had a sore throat, and it turns out she was right. The American Academy of Otolaryngology recommends warm salt-water gargles to soothe mild sore throats. Just mix one-fourth teaspoon of salt in a half cup of warm water for easy and inexpensive sore throat relief.

Clean a glass vase. To get your favorite glass flower vase sparkling clean, make a paste from one-third cup of salt and two tablespoons of vinegar. Apply to inside of vase, let stand for 20 minutes, scrub, rinse, and dry.

Remove rust. If you've let your household tools get rusty from disuse, get them back in tiptop shape with a little salt and lemon juice. Mix enough salt into a tablespoon of lemon juice to make a paste, apply to rusted areas with a dry cloth, and rub.

Make pantyhose last longer. Tired of buying expensive hosiery and getting a run the first time you wear them? Try this salty solution. Wash new pantyhose, and drip dry. Then soak for three hours in a solution of one gallon of water and two cups of salt. Rinse thoroughly and drip dry again. Your hose should be more run-resistant.

Remove fish odor from hands. You're the best fish-fry chef in three counties, but afterward, they can still smell the fish on your hands three counties away. Get rid of that lingering odor. Just dip a lemon wedge in salt, rub it on your hands, and rinse with water.

Make your own sculpturing clay. Mix one cup flour, a half cup salt, two teaspoons cream of tartar, one cup water and several drops of food coloring, if desired. Cook over medium heat, stirring constantly to avoid sticking. When it forms a lumpy ball, allow it to cool, and then add one or two drops of vegetable oil. Knead until pliable. The clay can be stored in a closed, plastic bag for later use. (Remind the kids that this clay is for artwork and not for eating.)

Preserve your wicker's natural color. Scrub natural rattan and wicker furniture with a little warm water and Morton's salt to keep it from turning yellow.

Add suds control. If you put too much detergent in the washing machine, over-sudsing can make it overflow. Stop the foaming action by adding half a cup of salt to the wash.

Clean your iron's bottom. Keeping your iron clean will prevent you from transferring any stains onto your clean clothes when you iron them. Get the iron hot on the dry (not steam) setting. Sprinkle table salt on a brown paper bag and run the iron over it. But don't clean your iron this way if it has a nonstick finish. Use a plastic scrubber instead, and make sure the iron isn't hot.

Easy-clean oven spills. Ever had a casserole bubble over in the oven? Or the extra cheese on your pizza make an extra-messy spill? If you sprinkle the spill immediately with salt, by the time your oven is cool, you'll have nothing but ash to wipe up.

A deadly seasoning for slugs. Kill slugs and snails instantly by sprinkling salt on them. You'll find them out and about mostly at night, so grab a flashlight and start shaking.

Kill a stubborn weed. If you have a large weed with deep roots that are difficult to dig out, reach for the salt shaker. But first, dig around the base of the root and cut it off below the ground. Sprinkle salt generously on the root, being careful not to get any on the surrounding soil. That weed won't return. (You can also use the brine left after making homemade ice cream.)

Deter fleas. Every couple of weeks, wash your doghouse with salt water. It will help prevent fleas from settling in.

The origin of the phrase "in the doghouse" came from the play *Peter Pan*. When Mr. Darling punished the dog/nursemaid Nana, the Darling children left home, and Mr. Darling lived in the doghouse as penance until they returned.

Lose the dandruff. Scrub away dandruff with everyday table salt. Just shake a tablespoon or so into your hair while dry. Rub it through your hair, massaging your scalp, then shampoo as usual.

Relieve dry skin. What's one of the best at-home treatments for dry skin? Would you believe salt water? Just dissolve one cup of ordinary table salt in your tub and take a normal bath. Sea salt, if you can find it, will give you even better results.

Test mushrooms. Never eat a mushroom if you have any doubt about its safety, but this is an interesting test. Sprinkle salt on the gills (the spongy part) of the mushroom. If it turns yellow, it's poisonous. If it turns black, it should be edible.

Toughen up your broom. Soak your new broom in a hot saltwater solution to make the bristles last longer.

Wash away stuck-on foods. Hardened pizza cheese or glue-like egg yolks can make dishwashing a culinary nightmare. Make the job easier by sprinkling the plates or pans with salt first. Soon, all your troubles will just wash away.

Tea for two without stains. If the spout of your teapot is stained, pack it full of salt and let it sit overnight. The next morning, pour boiling water into the pot and out the spout. The stain should rinse away, but if it's stubborn, use pipe cleaners or cotton swabs to give it a gentle scrub.

Easy-clean fireplace. Cleaning the fireplace is a messy and unpleasant job. You can eliminate some of that bother simply by throwing a handful of salt into your fire occasionally. It will reduce the amount of soot produced.

Because salt was such a valuable commodity, spilling salt has long been considered bad luck by superstitious people. The practice of throwing salt over the left shoulder was an attempt to "blind the devil by throwing a pinch at him," and avert misfortune.

Strengthen your glassware. There's an easy way to make your glassware less fragile. Bring a large pot of salt water to a *very* slow boil. Gently add your glassware and barely simmer. This will make all your glass stronger and less likely to break.

Invigorate your shower. For a refreshing, invigorating shower that smooths your skin, try this interesting homemade body scrub. Mix four tablespoons of salt with two teaspoons of vegetable oil and four drops of peppermint oil. Rub it into your skin while you're in the shower, and enjoy the wonderful, smoothing tingle.

Make an ant roadblock. Sprinkle salt across doorways or ant trails, and the little critters will make a fast detour.

Fry without splatters. Do you avoid frying bacon because you always get zinged with hot grease? Try adding a little salt to your frying pan, and say goodbye to dangerous popping grease.

Hold that stain. If you get a grease stain but can't treat it immediately, pour on a generous amount of salt. It should absorb the grease. Out of salt? Try cornmeal or cornstarch.

Get between the cracks. Add a few tablespoons of salt to boiling water, and pour it between the cracks in your sidewalk or driveway. This should spell the end for the stubborn weeds that seem to thrive in cracked pavement. To keep them from coming back, sprinkle more salt into the cracks after they're gone. But don't overdo it. The salt can damage your garden or lawn if the rain rinses too much of it in that direction.

Make baking-day cleanup fast and easy. Rolling out dough leaves a sticky, floury mess. When it's time to clean up, sprinkle salt over the area then wipe up with a sponge. Lumps and clumps will rinse right away.

Saltshaker

Easy garden sprinkling. In some cases, too much fertilizer can be as bad as not enough. Fill a large saltshaker with fertilizer for a light touch with tender seedlings.

No more waste on baking day. Do you end up wasting more flour than you use when you're preparing pans for baking? Instead of piling flour into a greased pan with a spoon, try filling a large saltshaker with flour. It makes "dusting" quick and easy.

Neat and easy cinnamon toast. Fill a large saltshaker with a cinnamon and sugar mixture. The next time you make toast, just sprinkle a little on for a warm morning treat.

Sand

Sparkling clean bottles. If you want the inside of a bottle clean, one way is to put some clean sand in it, add water and shake. The sand should supply enough abrasive to scrub the inside clean.

Whiten your wood floor. If you've got an unpainted wood floor in your house or on your porch, here's an easy way to clean and whiten it. Sprinkle a generous amount of clean, white sand on it, then walk on it as usual for a few days. Sweep it up, and your boards will look like new.

Sand was once used as a floor cleaner, especially in kitchens. The sandman — yes, he was a real character — would deliver a fresh supply about once a week. Before his arrival, the housewife would sweep out the old sand along with dirt and whatever else had dropped on the floor since his last visit.

Give yourself extra traction. If you're worried about getting stuck in snowbanks, throw some bags of sand in your trunk during the winter months. If you're ever stuck, a little extra grit under the wheels can often make the difference.

Dad's very own sandbox. A good way to keep your gardening tools clean and well-oiled is to prepare a sandbox in your toolshed. Mix 40 pounds of sand with one quart of motor oil, and keep it in an open box. After using tools, rub them through the gritty, oily mixture a few times to clean and lubricate them for storage.

Hands-free china repairs. If you've ever broken a plate, you know how difficult it can be to glue the pieces back together. Try this simple tip. Fill a large bowl with sand and set the largest piece of crockery in it so that the broken edge is up. Mound the sand around the piece until it can stand upright on its own. Then go to work on the repair. Glue one piece at a time, following the manufacturer's directions. To hold the joined pieces together while the glue is drying, try using a couple of clothespins.

Sandpaper

Slug it out. When you are finished with those sandpaper disks in your workshop, give them a second life in your garden. Cut them open to make a collar that you can slip around the base of your plants. Slugs won't crawl over them.

Give new life to scissors. Sharpen your scissors by cutting through sandpaper several times.

Remove ink stains from suede. You dropped your ballpoint pen, and it left a mark on your suede shoe. Try removing it by rubbing the stain carefully with fine sandpaper. This will work for scuff marks and other stains as well.

Clean up your tile floor. To lift stains from between floor tiles, use a fine-grade sandpaper to lightly rub the grout.

Make shoes less slippery. Whenever you buy a new pair of hard-soled shoes, run a piece of sandpaper lightly across the sole. This should roughen the surface just enough to provide more gripping power and perhaps prevent a fall.

Blend away a messy paint job. If you can't get all of the last coat of paint off before throwing on the next one, at least try to blend in the patches of old paint that remain. Use sandpaper to smooth down old paint so the new coat will look smoother.

Hold that pleat. Hold pleats in place while you iron by placing a coarse sheet of sandpaper underneath the fabric.

Sharpen your needles. If you're having trouble with your needle snagging or puckering fabric, it may be dull. Give it a quick fix by poking it through a piece of sandpaper several times.

De-ball your fuzzy sweater. Light-to-medium-grade sandpaper does a good job of pulling those annoying little fuzz balls off your favorite sweaters.

Remove scorch marks. You forgot to use a press cloth. Now you have a scorch mark on a tweed or heavy woolen jacket. If it's not too deep, you can remove it by lightly rubbing it with sandpaper.

Sandwich and freezer bags

Easy-does-it deviled eggs. A simple, no-mess way to make deviled eggs is to put all the ingredients for the filling into a zip-lock bag, seal, and mix by kneading the bag for a few minutes. Then just cut a small hole in one corner of the bag, and pipe the filling into the egg white halves — no bowl, spoon, or pastry tube to clean!

Keep cookbooks splatter-free. Slip your open cookbook inside a large clear freezer bag to hold open your place and protect it from spills while you're cooking.

Marinate meat. Zip-lock bags are the ideal no-mess method for marinating meat. You don't have to use as much liquid, and instead of having to turn or baste the meat, you just flip the bag over.

Save your cell phone from splashes. When you go to the beach or swimming pool, you can keep your cell phone or portable radio safe and water-free by keeping it in a zip-lock bag.

William P. Lear is most often associated with corporate jet airplanes. But earlier, he made his mark in car radios. And he launched the Motorola Company in the 1960s with the invention of the eight-track tape player.

No-mess greasing. If you do a lot of baking, you probably grease a lot of pans. If you keep a sandwich bag in your can of shortening, you can just stick your hand into the bag, scoop out some shortening, and grease the pan without ever getting your hand messy. Then you can just return it to the can and use it over and over.

Clean and easy shoe storage. A good way to store shoes is to slip them inside zip-lock bags. They'll remain dust free in your closet or attic. And if you're packing for a trip, bring out those baggies to keep the dirt from your shoes off the other items in your suitcase.

Economical cake decorating. If you've got leftover frosting, scoop it into a zip-lock bag and either refrigerate or freeze. When you make a fresh batch of cupcakes or cookies, defrost the frosting, add a bit of water to thin (simply mix in the water by squeezing the sealed bag for several minutes), snip off a small corner, and you have your own disposable icing bag.

Make crushed ice with no mess. Take a large zip-lock freezer bag and fill it with cold water. Zip it shut and lay it flat in your freezer on a baking sheet. Then next time you need crushed ice, take the bag from your freezer, and drop it on a hard floor until the ice is broken up.

Soak your shower head. If you have mineral deposits built up on your shower head, they can block the flow of water. To get rid of them without taking apart your fixture, fill a plastic sandwich bag with vinegar. Pull the bag up so that the shower head is completely immersed in the vinegar. Use a rubber band to attach the bag. Leave it to soak for several hours or overnight. Remove the bag and, if necessary, use an old toothbrush and toothpicks to clean all the holes.

No-odor way to chop onions. Turn a sandwich bag inside out, slip in your hand, and grab an onion. You'll get no onion odor on your fingers while you're chopping, and it's a simple matter to turn the bag right side out and store the leftovers.

Mark your garden well. All those seedlings seem to look the same when they are only a few inches high. Remember what you planted with colorful seed packets as markers. First staple the packet to the top of a popsicle stick. Then slip a plastic sandwich bag over it and staple again at the bottom. You'll have an attractive row marker that won't fade or fall apart when spring rains fall.

Screen doors and windows

Wash dirt from fresh produce. An old screen door placed over two sawhorses makes a great surface to wash, drain, and dry vegetables from your garden. Put it within reach of the water hose, but in the shade where the sun won't scorch the produce. And if you place it over a dry part of your garden, you can let the "wash water" do double duty and give your garden a drink.

Salvage old paint. Got some old paint that's a little lumpy? Although you can't break up the lumps, you can still save the paint. Just strain it through an old piece of screen into a new container. The lumps will magically disappear.

Introduce new pets. A screen door or a child's safety gate is a good barrier to separate pets that are about to become roommates. If they get a chance to see and sniff each other from a safe spot beforehand, their eventual introduction should go more smoothly.

In the garden of seedin'. The next time you spread seed in the garden or on the lawn, give the little guys a fighting chance. An old screen door or window laid down on top of the area will provide good protection against hungry birds as the new seed takes root.

A screen window's second career. Just because a screen window has too many holes to keep out even the birds doesn't mean it's useless. Cover it with heavy plastic, and it can go right back in as an extra storm window.

Shampoo

Starter solution for seedlings. Make it easy for your seedlings to get started. Water them with a solution of a teaspoon of baby shampoo and a quart of water. This mixture will keep the soil soft and moist so seedlings can break through easily.

> The word shampoo comes from the Hindi word champoo, which means "to massage."

Unshrink your sweater. Your favorite wool sweater shrank when you washed it, but don't give it to your 10-year-old niece just yet. Try soaking it in lukewarm water with shampoo mixed in the water. This may soften the fabric and allow you to reshape it. Dry it flat on a sweater rack or on a clean dry towel.

Say goodbye to ring around the collar. Rub shampoo into those stubborn collar rings and watch stains wash away.

Grownups don't like tears either. "No more tears" isn't just for babies. You can use baby shampoo to remove your eye makeup. Not only is it cheaper than specialty products, but it's gentle on your eyes.

Shoe bags

Get organized in every room. Hanging shoe bags, with their many little pockets, are great ways to organize clutter in the bathroom, your sewing room, even the kids' rooms. Hang them on a wall, in a closet, or on the back of a door and fill them with small toys, books or magazines, sewing supplies — anything that takes up valuable storage space.

Did you think the company that makes Weejun loafers gave them an Indian name because they look like Native American moccasins? In fact, it's not an Indian name at all. The cobbler, Henry Bass, redesigned a slipper made in Norway to create the modern loafer. He based the name on the last two syllables of "Norwegian."

Make cleanup fast and easy. Fill the pockets of a hanging shoe bag with various cleaning supplies and put it in a handy place. You can even carry it from room to room — it will hang from a shower rod or towel hook. You'll know at a glance which supplies need to be refilled on your next shopping trip.

Ease up on travel clutter. Going on vacation with the kids? Or do you have a lengthy commute with them every day? Either way, it's important to keep them entertained in the car, but that can mean toys and books all over the place. Try hanging a shoe bag on the back of the front seat and filling the pockets with their favorite items.

Stay organized when camping. A hanging shoe bag should be the first thing you pack on your next camping trip. This versatile item can save you from lost socks, misplaced toothbrushes, or cluttered piles of clothing. Hang one inside your tent or camper, and fill the bags with each person's necessities for the next morning. Use another one for bathroom items. Even if the family has to take turns in the shower, at least the shampoo, soap, etc. will all be in the right place.

Shoulder pads

Recyclable dust rags. Those shoulder pads you rip out of all your sweaters make great palm-sized dust rags. They're soft, washable, and reusable.

From shoulder to knee. Next time you need to scrub the floor, protect your knees with shoulder pads. That's right, just sew a couple of elastic strips to those useless shoulder pads and presto — you have useful knee pads.

Create sachets. Put potpourri or spices in old shoulder pads and tuck into your drawers for pleasantly scented clothing.

Make padded clothes hangers. No need to buy expensive padded clothes hangers for those delicate dresses. Just attach extra shoulder pads at the corners of plastic hangers.

Pad crutches and walkers. If you use crutches or a walker, you know the rubber hand and underarm pads can become irritating. Soften up those areas by taping shoulder pads on the hand grips or the tops of your crutches.

Socks

Clean louvered doors and blinds. Cleaning louvered doors and mini-blinds is always a challenge. Make your own specialized cleaning instrument with an old sock and a ruler or yardstick. Slip the sock over the ruler and secure it with a rubber band. Spray with a commercial dust-attracting spray or with rubbing alcohol, and wipe across each slat.

Protect shoes from paint spatters. You usually wear your socks inside your shoes, but on paint day, do the opposite. Pull an old pair of socks on over your shoes, and you'll protect your footwear from paint spatters.

Guard against drafts. If your house is a little drafty, you can keep some of that cold air out with an old sock. Just fill a long tube sock with sand, tie the end shut, and stretch it in front of the offending doorway.

De-feet dust. Make dusting furniture a fun and easy chore by slipping old socks onto your hands and spraying with furniture polish. Children love it.

Hand-y protection for road emergencies. Keep a few old socks in the trunk of your car, and use them instead of your good gloves when you need to change a tire or handle some other messy emergency.

Sock it to your next headache. Everyone has single or worn-out socks lying around. One way to still get some good use from them is to wet them and stick them in a zip-lock bag in the freezer. They make great compresses for headaches, bumps and bruises, or puffy eyes. You can even cut off the foot of the sock and just use the top.

No-scratch furniture moving. Slip old socks on the legs of your furniture on cleaning or moving day. No more scratches on your hardwood or vinyl floors.

Double-duty knee-pad holders. If you find yourself on your knees often, whether you're gardening or doing household chores, you might like this little trick to save wear and tear on your joints. Cut the tops off old, worn-out socks and slip them up (even over your pants) to your knees. These stretchy tubes make great holders for all types of pads, like sponges or shoulder pads.

A clean travel tip. Slip old, clean socks over shoes before putting them in your suitcase.

Bath-time fun for your toddler. When children decide they want to do everything for themselves, life can become more of a challenge for you. But here's an easy way to let them "help" in the tub. Take an old, clean, soft sock, and fill it with pieces of baby soap. Close the end with a rubber band or a piece of Velcro, and let baby scrub away. No more lost slivers of soap in the tub, either.

Save your upholstery. If you have little ones visiting that climb on your furniture or car seats, don't worry about dirty shoes. Slip an old pair of socks over their feet, shoes and all, and let them play. No more hassles with taking shoes off and putting them back on again.

Cover an ugly cast. Before six weeks are up, you're probably sick of looking at your cast — and it may be pretty grimy, too. Cut the foot off a large tube sock, and slip it on for an easy and inexpensive cover-up. If you like, you can buy different-colored socks to brighten your wardrobe. Kids, especially, will like this idea.

> You have 250,000 sweat glands in your feet, and they create up to a pint of moisture every day. And you wonder what you need socks for!

Make your car shine. Old socks make great hand mitts for waxing and buffing your car.

Protect your glassware. If you have to pack glass items, whether it's for a camping trip, a picnic, or a move, you worry about breakage. Old, clean socks are a perfect packing companion. Just slip the glass items into socks, and don't worry if they jostle next to each other. You can cut long socks into several pieces to get more use out of them.

Don't let a ladder scratch your siding. Old, thick socks make great booties to slip over the ends of your ladder before leaning it against your house.

Arm yourself against thorns. Briars can take the fun out of picking blackberries. Protect your arms with long cotton socks. Cut two holes in the toe of the sock — a small one for your thumb and a bigger hole for your fingers.

Soda

Perk up cut flowers. Fresh cut flowers beautify your home, so you want to keep them fresh as long as possible. When you bring your flowers home, you should cut about an inch off the end of each stem so it can soak up as much water as it needs. Then when you put water in your vase, add a little 7-Up (regular, not diet). Change the water every day, and add a little fresh 7-Up as well. These steps should help your flowers stay perky as long as possible.

Pop a top for better car care. Use a can of carbonated soda to wash away corrosion on your car's battery terminals. Simply pour it on, and watch it fizz away the rust and dirt.

Soda hasn't been around nearly as long as milk, water, or even tea, but it has become one of the most popular drinks in the world. Coca Cola was invented in 1886, and sales that year averaged nine drinks a day. Today, The Coca-Cola Company sells more than one billion drinks per day.

Remove spots from carpet. Do you automatically reach for soap to clean spots in your carpet? Next time, reach for club soda first. The carbonation loosens dirt so you can blot it up, and it doesn't leave a sticky residue like soap does.

Nourish your plants. You like to sip soda, but did you know your plants might also like an occasional soda? The minerals in club soda help nourish green plants, so give them a treat once in a while instead of water. Just let it go flat first.

Loosen rusty nuts and bolts. Have you ever been frustrated trying to remove a rusted-on nut? Next time, try pouring a little Coke on the stubborn nut or bolt. The bubbly carbonation will fizz away the rust and make removal much easier.

Fluff up pancakes. For lighter, fluffier pancakes and waffles, replace the usual liquid in your batter with club soda.

Clean your toilet bowl. Did you buy a lot of cola the last time your grandkids visited, and now it's all gone flat? You can still put it to good use. Instead of pouring it down the drain, pour it into your toilet bowl. Let it soak for about an hour, and you'll end up with sparkling porcelain.

Pop open oyster shells. Soaking oysters in club soda for about five minutes should make their shells easier to open.

Smooth out bitter coffee. If your brewed coffee has become bitter from sitting a bit too long, add just a touch of club soda (about one-fourth cup for every one and a half cups of coffee). Stir and enjoy.

Spices

Aromatic moth-proofing. If you hate the smell of moth-balls, just tuck some cloves into the pockets of your wool clothing, or make a clove sachet to hang in your closet. You'll keep moths away and make your closet smell pleasantly spicy.

Spice up your thermos. If you don't use your thermos often, store it with a couple of cloves inside, and you'll never have that musty smell again.

Keep ants at bay. You may like the smell of bay leaves, but ants don't. Keep them out of your house by crumpling a few leaves on your windowsills. You can also drop one or two into your flour and sugar containers just to be on the safe side.

Whiten those hankies. Your white handkerchiefs will wash out brighter if you put a bit of cream of tartar into the wash water.

> Pop-up tissues in pretty boxes may decorate your modern bathroom, but their origin is less than glamorous. The cotton wadding, which the Kimberly-Clark company called Cellucotton, served as super-absorbent surgical bandages and air filters for GI's gas masks during World War II. After the war, Kimberly-Clark tried selling leftover Cellucotton as Kleenex Kerchiefs, the "sanitary cold cream remover." After a marketing test showed more people were using them to blow their noses than remove makeup, they were repackaged as disposable handkerchiefs.

Bugs back off. Your flower garden can't flourish when your perennials are covered with insects. Discourage their foraging with a mixture of black pepper and pre-sifted flour. Sprinkle it on and around your plants. Bugs will beat a hasty retreat.

Spray away unwanted guests. Black pepper may be nothing for garden pests to sneeze at, but a few cayenne peppers will really burn them. Ants, spiders, caterpillars, and cabbage worms are just a few of the bothersome friends that won't appreciate the extra spice in their lives. To make an effective spray, just blend a few dried cayennes with water in a blender. Or if ants are your problem, grind up a handful of dried cayenne peppers and dump the hot powder into the colony. They'll evacuate the premises in no time.

Deer cayenne't stand it. Bugs aren't the only creatures turned away by spicy peppers. Bigger pests cringe at the taste, too. Keep deer and other leaf-chewers away from your bushes by spraying them with a cayenne and water blend.

Highlight your dark hair. Try this natural way to give your dark tresses some intriguing highlights. In a cup of water, simmer one teaspoon of allspice, one teaspoon of crushed cinnamon, and a half teaspoon of cloves. Strain and let cool. After shampooing, pour the solution on your wet hair, then rinse. If you have an allergy to cinnamon, which can be an irritant, you should not use this treatment.

Deodorize jars and bottles. You'd like to reuse a collection of glass containers, but some of them have unpleasant odors. Fill them with a solution of water and dry mustard. Let them soak for several hours, then wash and rinse.

Green means stop for red ants. Red ants hate green sage. If you want to make them unwelcome, sprinkle a dash of this handy spice in your kitchen cabinets.

Clean pots with cream of tartar. Brighten discolored aluminum with this mixture — two tablespoons of cream of tartar and one quart of water. Boil for 10 minutes.

Never store food in aluminum pots, because chemicals in the food can erode the metal. While this doesn't cause food poisoning, it does damage your pots and make them unsanitary to cook with.

General Basil to the rescue. Tomato plants under insect siege? Drive away flies and worms with a little well-placed basil.

Cabbage moths, you've been warned. Cabbage, broccoli, cauliflower, and brussels sprouts are all defenseless victims of the cabbage moth. Well, maybe not so defenseless. Add a little spice to your garden and a little protection against the cabbage moth by planting some mint, sage, dill, or thyme.

Steel wool

Make a pin cushion. Make a pin cushion by covering a steel wool pad with fabric. The steel wool will do double duty. It will keep your pins and needles in place, and it will keep them sharp.

> Have you ever noticed that there's a missing period in the name of S.O.S pads? However, it's not a typo. In order to avoid confusion with the famous distress signal, the inventor of S.O.S pads decided to give his product a unique spelling and register it with the Patent Office. His wife came up with the name, which stands for "Save Our Saucepans."

Keep bathtub drain clear. If you bathe your dog in the bathtub while he's shedding, you know the drain can quickly get clogged with hair. Put a piece of steel wool in the drain, and it will catch all that hair and still let the water drain.

Fix a sticky iron. If your iron is sticking to your clothes, it's time to clean the surface. First, give it a good rubdown using a rag and rubbing alcohol, then go over the surface with extra fine steel wool. Finally, wipe it down and buff it with a soft rag until it's smooth again.

String

Zip open boxes. When you pack for a move, before you seal your boxes, place a length of string where the tape will go. Leave a few inches hanging out at the place where the ends of the tape come together. Later when you are ready to unpack, a pull on the string will quickly rip the tape loose. No need for a knife or scissors.

Clean between the tines. Want to get your good forks squeaky clean? Wet a string and coat it with baking powder. Run it between the tines of your sterling silver forks to clean those hard-to-reach edges. You can use this method to polish tines as well. Just put your silver polish on a string, and rub away tarnish.

"Fork over that fork" may have been the cry of church fathers in 11th-century Tuscany when the two-tined fork appeared. They believed only the fingers, which were created by God, were worthy instruments to touch His bounty. Centuries later, forks were still not widely used. In fact, in the 17th century, a man was considered a 'sissy' if he used one.

Trim hedges straight. If your hedges usually look a little lopsided when you finish trimming, try this. Tie a string to a branch on one side of the hedge, and run it to the other side. Step back and eyeball it to make sure it looks straight, and then use it as a guide while you trim.

Make a wick to water your plant. You are going on vacation and have no one to water your plants. Take off your shoe to find a solution to your dilemma. A cotton shoestring can serve as a wick to slowly add moisture to the soil around your plant. Push one end deep into the soil around the roots, and put the other end into a container of water. You'll return home to a happy plant.

No more noisy drips. A drippy faucet can make sleeping a real nightmare. If the plumber has been delayed, here's an idea for a quick fix. Tie a piece of string, about two feet long, around the faucet letting the end hang down into the drain. The water will run silently down the string — sweet dreams.

Tighten up loose screws. Wrap a piece of thin string or thread around the screw threads before inserting it into a hole, and you'll have a tighter fit.

Can't think of anything to do with that leftover piece of string? Why not start a collection? That's what Francis Johnson did many years ago, and now he's the proud owner of the world's largest ball of string. Mr. Johnson's monster ball stands 11 feet tall and weighs more than five tons. And you were just going to throw it out!

Pretty flowers all in a row. Dampen a length of string, and dip it into your container of seeds — the seeds will stick along the string. Then stretch the string out in your garden and cover with dirt. You'll end up with a perfectly straight row of plants.

Styrofoam™

Get a head start on a birthday party. Make an ice cream cone holder by punching holes in a thick block of Styrofoam — like the kind you find in boxes protecting small appliances. Fill cones with ice cream, then stand them in the foam block, and place the whole thing in the freezer. At serving time there's no need to mess with scooping ice cream. Just take it out, and hand a filled cone to each excited youngster.

Protect fragile items in the mail. If you send pictures to Grandma or computer disks to your boss, you may get tired of buying special expensive padded mailers. Keep these important items from getting bent en route by slipping clean foam meat trays into regular envelopes first. You're recycling at the same time.

Perfect your pedicure. Save those little foam peanuts that are used as packing material, and use them between your toes during your next pedicure. No more smudged polish.

When the Dow Chemical Company developed the plastic foam it called "Styrofoam" in the 1940's, it was first used as flotation material in life rafts and lifeboats because it didn't absorb water. Then the company discovered it was an ideal insulation material and quickly found many more uses for this unique material.

Inspire a young Picasso. Every painter needs a palette. Your mini-Monet can have a disposable one made from a foam vegetable tray. Just cut a hole in one corner for his little thumb, and let the masterpieces begin.

When life hands you Styrofoam, make snow. Take any piece of Styrofoam. Add blender. Go. When the shredding is over, you've got yourself packaging material that will pad even the most delicate of items. This "snow" can also be used to beautify winter crafts.

Sugar

Keep your flowers fresh. To retain the beauty of your cut flowers, keep them fed and fresh. For each quart of water, add two tablespoons of sugar (for food) and two tablespoons of white vinegar (for freshness).

No more stale desserts. Keep your cake fresh and moist by storing it in an airtight container with a couple of lumps of sugar.

> You can just open a packet and shake pure white sugar into your coffee, but it hasn't always been that easy. Before the days of commercial refineries, a housewife had to refine sugar in her own kitchen. The sugar she purchased was black with molasses. To make it white, she would mix it with beaten egg whites and water, then boil it, skimming dark scum off the surface. When at last it looked clear, she would strain it and boil it again. She had to work for hours with four pounds of unrefined sugar to get one pound of the white stuff we take for granted today.

Just say no to nematodes. Here's a sweet solution to your problem with nematodes in your garden — till in three pounds of sugar per acre in early spring and again in late fall. You'll find no more damage from these bothersome worms.

Homemade fly trap. If you hate flies but hate commercial pesticides even more, here's a natural way to keep your kitchen fly-free all summer. Combine one pint of milk, a quarter pound of raw sugar, and two ounces of ground pepper in a saucepan. Simmer the mixture for about 10 minutes. Pour into shallow dishes, and set around your house or patio. The flies will flock to this treat and drown.

Give your family the fake bake. To give your kitchen a strong aroma of delicious baking without all the work, toss a few teaspoons of sugar and cinnamon into a pie tin, and burn it slowly on the stove. Don't be surprised if fooled parties start peeking their heads into the kitchen.

Gardeners, try this sweet cleanup. To get rid of dirty knuckles and ground-in soil on your hands, lather up with a teaspoon of sugar.

Tape

Pick up lint and hair. A wide piece of tape makes a great impromptu lint brush. Just wrap it (sticky side out of course) around your hand, and roll along your clothing. It also works great for getting pet hairs off your furniture.

Keep cats off counters. If your cat insists on jumping on your kitchen counters, you can discourage him even when you're not around. Just put a few strips of sticky-on-both-sides tape on your counters. Cats don't like the feel of the sticky tape on their paws, and after a few experiences with it, they'll find your counter-tops a much less attractive place to hang out.

Cut bangs straight. Your child's bangs have gotten a little long, but you don't want to spend money taking them to a salon for a haircut. You can cut them yourself with a little help from transparent tape. Just tape down the wet bangs and cut above the piece of tape, using the edge as a guide. You'll be able to cut straighter, and you have the added bonus of the loose hair sticking to the tape, so you can just toss it away.

> The average citizen couldn't buy transparent tape during World War II, because the military wanted it all for the war effort.

Repair shower curtains. You can repair torn ring holes in your shower curtain. Just put a piece of duct tape or heavy plastic tape on either side of the hole, and use a hole puncher to poke a new hole through the tape.

Keep paint cans neat. Before you pour paint from a can into a tray or other container, put masking tape around the rim. After you finish and pull the tape off, the rim of the can will be clean and paint-free, so you can put the lid back on without worrying about it sticking the next time you use it.

Hem jeans. Usually hemming a pair of pants isn't a big deal, but hemming thick denim jeans can be a lot of trouble. You can make a "fake hem" by folding up the legs to the desired length, pressing, and taping in place with duct tape. The tape won't show, and it will last through several washings. When it comes off, you just replace it with more duct tape, and no one will ever know.

> Levi Strauss sold cloth in New York before he decided to join the California Gold Rush of 1848. Once he got there, he found out the miners needed heavy work pants that would not wear out. He started making trousers out of canvas for them but eventually switched to a new fabric from Genoa, Italy, called "genes." Strauss changed the name to "jeans" and later to "Levi's."

Seal a small crack. For small leaks or cracks in an outgoing water pipe, wrap it with a few layers of electrical tape to keep things temporarily under control until you can replace or repair it.

Quiet a rattling window. Window air conditioning units can get pretty noisy, but it's not always their fault. After making sure the unit is securely fastened in the window frame, check the window itself. If the glass is just a little loose, that could be causing the rattle. To silence this culprit, put a few strips of tape between the frame and the edge of the window.

Replace freezer tape. Masking tape works as well as the more expensive freezer tape. You can write on it, and it sticks tight. Cellophane tape, on the other hand, won't hold when frozen.

Protect prying surfaces. If you need to pry something open with a putty knife or screwdriver, first put a piece of masking tape along the prying edge. This doesn't matter, of course, if you're opening a can of paint, but if it is something you care about, like the top of your washer/dryer, protect the surface by taking this extra step.

Picnic wind insurance. You're having a picnic, and you've covered the table with a pretty tablecloth, but the wind keeps blowing the cloth around. If you don't want a corner of the tablecloth in your baked beans, just use some two-sided tape to hold that cloth in place.

Watch out!

Don't use transparent tape on paintings or other artwork on paper. It can leave permanent brown stains.

Improve your drill's aim. If you're drilling into a slick surface, such as sheet metal, put down a piece of masking tape where your hole will go. The rougher texture of the tape will help keep your bit in place while you drill.

End plastic wrap frustration. When you want to tear off a piece of clear plastic wrap, it's sometimes impossible to find the edge of the roll. Tape can make the job easier. Wrap a piece — sticky side out — around your finger. Then dab at the roll until it lifts the edge.

Put a screw in the smallest corner. If you need to put a screw in a corner, but you can't get both your hands back there to hold it in place, use a little masking tape. Cut an inch-long piece, and make a slit down the center. Place the tape sticky side up, and

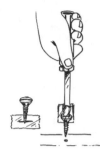

put your screw through the slit, then fix your screw driver into the screw's slot. Once in place, fold both sides of the tape up over the screw head and onto the head of the screwdriver. Now you can put that screw in anywhere you want.

Make a clean joint. Paint isn't the only thing masking tape can protect against. A glue job can be just as messy if you accidentally use too much. Keep extra, squeezed-out glue from marring an otherwise neat job by putting masking tape along the edges where glued pieces come together.

Seal in salt and pepper. You're unpacking your picnic lunch when you find the salt and pepper have fallen over and emptied into your picnic basket. Next time cover the holes with tape. The salt and pepper will stay put until you are ready to sprinkle them on your potato salad. This also works to hold salt in when refilling shakers.

Clear away the cobwebs. Wrap tape, sticky side out, around the end of a broom handle or yardstick. You'll be able to reach those spider webs near the ceiling, and they will stick to the tape. It's also a good way to get that hard-to-reach dirt out of the track of sliding doors. Or retrieve coins or other small items that have fallen behind the clothes dryer.

Soothe the back of your neck. Does a scratchy label keep you from wearing your favorite shirt? No need to cut it out. You can end the irritation by covering it with enough transparent tape to make it lie flat.

Caulk a straight line. Use a strip of tape as a guide when you caulk a bathtub or shower. When the job is done, just pull it up. You'll have a nice, neat edge.

Slide on sheers without the snags. Place a piece of tape over the end of your curtain rod, and thin curtains will slide right over the rough edges without snags or tears.

One-handed magic. You have a special bracelet you want to wear, but it's hard to clasp, and there's no one around to help you. Don't put it back into the jewelry box just yet. Get out the tape, and use a piece to paste one end of the bracelet to your wrist. Now you can easily attach the clasp with one hand. Remove the tape and off you go, looking great.

Keep a tight lid on lipstick. A loose cover on a lipstick case can come off in the bottom of your purse, and — yuck! — what a mess. Don't take that chance. Wrap clear tape around the tube. The cap will fit snugly, and your purse will stay clean.

Your picture's in the mail. You've just sealed and stamped the letter to your friend when you realize you forgot to enclose the picture you promised. Just cut off the end of the envelope, slip in the picture, and reclose it with a piece of transparent tape. Now it's ready to go.

Arrange flowers artfully. Transparent tape can come in handy when you arrange cut flowers. Wrap stems that bend easily with tape to keep them straight. They'll stay fresher because water can rise up to the blossoms more easily. And you can use tape to keep flowers upright, even if the vase is a little too wide. Wrap tape around the bunch of stems below the top of the vase. Or criss cross tape across the mouth of the vase to keep them straight with a little more separation.

This is for the birds. Make a quick, cheap birdfeeder for your feathered friends. Wrap strips of tape, sticky side out, around a tree branch. Sprinkle with birdseed, and pat it a little to help it stick. The birds will flock to the feast in no time.

Design a T-shirt. To make a geometric pattern on a T-shirt, criss cross transparent tape on the front. Dab on fabric paint with a sponge or brush. Let dry, then remove tape.

Bookmark it. Create an original floral bookmark by placing small flowers on the sticky side of a piece of wide, clear tape. Cover it with a pretty piece of ribbon, a little bit narrower than the tape. Add another piece of tape, sticky side toward the ribbon, to form the back. Turn it over to see the flowers against the ribbon background.

Clean a file. Use a piece of tape to remove embedded sawdust from a metal file.

No more lost screws. Lay a piece of double-stick tape near a work surface. Use it to keep small parts from rolling around and getting lost.

Avoid messy cracks. When driving a nail through plaster, use two pieces of cellophane tape to mark the spot with an X. This will keep the plaster from splitting or chipping into an unsightly crack.

Help the blind. Busted one of the slats on your Venetian blinds? No problem. Just use tape to join it back together on the wall side, then cover any cracks with the right color shoe polish.

Tea and tea bags

Ease achy eyes. When your eyes ache from reading or staring at a computer all day, pamper yourself with some tea. You can drink a cup of course, or you can wet two tea bags with warm or cool water, and lie down with one tea bag on each eye. Relax for at least 15 minutes, and your eyes (and you) will feel invigorated. Chilled chamomile tea bags are particularly effective against puffiness.

Feed your houseplants. For lush, luxurious ferns, give them an occasional spot of tea. Use tea instead of water once in a while, or work wet tea leaves into the soil.

Soothe burns and sunburns. You stayed out on the beach just a little too long, and even your sunscreen didn't keep you from getting an uncomfortable sunburn. Wet tea bags can take out the sting. Just pat them onto affected areas or keep in place with gauze. You can also put tea into your bath water. This works for other types of burns as well.

Tenderize meat. If you can't afford expensive cuts of meat, try marinating or cooking your meat in tea. The tannins in tea work as a tenderizer to make the meat tasty and delicious.

> In Great Britain alone, 150 million cups of tea are made from tea bags every day.

Stop bleeding gums. If you've just had a tooth pulled, or if you have a youngster who just lost a tooth, tea bags can help stop the bleeding. Just wet a tea bag with cool water and press into the spot the tooth came from.

Keep the dust down. Sprinkle damp tea leaves over the ashes in your fireplace before cleaning it out. The tea will help keep the ashes from rising and getting all over the place while you lift them out.

Dye lace for an old ivory look. Soak white lace in cold brewed tea to get a beige, ecru, or ivory color.

Remove old furniture polish. Boil two tea bags in a quart of water and let cool. Soak a soft cloth in the tea and wring out. Wipe off dirt and old polish, let dry, buff, and then decide if you need to reapply polish.

> Before the invention of tea bags, tea was brewed loose-leaf and then strained. If you wanted just one cup of tea, you could put a small amount of tea in a "tea bell" and submerge it in your cup. A tea wholesaler decided to make his own version of a tea bell out of gauze so he could send his customers small samples. He was surprised when he received large orders for tea — in the sample containers. He'd invented the tea bag.

Mirrors that sparkle and shine. Brew up a batch of strong tea, let it cool, then use it to clean your mirrors. Buff it dry with a soft cloth for a great streak-free shine.

A tea party for your roses. Tea leaves sprinkled under your rose bushes will give them a new lease on life in mid-summer. Tea provides tannic acid, which roses love.

Darken gray hair. Make a natural dye for dark hair that's going gray. Steep three regular-size tea bags in a cup of boiling water. Add a tablespoon of fresh or dried rosemary and a tablespoon of fresh or dried sage. Let it stand at least three hours — overnight is better — and strain. Shampoo your hair. Then, wearing old clothes because it can stain, pour or spray the mixture on your hair, saturating it thoroughly. Blot with a towel and dry. Don't rinse it out. You may have to repeat the process a few times before the gray hair turns dark.

Take care of a messy shave. A wet tea bag is a soothing way to treat shaving nicks and cuts.

Freshen your breath. A cup of mint tea is a good-tasting breath freshener for after meals, especially if you can't brush your teeth, or don't like gum or candy mints. Carry a few mint tea bags with you so you'll always be prepared.

Seed your lawn with a tea bag patch. Sow grass seed in small bare spots with a used tea bag. Make sure the bag is moist, and place it on the dirt where you want the grass. Sprinkle it with seed. The bag will hold moisture and gradually decompose.

According to legend, tea was discovered by a Chinese emperor named Shen Nong, often called "The Divine Healer." Some tea leaves accidentally fell into boiling water, and he tried it and found it invigorating. Today, tea is the most popular beverage in the world.

Out of the teapot and into potted plants. Place a few used Tetley tea bags in the bottom of a planter, on top of your drainage material (gravel, Styrofoam, etc.). Add soil and your plants as usual. The tea bags will hold moisture and gradually leach nutrients into the soil.

Tennis balls

Rustproof your trailer hitch. Chrome trailer hitches get scratched almost every time you hitch them to something. Those scratches then let in moisture, which of course leads to rust. You can keep the moisture out, and the rust away, by splitting a tennis ball and slipping it over your hitching ball.

Serve up a winning solution to snoring. Sew a tennis ball to the back of your pajamas and — presto! — no more snoring.

Massage your own back. A back massage is relaxing and therapeutic. All you need is a long tube sock and a few tennis balls, and you can do your own. Just put the balls in the sock, tie the end shut, and stretch your massager around your back, like you do when you're toweling off after a shower. Ahhhh.

Fluff up your down. Whenever you dry down-filled items like comforters, pillows, vests, or jackets, toss a couple of tennis balls or a pair of tennis shoes in the dryer, too. The balls will help fluff up the down as it dries.

Give your feet a treat. If you've worn out your poor feet from working or perhaps playing tennis, sit down and roll your bare feet over a tennis ball. It will give your feet a soothing massage.

Get a better grip. Cut a slit in a tennis ball, and slip it over a screwdriver handle to get a better grip and turn those stubborn screws more easily.

211

The game of tennis originated in medieval France. It was first called "jeu de paume" and was a type of handball ("paume" means "palm.") Eventually, it was played with rackets, and the server would cry "tenez!" ("here!") to let the other player know he was about to start. That's where the word "tennis" comes from.

Sand those curves. When you're refinishing furniture, a tennis ball wrapped with sandpaper is ideal for sanding out curves.

Tires

Protect trees from the lawn mower. Recycle your used tires as bumpers to protect your trees from lawn mower scrapes. Make two from one tire by splitting it crossways, like slicing a bagel. You can place them over small trees without cutting the sides. For larger trees, you'll need to cut them so they'll stretch around the trunks. If you don't like the look, you can remove the tires when you finish cutting the grass. Just store them until the next mowing. If you want to make them a permanent addition, they can serve a double purpose. Place them open side up, and punch some holes in the bottoms. Fill with composted manure, and when it rains you'll have manure tea to fertilize your trees.

Be a swinger. You haven't forgotten that old tire swing in your grandmother's yard, have you? Why not put an old tire to good use in your yard? Drill a couple of holes in the bottom for water to drain, paint it white so it won't get too hot in the sun, and attach it with sturdy chains. Then sit back and watch the kids have fun, or better yet, give it a swing yourself.

Throw the squirrels a bone. What's the best way to keep squirrels away from the bird feeder? Give them a squirrel feeder to play with. You can make an easy squirrel house by making a few simple cuts on an old tire and folding one side in to close off the other. Drill a hole into the bottom section to allow water to drain. Hang this rubber condo at a safe distance from the birds, then do your best to squirrel-proof the rest of the feeders.

Watch your step. The treading from old tires can add safety to your dock, slippery stairway, or oily garage floor. Just attach several sections in extra slick spots, and your path will be a safer one.

Shoes for your car and you, too. An old tire can join your wardrobe as a pair of sandals, if you want it to. Use a linoleum knife to cut sections from the tread that are about the size and shape of your feet. Cut a slit through these soles on each side, toward the heel. Then thread the ends of a V-shaped stretch of inner tube through the slits and staple them to the bottom. Bring the V of the tube to the front of the sole and staple it to one side for your toes to fit through.

Ernest Hemingway reportedly once made a pair of sandals out of tire treads. It was wartime, and the patriotic writer wanted to do what he could to further the conservation effort. So if a famous writer can wear them on his feet, surely you can find something to do with your old tires instead of adding them to the landfill. Who knows? Thick rubber sandals might be quite comfortable.

213

Protect your car and garage walls. If your garage is less than spacious, it may be hard to park without bumping the back wall. And you might find it a tight squeeze when you open your doors. You can protect your car and recycle your old tires at the same time. Cut the tires into rubber strips, and nail them to your garage walls where your bumper or car door might hit.

Tame a wild axe. Next time you're splitting firewood, try this safety tip. Arrange as much wood as will fit, on end, inside an old tire. The tire will keep the wood in place and serve as a buffer if your swinging goes awry.

Prevent moisture damage to lumber. You have lumber stored in your basement that you fully intend to use in a project — someday. But in the meantime, the moisture down there could damage it. Air will circulate around it better, and it will stay drier, if you stack it on a couple of old tires.

> The tires on your car are probably black, but originally, all tires were white. Then the Goodrich company added carbon pigments made by Binney and Smith, the company that makes Crayola crayons. They discovered that not only did the pigment change the color of the tires, it made them five times more durable as well, so black tires soon became standard.

Tomato juice

Get out the green. Chlorine from a swimming pool can give blond hair an unattractive green tint, but you can neutralize it with tomato juice. Just rub some juice in your hair, leave on for a couple of minutes, and shampoo.

De-skunk your dog. Tomato juice is the age-old remedy for skunk stink. Douse the sprayed area with undiluted tomato juice, or try a solution of half vinegar, half water. Then scrub him down with soap and water, and repeat if necessary. This might not get rid of all the odor, but every little bit helps.

Wash away a putrid smell. The power went off while you were on a trip. You returned home to find spoiled meat in your freezer. You disposed of the meat, but how do you get rid of that awful smell? Perhaps easier than you think. Just rinse inside the freezer with tomato juice or vinegar.

Toothbrushes

Brush your grater's teeth. Use a toothbrush to pick the leftover bits of cheese or whatever you grated out of the grinding surface of your grater to make things easier on your dishwasher.

Get at that stain. When treating a stain that has soaked into the fibers, use a soft-bristled nylon toothbrush to dab at the stain, gently working the stain removing agent — bleach, alcohol, vinegar, or whatever you are using — into the fabric.

The first nylon-bristle toothbrush appeared on the market in 1938. It was known as "Dr. West's Miracle Tuft Toothbrush." The real miracle was that people had survived with reasonably healthy gums after centuries of using brushes made of hog bristles and other animal hair.

Clean your ears. Ears of corn, that is. To get all those clingy strands of silk off fresh corn, take an old toothbrush and rub down the cob gently.

Help Velcro keep its cling. The clinging power of Velcro fasteners is amazing. However, those fasteners don't work nearly as well when they get lint stuck in them. Use a stiff toothbrush to clean out the lint, then fasten up.

No waffling with your waffle iron. Use a clean, soft toothbrush to oil and clean your waffle iron.

Clean your teeth, then everything else. When your toothbrush loses its oomph, don't toss it just yet. You can use it to clean a whole host of things — the tiny spaces around faucets, tile grout, your fingernails after gardening, mud from the grooves on the bottom of your sneakers or hiking boots, small plastic or wooden toys (especially those from garage sales), can openers — and whatever else you can think of.

Toothpaste

Make metals shine. If you don't have any silver polish handy and need to shine silverware or jewelry, toothpaste will work well. Use a very soft brush or cloth, and rinse thoroughly. This will work on other metals like copper and gold as well.

Rub out glass stains and scratches. Non-gel toothpaste provides just enough mild abrasive to rub out tiny scratches on glassware or acid-rain stains on windows.

> The white part of toothpaste is made mostly of finely powdered chalk.

Clear up acne. If you have a flare-up of acne, just dab a bit of toothpaste on each troublesome pimple at night. The toothpaste will work to dry out that blemish.

Fill nail holes. You can use toothpaste in a pinch to fill in nail holes in a plaster wall. Just squeeze some in, smooth, and let dry. You can then paint over it.

Clear away scratches on CDs. For both smudges and scratches on discs, a non-gel toothpaste will do the trick. Just rub a little on, then remove it with a damp cloth. It may leave a few tiny scratches on the surface, but they won't affect the sound.

Clean fireplace grout. To clean the grout between the stones or bricks of your fireplace, rub it with smokers toothpaste. Wipe off the excess with a damp cloth.

Put a sparkle on your piano's smile. The keys on your piano were once an elephant's tusks, so what do you do if they turn yellow? That's right. Brush them with toothpaste. Rub very gently with a soft cloth and use as little as possible, being careful not to get any paste stuck down between the keys. When you're done, buff the new pearly whites back to their original glory.

Clean white leather. Clean dirty white leather shoes with a white, non-gel toothpaste. Rub it on, rinse it off, and wipe shoes dry.

End of the line for fishy hands. Get rid of that fishy smell on your hands by washing them with toothpaste.

Hang art without poking holes. To stick lightweight posters or other artwork to walls, put a dab of toothpaste on each back corner. Press it firmly against the wall. Later, when you take it down, just wipe away the dried paste. It's quick and leaves no hole in the wall or your poster.

Make your diamonds sparkle. Clean your best friends with a bit of toothpaste and a small brush. Rinse with cold water and watch them shine.

Toothpicks

Fry sausages evenly. If you love those little link sausages but hate frying them because they roll around and cook unevenly, try connecting two of them with toothpicks. They won't roll around, and you just have to flip them over once to brown them.

Tighten a loose screw. Probably the easiest way to tighten a loose screw is to replace it with a larger one, but if this isn't possible, try inserting a couple of toothpicks into the hole, then screwing the original screw back in. The wood will give the screw something to bite into and will also "shrink" the hole itself.

Keep toast from disappearing. If you have a small piece

of bread that disappears into the toaster, making it almost impossible to remove, stick a toothpick through the top of the bread. The toothpick will lie across the top of the toaster and keep your bread from falling down where you can't reach it.

Rehang pictures after a paint job. Don't worry about getting your pictures back in the right spot after painting a room. Stick a toothpick into the nail hole, and paint as usual. After the paint dries, remove the toothpicks and rehang your pictures.

Stop a leak. Make a quick, temporary repair to a leaky garden hose by pressing the point of a toothpick into the hole. Water will cause the toothpick to swell, plugging the hole. Break off the rest of the toothpick, and wrap the area with duct tape.

One average tree produces about 400,000 toothpicks.

Make a cake "tent." If you're going to wrap a cake or other food item with plastic wrap, but you don't want the wrap to touch the surface of the food, poke toothpicks into strategic areas to form a "tent" that keeps the plastic elevated.

Help with hang-ups. Here's a handy way to help your picture stay straight after you hang it. Wrap masking tape, sticky side out, around a toothpick. Attach it to the bottom of the back of the frame. It will be just sticky enough to steady the frame without leaving a mark when you want to move it.

Twist ties

Quick-fix eyeglasses. If you lose the tiny screw that holds the earpiece onto the rest of your eyeglasses, you can poke a twist tie through the hole. Twist the ends and cut off the excess. It should hold until you can get a new screw.

Keep cords untangled. Entertainment has come a long way from the old Victorola. Today, it always seems to involve lots of electrical cords. You might have an entertainment center with a television, video recorder, stereo, video game player — even a computer. All those wires can get confusing and unruly. Keep them neat and organized with a few twist ties from bread bags. You can group all the cords from one appliance together, so if you ever decide to move one component, it won't take you an hour to figure out which cords to unplug.

Tie up plants. Use twist ties to fasten the stems of plants to stakes. Be sure you fasten them loosely so the twist tie doesn't injure the plant as it grows.

Tighten loose screws. If you have a loose screw, here's a cheap and easy way to fix it. Take a couple of twist ties, cut them as long as the screw hole is deep, stick them in the hole, and reinsert the screw. The twist ties will make the hole smaller so the screw should hold tighter.

Unclog caulk guns. If you ever use a caulk gun, you know the tip can get clogged up. Before you put your gun away next time, push a twist tie into the tip. Then, when you're ready to caulk again, you can just pull out the plug of dried caulking with the end of the twist tie.

Umbrellas

Neat and easy chandelier cleaning. Not only will an umbrella keep raindrops from falling on your head, it can also keep cleaning solution from falling on your table when you clean your chandelier. Open the umbrella, and hang it upside down from the center of the chandelier. Spray cleaner generously on the chandelier, and the umbrella will catch the drips. You can make your own cleaning solution by mixing two teaspoons of rubbing alcohol in a pint of warm water.

Catch a mouse. If you don't like the idea of mousetraps or poison in your home, but want that mouse out of your house, get out your umbrella. The next time you see the little creature scurrying about, open a black umbrella, and hold it to the floor at an angle. Have someone else chase the mouse, and since mice are drawn to dark places, it will probably head right for the black umbrella. As soon as it runs in, shut the umbrella, take it outside, and free your furry little friend.

Make a trellis. You can make a unique and beautiful trellis for your morning glories or other climbing plants. Remove the fabric from an umbrella, and bury the handle in the ground.

Vinegar

Zap bacteria. Cutting boards can harbor bacteria, particularly when you cut up meat. Sanitize them by spraying lightly with vinegar, followed by hydrogen peroxide. This combination can kill bacteria from meat and produce.

Get the yellow out. Some articles of clothing never go out of style, so you can keep wearing them for years. However, sometimes they yellow with age. To remove those yellow age spots from washable wool or silk items, try sponging them with a mixture of one tablespoon of white vinegar in a pint of water. Rinse and wash according to label directions.

> The word vinegar comes from two French words, vin, which means "wine" and aigre, which means "to sour."

Nourish azaleas. Azaleas grow best in acidic soil, so for really beautiful plants, add some vinegar occasionally when watering them. Use two tablespoons of vinegar to one quart of water.

Cheap and easy wall cleaning. Here's a natural solution for cleaning painted walls and other surfaces — mix a half cup of white vinegar, one cup of ammonia, one-fourth cup of baking soda, and a gallon of warm water.

Polish metals. To clean brass, copper, bronze, or pewter, dissolve a teaspoon of salt in a cup of white vinegar. Mix in enough flour to make a paste, coat the item, and let it stand for 15 minutes. Rinse with warm water, and dry with a soft, clean cloth.

> Vinegar is made from ethyl alcohol. A bacteria that feeds on the alcohol converts it into vinegar.

Clean toilet bowls. For general cleaning, pour white vinegar into the bowl, and let it remain for an hour or so before flushing. To get rid of lime deposits, first close the valve to the tank and flush to empty the bowl. Line the discolored area with white paper towels, and soak with white vinegar. After a while, scrub any remaining stain with a plastic brush.

Shine your hair. Put an apple-fresh shine in your hair with an apple cider vinegar rinse. Mix a half cup of apple cider vinegar with two cups of warm water, and pour over your freshly washed hair.

Relieve itching. You decided to go hiking and had a great time except for all the bug bites you came home with. Douse those itchy spots with a cotton ball soaked in vinegar. It should bring you relief.

Even your dishwasher needs cleaning. To get rid of the hard-water film in your dishwasher, pour a cup of vinegar in the bottom and run it. Fill it with glassware to clean them at the same time.

Rinse away the annoying smell of new perms. Mix about one-half cup of apple cider vinegar into two cups of water. Use this mixture to get rid of that new perm smell. Follow it with a rinse of clear water.

Clean out your coffee maker. For best care and the best coffee, clean out your drip coffee maker about once a month. Fill it with equal parts water and distilled vinegar, then run it through the brew cycle. Rinse it out with another cycle using just plain water.

Watch out!

If you wait until calcium deposits have built up in your coffee maker and then run vinegar through it, the loosened calcium deposits may block your tubing and cause leakage. Make sure you start using vinegar before you have a problem.

Remove stains from ice trays. Soak plastic trays in vinegar — full strength — for several hours to remove hard-water stains.

Bring a bright polish to chrome. Gently shine chrome surfaces with a soft cloth dampened with apple cider vinegar. For the insides of chrome teapots, dip a vinegar-moistened cloth into some salt and scrub.

Say good bye to soap scum. Attack soap scum on ceramic tile with a solution of four parts water to one part vinegar.

Effortless microwave cleaning. Remove cooked-on food from your microwave the easy way. Put one-fourth cup of white vinegar and one cup of water into a glass bowl, and microwave on high for about five minutes. The moisture from the vinegar water will soften food splatters while it deodorizes the interior of your microwave. Let the water/vinegar mixture cool, and use it to wipe off the softened mess.

Improve boiled eggs. Don't you just hate it when an egg cracks while it's boiling? If you add a couple of tablespoons of vinegar to your water before you boil, you can prevent that, and the eggs will peel more easily when they're cooked, too.

Watch out!

Don't beat egg whites in aluminum bowls because eggs tend to darken.

Tackle athlete's foot. The itch of athlete's foot can drive you crazy. You can cut down on this by soaking socks in a solution of one cup vinegar and four cups of water, then washing them as usual. Soaking your feet in full-strength apple cider vinegar may also help relieve the itching.

Unclog your shower head. When mineral deposits build up inside your shower head, getting in there to clean them out might seem like a big hassle. But it shouldn't be. Simply unscrew the shower head from the wall, then unscrew each piece of it one at a time. Soak all the pieces in a bowl of vinegar until the deposits soften and can be easily brushed away.

Bring a shine to stainless steel cookware. It's supposed to be stainless. Put that's not always 100 percent certain. If stains do appear on your stainless steel cookware, scrub them with a stainless steel pad dipped in undiluted white vinegar.

Remove fabric stains. Vinegar is good for removing fruit, beverage, and grass stains from most washable fabrics. Mix it in equal parts with dishwashing liquid and water in a plastic squirt bottle. Squeeze it onto the stain and work it in. Leave it for several minutes and then rinse.

Watch out!

Don't add vinegar to chlorine bleach. This mixture could produce toxic fumes and make you extremely sick.

Wipe down your "in-shield." Get haze and grime off the inside of your windshield by wiping it down with vinegar. New cars often have a residue of plastic fumes on the inner windows that will come right off with a sponge.

Instant conditioner for thicker hair. For a good, deep conditioning at home, combine a teaspoon of vinegar with three beaten eggs and two tablespoons of olive or safflower oil. Rub the gook into your hair, cover with a shower cap or plastic wrap, and let it sit for half an hour. Shampoo when you're done.

Firm up molded salads. To keep your gelatin dishes "in shape," add a teaspoon of white vinegar along with the usual ingredients.

> When P.B. Wait invented a new product made from fruit syrup and gelatin, it did not appeal to 19th-century consumers. He sold out to a cereal manufacturer, but it still was a flop — that manufacturer couldn't even sell the business for $35. Then a few cooking experts discovered the product and decided it was a very elegant dish. That changed everything, and today Jell-O is a favorite all over the world.

Kill unwanted grass. Do you have grass growing between the cracks in your sidewalk or other hard-to-reach places? If you hate using harsh chemicals, you can just pour a little white vinegar in the cracks, and it will kill that unwanted greenery.

No smoking, please. If you've got the lingering odor of cigarette or fire smoke hanging about, banish it with vinegar. Fill a dish and let it sit in the room, or put some in a humidifier. You'll be surprised at the results.

Keep glue soft. You can still use all those hardened bits of glue in the bottom of the container by mixing in a bit of vinegar. If your glue is too thick, just put a few drops of vinegar in the container and shake it, and it will turn soft and easy to work with.

Hair care for Fido. Give your dog glossy, thick hair by adding just a bit of apple cider vinegar to his drinking water. It will also help get rid of doggy odor.

Perfect poached eggs. To make your poached eggs come out perfectly shaped every time, add a few drops of vinegar to the poaching water.

Banish the smell of icky veggies. Simmering a small pot of vinegar on a spare burner will help get rid of ugly odors from cooking certain vegetables, such as cabbage or sauerkraut.

Resurrect a crusted brush. You let the paint dry on your brush, didn't you? Well, all is not lost. Simply let it soak in hot vinegar for a while, then wash as usual.

A freshening tip for oily skin. Fill a spray bottle with apple cider vinegar. After washing your face, spritz the vinegar on and let it air-dry.

Although vinegar is quite handy and versatile around your house, it isn't a good cleaner for most household grime — at least not by itself. That's because most of the soils in your home contain fats or oils, which need an alkaline solution (like baking soda) to break them up so they can be wiped away. Vinegar is acidic, which makes it good for cleaning water stains and lime deposits, and it's a great rinsing agent because it dissolves soap scum. Vinegar may work wonders on some jobs, but make sure you're using it to its best advantage.

Give your outdoor decking new life. If you've got moss growing on your deck, pour apple cider vinegar on it, and let it sit for an hour. Rinse off and enjoy a like-new deck.

Stretch the soap. You can make your dishwashing liquid go further by adding a few tablespoons of vinegar to the dishwater. This works with even the cheapest brand.

It's curtains for mildew. Don't let unsightly mildew build up on your shower curtain. Wash it now and then with a load of towels. They'll give it a good scrubbing. Then add a cup of vinegar to the rinse cycle for a sparkling clean spin.

Water

Keep drains clear. Clogged drains can complicate your life and sometimes lead to expensive plumbing bills. Keep that from happening with just a little free prevention. Pour boiling water down your kitchen drains about once a month. To keep from cracking the porcelain, make sure you pour it directly into the drain.

Separate glasses. When two drinking glasses get stuck together, here's an easy way to separate them without danger of breaking them. Fill the top glass with cold water, and then dip the bottom glass in hot water. They should come apart easily.

> Ever wonder why the cold faucet handle is always on the right, and the hot on the left? Until the hot water heater was invented, there was no need for a hot water faucet, and the cold knob was placed on the right because most people are right-handed. When there became a need for a hot water knob, it was placed on the other side — the left.

Squelch bad behavior with a squirt. If your dog or cat won't behave, keep a water pistol loaded and handy. Each time they do something bad, give them a quick squirt of water. It's not pleasant, but it won't hurt either, and it lets them know that bad behavior has unpleasant consequences.

Fix saggy chairs. You love that old cane-bottom chair on your front porch, but now the seat sags so much you're thinking of throwing it out. Don't give up on it just yet. Remove the caning and put it in a bathtub of steaming hot water with a little lemon oil. Let it soak, and then put it in the sun to dry. As the seat dries, it will return to its original shape. Rub it with some lemon oil to help keep it supple, and reattach it to the chair frame.

Quick-dry nails. If you always seem to mess up your nail polish about 10 seconds after you finish polishing, you may be tempted to buy one of those quick-dry sprays. Try this instead. Immediately after polishing, dip your fingers into a container of ice-cold water, being careful not to touch the sides of the container. Your nails will be dry in no time.

> You could survive for about a month with no food, but you'd only live five to seven days with no water.

Anchor wobbly candles. If your candles are forever listing to starboard, secure them with this easy tip. Pour hot water into the candle holder and let it stand for a few minutes. When the holder is heated, pour out the water, and immediately fit in your candle.

Say goodbye to pesky weeds. Keep unwanted weeds from sprouting in the cracks of your brick or flagstone patio. Pour boiling water on them, and watch them shrivel up and die.

From fish to plant. When you clean your aquarium, don't just throw out the water. Use it to water your houseplants. It makes great fertilizer.

The great flood. Ant hills a problem? Send them a message of biblical proportion. A nice tidal wave of boiling water, right down the hatch, will make them think twice about putting up another condo in your yard.

Steam out those wrinkles. For a quick iron job, hang your clothes in the bathroom, and turn on the water as hot as it will go. Close all doors and windows, and let the steam go to work on the wrinkles. Be sure to give the clothes enough time to dry out before you wear them, because the steam will get them a little damp.

Wax paper

Protect iron skillets from rust. Iron skillets are so durable they often become heirlooms, handed down through generations. The one thing that might destroy their beauty and durability is rust. To prevent this, rub your skillets with wax paper inside and out. This puts a thin layer of wax on the skillet that keeps air from interacting with the metal and moisture. If you store your iron cookware stacked inside each other, separate them with pieces of wax paper.

Make defrosting a snap. If you have to defrost your freezer, you know what a messy, time-consuming job it can be. Get a jump on this chore by layering a few pieces of wax paper on the newly defrosted freezer shelf. When defrost time rolls around again, you'll find the ice comes right up.

Lube up a sticky iron. Your iron is coated with a nonstick surface that's supposed to make it, well, not stick. But it's sticking anyway. Here's an easy solution. With the iron just a little warm, lay some wax paper on the ironing board and run your iron over it several times. Remove any residual wax by running it over an old cloth. This should smooth things out a bit.

Keep the microwave clean. When heating a taco or a slice of pizza, there's no need to bother with a messy clean-up job. Line the bottom of the microwave oven with wax paper. When the food is ready, just remove it and toss the paper.

Store candles. Pretty colored candles can get scuffed up during storage so that the next time you use them they're not so pretty anymore. To prevent this, roll your candles up in a piece of wax paper, twist the ends to seal, and store.

Unstick your waffle iron. Has your waffle iron lost its non-stick ability? You can restore it by inserting two sheets of wax paper into the waffle iron and letting it heat. When the paper gets dark brown, remove it. Now your waffles should come out easily again.

A memento of fall. If you love the beautiful colors of leaves in the fall, save a few of them. Just lay the leaf between two pieces of wax paper, and put the wax paper between two pieces of brown paper. Then press with a warm iron.

Preserve your heirloom lace. Store lace articles in layers of wax paper to keep them from rotting.

Wax your floor with paper. If you can clean your oven with tin foil, of course you can wax your floor with wax paper. For a quick mini-wax, push a piece of wax paper around on the floor with a mop. It's important to sweep up first, though, no matter what kind of hurry you're in. Dirt and grit that's pushed around under the paper can scratch your floor something fierce.

Pop your cork with ease. Wrap a bit of wax paper around a cork, and next time it will come out of the bottle without the usual effort.

A sticky situation. What can you do if your clamps or wood blocks are stuck to the project you've glued? Start your project over, probably. It's enough to make you come unglued yourself. To keep this from happening, always slide a sheet of wax paper between your project and your clamp or block.

Guarantee good reception. Many new cars have antennas that automatically raise and lower when needed. Keep yours in good working order by rubbing a piece of wax paper up and down it occasionally.

Wheelbarrow

Make a portable grill. If you don't have a charcoal grill, you can still cook out if you have a metal wheelbarrow. Just put the charcoal in the wheelbarrow, and put an oven rack on top of it, and have "grilling to go."

No ice chest needed. For your next barbecue or outdoor celebration, don't bother with that unwieldy cooler. Fill a wheelbarrow with ice, add a bit of water and — presto — a great mobile way to keep drink cans and bottles cold.

Gardening on the go. If you have a small yard or even no yard at all, don't despair. You can still enjoy flowers and even some vegetables. Just prepare a wheelbarrow like you would any other container, and plant away. It's easy to move from sun to shade as needed, and when winter rolls around you can dump it out and store as usual.

Yogurt

Give ivory a new luster. If you have genuine ivory pieces, you need to clean them carefully. Mix one tablespoon of lemon juice into one-fourth cup of plain yogurt. Rub this onto your ivory, and let it sit for a couple of minutes. Rinse off, and enjoy the new luster to your old treasures.

Soothe sunburn. Cool, creamy yogurt can soothe your sunburn pain. Just smear on, leave for about 20 minutes, and rinse off with lukewarm water.

> The medicated cream Noxema started out as "Dr. Bunting's Sunburn Remedy." While the inventor was looking for a catchier name, a customer happened to mention that the cream had cleared up his eczema. Thus the name "Noxema" was born.

Prevent vaginal yeast infections. A bacteria called *Candida albicans* can cause annoying yeast infections, but yogurt contains a "good" bacteria called *Lactobacillus acidophilus* that can help fight yeast infections. Medical research finds that eating yogurt regularly can greatly reduce your risk of yeast infections. Applying yogurt directly on the inflamed area can also relieve a vaginal yeast infection.

Make cheese. Yogurt cheese can be a natural, low-fat alternative to cream cheese. You make this tasty cheese by removing the liquid from yogurt. Put 8 ounces of plain low-fat or nonfat yogurt that doesn't contain gelatin into a strainer lined with cheesecloth or three coffee filters. Don't try to use yogurt with fruit because the fruit tends to clog the strainer. Place the strainer over a bowl to catch the draining liquid. Cover and refrigerate for 24 hours. The liquid will drain into the bowl and leave behind a versatile yogurt cheese. You can season it with herbs and spread it on a bagel, or use it as a dip for chips, crackers, or veggies. You can even use it in place of cream cheese in your favorite cheesecake recipe. Make it with lemon yogurt to give your cheesecake a tangy twist.

Slow down diarrhea. According to research, yogurt can kill the kind of bacteria that is often responsible for diarrhea. You should also be sure to eat plenty of yogurt whenever you're taking antibiotics, because antibiotics often kill "good" bacteria along with the bad kind, which can also lead to diarrhea.

Uncommonly Good Ideas to Make Your Life Easier

Automotive

Be prepared for emergencies. If you've ever had to change a flat tire while wearing high heels or your best suit, be better prepared next time. Keep an old set of sweat clothes and tennis shoes in the trunk.

A giant-sized ice scraper. A plastic dustpan makes a great ice scraper. Because it's so big, it whisks ice off in a jiffy, and it won't scratch your windshield.

Prevent frozen keyhole. The next time the temperature dips below freezing, place a refrigerator magnet over your car door's keyhole so your car is ready to go when you are.

Save your carpet. If you wear high heels while driving, you could eventually wear a hole in your car's carpet. If you don't want to change your shoes when you drive, put a small carpet remnant under your heel.

Keep your hands clean. If you have to tinker under the hood but hate to get your hands and fingernails dirty, get some surgical gloves from the drugstore. They are thin and flexible enough to allow you to turn those screws but will still keep your hands clean.

Take it easy. If you want your car to last longer, take it easy when you first start driving. Since most engine wear occurs while the cold engine is warming up, accelerate gently until your engine reaches its normal operating temperature.

Have you ever referred to something or someone as being a "doozy" and wondered where the term came from? In 1929, Duesenberg introduced a car that boasted an impressive 265 horsepower engine, and the expression "it's a Duesy" was born.

Set the brake. You'll take some strain off your transmission and help it last longer if you get into the habit of setting the emergency brake whenever you park. You should do this whether your car has a manual or automatic transmission.

Don't get shocked. Does everyone who rides in your vehicle get a shock when they get out? If so, it could be your fabric seats. Just spray your seats liberally with aerosol fabric softener or a static-reduction spray found at electronics stores.

Safe jump-starting. If you ever have to jump-start a vehicle, do it right so you won't damage your car or injure yourself. Connect the two positive terminals (the posts with the "+" mark) together with the red cables. (Make sure you don't connect a positive post to a negative post.) Put the black cable on the stalled car's negative battery terminal (the post with the "−" mark). Next, connect the last clamp to a good ground, like a bolt on the engine or other unpainted, metallic surface on the donor car — not the last battery terminal. That way, if any sparks are created, they'll be away from any hydrogen gas given off by the battery. Then start the donor car and let it run for a few minutes before you try to start the stalled car.

Keep an eye on the antifreeze. Antifreeze helps keep your car running well, but did you know it also helps prevent rust and corrosion? To make sure your antifreeze works its best, have it changed every two years or 24,000 miles, whichever comes first. If you change it yourself, use a 50-50 antifreeze-water mix, using distilled water, not tap water.

Buy the book. One of the most important things you can do for your car is read the owner's manual. It's the most reliable source of information about caring for your car. If you don't have an owner's manual, call a dealership that sells your kind of vehicle, and order a manual from the parts department.

Check your tires. Before you put air in your tires, check your owner's manual to find out how much air your tires need. To be sure you're putting in the right amount, use a tire gauge. Too much air or not enough can cause problems. If your tires are wearing out in the middle, you probably have too much air in them. If they are wearing out on both edges, they are probably underinflated. If you have excess wear along one edge of your tires, your vehicle could be out of alignment.

Leave the detergent under the sink. Detergents meant for washing dishes or clothing have a pH content designed to cut grease. This could also cut through your car's wax coating and harm its clear-coat finish. Use specially formulated car wash products instead. It's also important to rinse your car before washing it because dirt and grit caught under your sponge or towel can scratch the paint.

Save gas, your tires, and the environment. You can accomplish all three of these goals just by keeping your tires at the correct air pressure. Underinflated tires wear out more quickly, and they cut fuel economy by as much as 2 percent per pound of pressure below the recommended level.

This little light of mine. Keep a penlight and a couple of rubber bands with your emergency tool kit. If you ever need to go under the hood at night, you can rubber band the light to whichever tool you're using. This is a lot easier than trying to balance a regular flashlight in your mouth or under your arm.

Keep your hand off. Don't rest your hand on your gearshift knob while driving. It can eventually cause damage to your gears.

Ford wasn't first, not even in America. The first American automobiles were built by Charles and Frank Duryea in 1892. Duryeas became the first horseless carriages regularly manufactured in the United States when the Duryea brothers made 13 of the same model in 1896. Henry Ford didn't sell his first production car, a 2-cylinder Model A, until July 23, 1903.

Recycle used motor oil. If you change your own oil, make sure you recycle it. According to the Environmental Protection Agency, oil from one do-it-yourself oil change can ruin a million gallons of fresh water. That's enough for 50 people for a year. People changing their own oil drain about 200 million gallons from their cars every year. Check with local service stations, recycling centers, transfer stations, and auto parts stores to see if they take oil and oil filters for recycling.

Getting it out of PARK. If you have an automatic transmission, you may have had trouble shifting out of PARK on a steep hill. This is because your wheels are locked, and your transmission is resisting your vehicle's tendency to roll. If your shift lever is truly stuck, the vehicle will need an uphill push or pull to release pressure on the transmission. To prevent this, whenever you park on a steep grade, don't put your car in PARK until — with foot brake still on — you secure the emergency brake. Then, when you're ready to drive away, apply the foot brake and move the shift lever to NEUTRAL or DRIVE before releasing the parking brake.

Keep a log book. Businessmen who write off automotive expenses on their taxes probably keep a detailed log book. You can also benefit from a log book. Keeping a record of gasoline and other fluid consumption can tip you off to a leak or other repair problem and remind you when it's time for a tune-up or other maintenance. And if you decide to sell your car, potential buyers will appreciate knowing exactly how well your vehicle has been cared for.

Choosing the right mechanic. The National Institute for Automotive Service Excellence (ASE) is an independent, non-profit organization dedicated to improving automotive service and repair by testing and certifying the competence of mechanics. Ask if your mechanic is ASE certified, and in what areas (brakes, engine repair, etc.). For free information about ASE technician certification, send a business-sized, self-addressed, stamped envelope to: ASE Consumer Brochure, Dept. CCC-F95, P.O. Box 347, Herndon, VA 22070.

Do-it-yourself car care tips

For this ...	Do this ...
inexpensive floor mats	*pick up carpet remnants or samples from local carpet store*
cleaning corrosion off battery terminals	*paint with paste of one cup baking soda and one cup water, let sit for one hour, then rinse; or pour a can of carbonated soda over them*
cleaning winter dirt from your car's undercarriage	*set a sprinkler under your car for a half-hour*
cleaning your car doors' drainage holes	*unclog with a wire hanger*
covering dings in paint job	*paint with clear nail polish*
covering scratches	*color match a crayon to your paint and rub it on*
de-icing windows and thawing frozen door locks	*keep windshield wiper fluid in a spray bottle*
emergency light or heat	*keep an empty coffee can, candle, and matches in your trunk*
keeping frost off your windshield	*spray with rubbing alcohol*
maintaining automatic antennas	*rub with wax paper occasionally*
messy emergency car repairs	*carry a carpet remnant to kneel or lie on*

continued ...

For this ...	Do this ...
messy emergency storage	*stuff an empty tissue box with small plastic grocery bags and keep in trunk*
messy road emergencies	*keep old socks in your trunk to use instead of good gloves*
organizing travel clutter	*hang a shoe bag on the back of the front seat*
preventing corrosion on your battery terminals	*coat with petroleum jelly*
preventing your trunk from freezing	*rub gasket/seal with vegetable oil*
protecting your car door from hitting garage walls	*cut strips from old tires and nail to walls*
removing bugs easily	*spray cooking oil onto clean bumper and grill*
removing haze and grime from the inside of your windshield	*wipe with vinegar*
repairing small holes in your windshield	*paint with clear nail polish*
safer travel in ice or snow	*fill clean plastic milk jugs with sand or cat litter and store in trunk for added weight or better traction*
starting a cold, sluggish car	*blow hot air from your hair dryer on the carburetor for a few minutes*
stuck in snow	*keep old carpet remnants in your trunk, put under tires to increase traction*
thawing a frozen lock	*heat your key with a match, then put in lock*
waxing and buffing	*use old socks as hand mitts*

Cleaning

Be careful with crystal. If your crystal glassware has deep etchings, lather it up with an old-fashioned shaving brush. The bristles are stiff enough to get into those hard-to-clean crevices but gentle enough not to cause any damage.

Make copper cookware gleam. Mix equal amounts of ketchup and water, and rub it onto your copper with a soft cloth. Wipe off, and smile at your reflection.

Wipe away crayon marks. Use a little silver polish to rub your tyke's crayon masterpiece off a vinyl wall covering. Don't worry — he can draw another on paper.

Tidy your toilet bowl. For space-age cleaning that adds a citrus freshness to your bathroom, sprinkle about a half cup of Tang drink mix in your toilet. Leave it for a couple of hours, then flush.

Small-mouthed glasses sparkle. Glasses, jars, and vases with openings too small to get your hand into can be a nightmare to clean. Just put in a handful of rice, add some water and dish detergent, shake it around, and rinse it out. The rice will help scrub it clean.

Give candlesticks a veggie scrub. A leaf of raw cabbage or leek will clean tarnish from pewter ware. Just give it a good rubbing, then rinse and dry it.

Baby old books. When dusting your antique volumes, hold each book closed by the front edge. Softly brush the top of the pages with a shaving brush. The cleaning will be gentle, and dust won't get inside.

Watch out!

A dusty old painting that has been hanging on your wall for many years may be more valuable than you thought. But don't rush to clean it. Common household cleaners and solvents — even linseed oil, which is sometimes recommended — could do permanent damage. Try dusting it with a sable or camel's hair paintbrush. If it needs more than that, find someone who cleans and restores paintings professionally.

Clean your garage and the rest is easy. Strange as it may sound, waxing the floor of your garage could help you keep a cleaner house. Sweeping, mopping, and cleanups will go faster, so you'll do it more often. And you'll cut down on the dust and grime you track into the house.

Back away from mirror damage. Spray glass cleaner onto a cloth, and then wipe your mirror. Don't spray it directly on the glass. It could get to the back and damage the reflective coating.

Mop up two messes at once. Next time you mop the floor, use your kitchen trash can as your suds bucket. You'll be cleaning two birds with one stone.

Cotton swabs aren't just for your ears. Use them to clean dust out of the corners of windows and picture frames. And they're particularly handy for surfaces with lots of small pieces, like a keyboard or the face of a radio.

In the 1920s, a Polish-born American named Leo Gerstenzang saw his wife cleaning their baby's ears with a piece of cotton on the end of a toothpick. Fortunately, he got the idea for a safer cotton swab before his wife's hand slipped. Otherwise he might have had to work on a hearing aid for his child. He called his invention Baby Gays. Mothers today know them as Q-Tips.

Say ta-ta to tarnish. Clean silver as soon as possible after it comes into contact with eggs, olives, vinegar, salad dressing, or salty foods. These substances can cause it to tarnish more quickly. They can even damage the surface if left on too long. And rubber can corrode silver as well. So don't store silver flatware on a rubber surface or wear rubber gloves when polishing a silver teapot.

Wait for cool weather to wash windows. Clean windows let in more warmth from the sun. So wash them, and save on your winter heating bills. But let them gather dust in summer, and you'll save on cooling costs.

Mop up spills on marble. Quickly clean up anything oily that is spilled on marble. Dust it with talcum powder or plaster of Paris, and blot it.

Sample this. If your antique sampler needs cleaning, here's a way to do it. Warm some dry potato flour in a double boiler. Cover the sampler with it, about one-fourth-inch deep. Brush it off before it cools.

The 17th century was known as the "Golden Age" of sampler making. Needleworkers employed a great variety of stitches, many of which are no longer used today. Among the most popular themes of that time were acorns and oak leaves, flowers, and lovers bearing gifts.

Polish off your bath. Tired of constantly scrubbing mold and mildew off your bath tile and grout? Then seal it with car wax. Cleanup will be quick and easy. And you'll only need to reapply the wax about once a year.

Give windows a 'sill' of approval. A lot of dirt and grime can accumulate on those windowsills. But you can clean them in a snap if you give them a quick coat of wax. Most dirt won't stick, and any that does will wipe away easily.

Is cleaning bronze a good idea? You bought a corroded piece of bronze sculpture at the flea market. Now how do you clean it? Maybe you don't. If it is an antique, cleaning it may lower its value. But if you are sure you want it clean, use a brass-wire brush to remove any flaking. And to get rid of the green color, soak it in a weak solution of vinegar and water. Rinse and let it dry. (Do not use ammonia to clean bronze.)

Treat fine china with care. A dishwasher is a great time saver, but when it comes to your fine china, you're better off taking the time to wash and dry by hand. The heat from the drying cycle can damage it. Save the dishwasher for your everyday dishes.

Extend your reach. Cover a straightened coat hanger with a sock or other fabric. Attach it with some sturdy tape. Use the hanger to clean hard-to-reach areas such as the space between the refrigerator and cabinet.

Vacuum smart. There's no need to vacuum every inch every week. Instead, vacuum the high traffic areas more frequently and the out-of-the-way places once a month.

> Make a great boot scraper with plastic bottle tops or the metal caps from glass bottles. Simply nail a bunch of them, topside down, to a heavy log or block of lumber. Secure it to the ground near your patio or deck. By using the rough edges to scrape the caked-on mud off your shoes, you won't track it onto the patio or into the house.

Use utensils twice. When cooking, measure dry ingredients first, then liquid ingredients in the same measuring cup or spoon. This strategy will speed your cleanup.

Charge on. Use an expired credit card to remove cooked-on food from a cookie sheet or baking pan. It's tough enough to scrape up the stuck particles without scratching the surface of the bake ware.

Starch your silverware. If you are out of silver polish, you'll find a good substitute in the pot where you cooked potatoes. Soak your silverware in the starchy water for an hour, and watch tarnish disappear. Next, wash it in warm, sudsy water. Rinse and dry, and you're ready to set your table.

Must books stay musty smelling? No, not when there's baking powder in the house. Put the offending book in a brown paper bag with a bit of baking powder. Leave it for a week, and say hello to a sweet-smelling tome.

Whiz dirt off whitewalls. Just wet your wheels and spray on oven cleaner. Brush for about 30 seconds and rinse.

Clothing and accessories

Oust mothball odors. Put garments with a mothball smell in a garbage bag or suitcase with a few fabric softener sheets. In a few days most of the odor should be gone. Air them out for a day or two, and they'll be ready to wear. If you need to wear an item right away, use your clothes dryer to speed things up. Put the item in the dryer with a couple of fabric softener sheets. Toss it with cool air, no heat, for 15 to 20 minutes.

Sharpen your eyesight. Out of eyeglass cleaner? A drop of vinegar is a safe substitute.

Protect the luster of your pearls. Wearing your pearls is good for them. The oils from your body helps keep them lustrous. If you have no place to wear them during the day, do what your grandmother did — wear them to bed. They may make you feel romantic, but leave off the Chanel No. 5. The alcohol in perfume can damage pearls. For the same reason, keep hairspray far away as well. And don't use any kind of jewelry cleaner that contains alcohol or ammonia. They can remove the finish.

Read it and stuff it. Cram hats and leather handbags with newspaper so they'll keep their shape in storage.

Cut buttons off carefully. To update the look of a favorite jacket, you might want to replace the buttons. When you remove the old ones, make sure you don't cut the fabric. Slip the teeth of a pocket comb between the button and the garment. Place the sharp edge of a razor blade between the button and the comb, and slice the threads.

Looking for the perfect fit? Wait until the afternoon or later to shop for shoes. Feet tend to swell as the day goes on. To get the size that will be most comfortable, you need to try on shoes when your feet are their largest.

Preserve valuable ivory. To protect the ivory settings in jewelry, rub them with a little almond oil on a soft cloth. Never clean ivory with water. It can make it crack.

Away with wet sneakers. Use the floor in front of the refrigerator grille as a dryer. The fan in the fridge will dry tennis shoes overnight.

Don't keep losing your mittens. Sew buttons the size of your coat buttons on the wrists of your gloves. When you take them off, button them to the front of the coat. They'll stay put until you are ready to wear them again.

Did you ever wonder why women's blouses and men's shirts have buttons on opposite sides? There's a logical explanation. Just like today, when buttons first came into use, most people were right-handed. So it was easier for them to button from right to left. Early buttons were expensive, but even wealthy men tended to dress themselves. On the other hand, maids performed most of the buttoning tasks for the ladies. It was easier for the maid to button left to right while facing the front of the garment.

Tighten loose shoes. If your shoes are falling off your feet, try shrinking them. Wet the insides, then dry them outside in the sunlight.

Make hangers glide. If your clothes hangers stick, it can be difficult to flip quickly through your wardrobe. To make it easier, rub a piece of wax paper along the clothes rod. Hangers should slip smoothly along.

Turn a button into a bauble. Got a fancy old button that no longer has a home? Give it new life by making it into a decorative pin, tie tack, or broach. Just glue a safety pin to the back. Or you can use a pin-making kit, available at arts and crafts stores.

So many shoes have so little room. Make more shelf space for your footwear. Use bricks or stacks of books to support a board or two. Place shoes both on the shelves and on the floor underneath.

Do away with wrinkles. Before folding clothes made of very thin fabrics, stuff them with tissue paper. This will help them keep their shape and avoid wrinkles.

The reptile on a Lacoste "alligator shirt" isn't an alligator at all. French designer Rene Lacoste, a former tennis star, was called "le crocodile" by his teammates. And that's a crocodile he put on the famous tennis shirts.

Make a cedar closet for pennies. For a great-smelling closet, fill the toe of one leg of an old pair of pantyhose with cedar chips. Tie the top to your closet rod, and — just like that — you're done.

Travel wrinkle free. To cut down on wrinkles when you travel, roll up your clothes in your suitcase instead of folding. Unpack as soon as possible.

Steam away a smoky smell. You can remove the odor of smoke from your clothing without washing or dry cleaning. Just hang it in the bathroom. Run a tub of hot water and add a cup of vinegar. The steam will take the odor away.

Save $ on pantyhose? Cool. Don't you hate throwing away pantyhose because they've gotten a run after just one wearing? Make them last longer by freezing them. Rinse and wring them out first, then place them in a zippered plastic bag. The night before you need them, thaw them out and hang them up to dry. You'll be amazed at how much stronger they'll be.

A walk in the garden can dirty your shoes. But if you are growing hibiscus flowers, you may be able to get the shine right back. In the West Indies, they call it "the shoe flower" because they say its blossoms are good for polishing black shoes.

Freshen drawers on the cheap. When you unwrap a new bar of soap, don't throw away the wrapper. Instead lay it inside a drawer, closet, or even a shoe box. You'll have a nice fragrance for free.

A closet can be your jewelry box. Put small hooks on the back of your closet door. Use them to hang bracelets, necklaces, and beads.

Make a case for recycling ties. It may be hard to throw away out-of-style neckties — especially when they are still colorful and pretty. Since ties are already tubes, you can quickly convert them into holders for eyeglasses, umbrellas, or other narrow items. Simply measure the object you want to store. Then measure that same length on the tie, starting at the wide end. Add a few inches and cut the tie to that length. Turn it wrong side out and sew the small end closed. Turn it back the right way. Fold over the tip, making a flap. Sew on a snap to hold the flap closed.

Find a substitute for a lost screw. Losing a screw from your eyeglasses can put you in a real bind. In an emergency, use a stud earring, a paper clip, or the wire from a bread twist tie to hold them together.

No need to hold your nose. You can take the smell out of your shoes by filling them with baking soda. Leave them overnight, then remove the powder. They'll be fresh and ready to wear.

Linen is one of the strongest natural fabrics. So strong, in fact, it was once used in making masts for sailing ships. And it's long-lasting as well. Linen cloth, still in good condition, has been found in Egyptian pyramids.

Protect your purse. Never let a leather handbag get wet. Keep a plastic bag inside to pull out and use as a cover in case of rain.

Repair instead of replace. You can often save money by repairing shoes instead of buying a new pair. But don't wait too long. The point at which shoes are too damaged to repair may come quicker than you think.

Clutter control

Simplify storage in your sewing box. Keep extra buttons handy by slipping them onto large safety pins. You can even color code them for easier matching.

Find tape quickly with a giant dispenser. If you have rolls of duct tape, electrical tape, masking tape and more in a disorganized jumble, try this clever way to get organized. Buy a paper towel holder that comes with a rod or dowel. Attach it to your workshop wall. Slip rolls of tape onto the dowel, and you'll never have to hunt for the right kind of tape again.

Hang a cool kid's shelf. A skateboard makes an instant bookshelf or storage space for toys in a child's room. Just position it on two shelf brackets.

Put pin-ups in your workshop. Use extra-large safety pins to store washers and bolts. Loop them through the pin, close it up, and hang it from the peg board over your bench.

Make a desk for your home office. Lay an old, hollow door across a couple of sturdy wooden crates, and you've got an instant desk. This works just as well with a pair of filing cabinets, and it maximizes your storage space.

Wrap ribbons smoothly. A good way to store hair ribbons is to wind them around hair curlers. They'll stay tangle free until you are ready to use them.

Remember to return library books. Hang a plastic bag near a calendar. When anyone in the family checks out books, have them remove the check-out slips from the pockets and put them in the bag. Also mark the due date on the calendar. You'll not only be reminded to return them, you'll also know what titles you are looking for when searching for missing books. Just remember to put each slip back into the appropriate book before you take them back.

Tuck away your garden tools. Maybe your yard is too small for a toolshed. But you can still have your gardening hand tools close by. Just paint an old mailbox to fit your garden style, and install it. Keep gloves, a trowel, pruning shears, and other small tools neatly inside until you need them.

Beat bath-time cleanup blues. If you have little ones at home or visiting on weekends, you know that bath time means lots of toys in the tub. To make cleanup and storage hassle-free, buy a mesh bag with a drawstring top. Load up all the bath toys when the bath is done. Give them a quick rinse under the faucet, then hang the bag from the shower head to drip dry.

Be seasonal about magazines. If you save your home and garden magazines, store them by seasons instead of titles. In springtime, you'll likely be looking for articles about starting your garden. In winter, you'll want to find recipes for hearty winter meals or articles on holiday decorating. So putting them together this way is more useful.

Who do you thank when your mailbox is overflowing with advertisements addressed to "occupant?" Lunsford Richardson of Selma, N.C., that's who. Around the turn of the century, he persuaded the U.S. Postal Service to let him mail ads for Vick's Vaporub addressed simply to "box holder."

Make your own wine rack. Cut 6-inch diameter PVC piping into 14-inch lengths. Stack the pipes inside a crate, cupboard, box, or storage unit. You have instant storage for wine or soda bottles.

Recycle for a disposable tote bag. Gather together several unbroken plastic rings from six-packs of soft drinks. Tie them to each other with string or fishing line in the shape of a carryall. Cut one in two to make handles. It's great to take to the lake or beach, and nobody cares if it gets lost.

Hold your hoses. If you bring your garden hoses in for the winter, here's a neat way to store them. Cut a plastic garbage can down until it's only a few feet high. Then simply coil your hoses inside, and store them in your basement, shed, or garage.

Clear your closet as you go. Keep a hand-me-down box in your closet. When you put something on and find it no longer fits, or you just don't want to wear it anymore, place it immediately into the give-away box. You won't have to rifle through these to find wearable items. And you'll have more room to hang the new replacements.

Watch out!

Don't store your bicycle near a refrigerator, freezer, or electric heater. They give off ozone, which can cause the rubber tires to crack.

Tidy your drawers. Bottles of nail polish or office supplies tip and slide every time you open and shut a bathroom or office desk drawer. To fix this problem, tack a piece of sewing elastic across the inside of the drawer at just the right depth to keep these items snug.

Store shoes instead of wine. A wine rack once seemed like a good idea, but now you find those bottles of burgundy are easier to reach in the kitchen cabinet. Put that wine rack to better use in your closet as a handy shoe holder.

Never lose your glasses at night. With Velcro, attach an eyeglass case to your night stand. Then, no matter what, you'll always know where your glasses are in the morning.

Take a long look at these hang-ups. What do you do with all those long, thin items you need to store — like pipes, light lumber, or molding? Consider this inexpensive solution. Buy lengths of vinyl or aluminum gutters, and attach them to garage, shed, or workshop wall studs. Then simply lay your items inside. You can even mount several lengths of gutters at different heights for maximum storage.

Hook up your towels. Does your bathroom floor or laundry basket seem to stay full of damp bath towels? Your family members are more likely to hang and reuse towels if you make your bathroom more functional. Take down the towel bar, and put up several hooks instead. Assign each family member a hook to hang his towel on.

Provide a place for everything. Get the stuff in your drawers organized cheaply. Wash and dry plastic yogurt or pudding cups. You can use them for storing pantyhose, jewelry, hair accessories, baby socks, office items — the possibilities are endless.

Organize your deep-freeze. Do you have a large freezer that's become a mixed-up jumble of frozen foods? Organize it with plastic milk crates. They're easy to stack and lift. And you can even sort your foods by color — perhaps green for vegetables, red for meats, and a yellow crate for your frozen fruits.

According to the 1998 Guinness Book of World Records, John Evans of Marlboro, England balanced a record 94 milk crates on his head for 16 seconds. Since each crate weighed three pounds, that totalled a whopping 282 pounds.

Speed up selection in your linen closet. Instead of pawing through stacks of mismatched sheets when it's time to change your bed linens, try this handy tip. Fold matching fitted and flat sheets, and slip them inside the matching pillowcase. Fold over the end and stack in the closet. Next time your bed needs a change, just grab and go.

Get the rap on neat wrapping paper. There's no need to waste wrapping paper by letting it unroll and get crumpled. Cut the foot and panty off an old pantyhose leg, and slip the hosiery tube over the paper. You can secure the ends, if you like, with bread wrapper tabs or twist ties.

Keep coloring books under control. An ingenious way to keep coloring books and other art supplies neat in your child's room is to buy a bright dish drainer. The plate separators will hold the coloring books upright. And the silverware holder can store pens, pencils, and paintbrushes.

Neaten up your photos. Don't spend money on expensive photo organizers. Create your own from shoe boxes. Cover them with pretty wrapping, contact, or wallpaper. Stand your photos in order, separating them in groups with tabbed dividers. Put a date label on the front, and add an envelope for negatives.

Watch out!

Don't feel guilty about those boxes of family photographs you never got around to putting into albums. Pat yourself on the back instead. Your photos are much better off in cardboard than they would be stored in most albums. Low-grade paper, acidic adhesives, and plastic dividers speed up the decay of your photos. Magnetic albums may be the worst of all. The plastic-coated cardboard pages give off peroxides and gases that stain and destroy images. To best protect your treasured pictures, use archival albums. They are made of non-polyvinyl materials and are worth the extra expense.

Cooking

Boil eggs without the shell. Sometimes removing the shell from hard-boiled eggs can be a pain. Next time shell them before you boil them! Sound crazy? Simply poach your eggs until well done, spoon out, and mince for your favorite recipe.

Chop without tears. Partially freeze your onion before you start to cook. It will be easier to slice or chop, and you won't shed a single tear.

Instant salad dressing. Don't toss out that almost-empty ketchup bottle. Pour in a little salad oil and your favorite vinegar, and give it a shake. You'll have a great homemade salad dressing.

Whip up a fluffier omelet. Do you like your scrambled eggs or omelets super fluffy? Add one-fourth teaspoon of cornstarch for every egg you're beating.

Bake better potatoes. If you insert a tenpenny nail into one end of a potato, it will conduct heat to the inside and bake your potato more quickly. Of course, don't do this if you're baking your potato in a microwave.

People in the United States consume about 54 pounds of potatoes apiece each year. That's a lot of french fries!

Make meatloaf without the mess. Put the hamburger meat and all the other ingredients into a zip-top bag. Push out most of the air and close it. Knead and blend the mixture by squeezing it inside the bag with your hands neatly on the outside. Once it's mixed thoroughly, shape it into a loaf. Remove it from the bag, and place it in the baking pan.

Homemade bread gets a new twist. If you make your own bread, be bold. Experiment with different liquids in your recipes. You can substitute milk, fruit juices, even meat or vegetable broth for water. It will give your bread a wonderfully distinctive flavor.

Soften up for half the cost. You can make your own soft spread to butter up your fresh bread. Bring a stick of butter or margarine to room temperature. Whip it with eight tablespoons of cooking oil, adding one tablespoon at a time.

Enjoy your eggs, Benedict. If you like poached eggs but don't own a poacher, try this neat trick. Cut both ends off a tuna can, and place the ring in a pan of simmering water. Poach away.

> Six average-sized lemons will yield just about a cup of juice.

Beat the mixing blues. When creaming butter or shortening, keep it from sticking to the beaters of your electric mixer. Just put the blades in hot water for a few minutes before you use them.

Hooked on shrimp? If you need a shrimp deveiner, go to your sewing box. A small crochet hook makes a good substitute.

Keep the flavor, lose the fat. Skinless chicken is lower in fat, but the skin seals in flavor, vitamins, and moisture. So cook it first, then remove the skin.

Grill a fresh and fruity treat. Make a wonderfully easy summer dessert next time you barbecue. Place whole, unpeeled bananas right on the grill, and cook them for about eight minutes, turning often. Slice open, top with sauce or ice cream, and enjoy!

> What does it mean if your recipe calls for "stock?" Stock and broth are the same thing — water with vegetables, beef, chicken, or fish cooked in it. If you don't have any stock on hand, you can make it from bouillon and water. You can buy bouillon in cubes or granules at the grocery store.

Make your own designer honey. Slowly boil one cup of honey with a half teaspoon of ground cloves. Cool and use to top waffles, ice cream, or your favorite dessert.

Cover bowls for a clean mix. With a clean shower cap, mixing can be splatter free. Just poke a couple of holes for the mixer blades, insert them, and cover the bowl. Whipped cream or cake batter will stay inside, while you and your countertop stay clean. Shower caps also make good covers for lidless bowls of leftovers.

This homemade mayo is a delicate delight. When making your own mayonnaise, use rice wine vinegar. You'll end up with a deliciously delicate flavor.

Watch out!

Don't use a vinegar-based dressing if you're serving on a painted plate. The acidity of the vinegar could ruin the plate. Even worse, it may leach lead from the paint into your food and make you sick.

Grab a turkey by the drumsticks. The hardest part about fixing a turkey or roasted chicken is getting it out of the pan and onto the serving platter. The job will be easier and neater if you slip on a pair of rubber gloves and simply grab the bird. No more slipping, sliding, or splattering.

Skin garlic cloves. The simplest way to quickly remove the skin from garlic cloves? Zap them in the microwave for about 15 seconds.

Sweeten up a lasting fluff. Your fresh whipped cream will stay fluffy longer if you sweeten it with confectioners' sugar instead of the granulated variety.

Mash for faster juice. In a hurry for juice? Soften the frozen concentrate with a potato masher, and it will thaw faster.

Some say the best mashed potatoes are made from baked potatoes rather than boiled. And since potatoes cooked whole contain more nutrients than those that are cut up, they may be healthier, too.

Adjust for nutrition's sake. If you want to cut back on the amount of fat, salt, or sugar you eat, try adjusting your recipes. First cook the dish the way the recipe is given to get a sense of the full taste. Then cut these ingredients in half. If it still tastes good, make those changes a part of the recipe. If the taste or texture falls far short of the original, try again, cutting back one-fourth. More often than not, with just a few attempts, you will get the recipe to fit your needs.

Slicing is simple. Use an egg slicer for fast and easy sliced mushrooms.

Substitutes serve the purpose. Are you waiting to make a recipe because you don't have the right wine? Cranberry juice or red grape juice both work in place of red wine, while white grape or apple juice can substitute for white wine.

In case you didn't know, coriander, cilantro, and Chinese parsley are the same thing — more or less. Cilantro and Chinese parsley are names for the herb as well as the leafy part you use in cooking. Coriander is the spice made by grinding the seed.

Sour your own milk. Why spend money on buttermilk? Add a tablespoon of vinegar to each cup of regular milk. Wait half an hour before using.

Ingredient substitutions

Ingredient	Amount	Substitution
allspice	1 teaspoon	1/2 teaspoon cinnamon and 1/2 teaspoon ground cloves
apple pie spice	1 teaspoon	1/2 teaspoon cinnamon, 1/4 teaspoon nutmeg, and 1/8 teaspoon cardamom
arrowroot	1 1/2 teaspoons	1 tablespoon flour or 1 1/2 teaspoons cornstarch
baking powder	1 tablespoon	1 teaspoon baking soda and 1 teaspoon cream of tartar
baking powder	1 teaspoon	1/4 teaspoon baking soda and 1/2 teaspoon cream of tartar or 1/4 teaspoon baking soda and 1/2 cup sour milk or buttermilk (decrease liquid in recipe by 1/2 cup)
brown sugar	1 cup	1 cup white sugar and 1 1/2 tablespoons molasses
buttermilk	1 cup	1 cup plain yogurt; 1 cup sweet milk and 1 3/4 teaspoons cream of tartar; or 1 cup minus 1 tablespoon warm milk and 1 tablespoon vinegar or lemon juice, let stand for 5 minutes
cake flour	1 cup	1 cup stirred all-purpose flour minus 2 tablespoons
catsup	1 cup	1 cup tomato sauce
catsup (for cooking)	1 cup	1/2 cup sugar and 2 tablespoons vinegar
catsup	1/2 cup	1/2 cup tomato sauce, 2 tablespoons sugar, 1 tablespoon vinegar, and 1/8 teaspoon ground cloves
chili sauce	1 cup	1 cup tomato sauce, 1/4 cup brown sugar, 2 tablespoons vinegar, 1/4 teaspoon cinnamon, and a dash each of ground cloves and allspice
chocolate chips	1 ounce	1 ounce sweet cooking chocolate

continued ...

Ingredient	Amount	Substitution
chocolate chips	1 ounce	1 ounce sweet cooking chocolate
chocolate, semisweet	1 2/3 ounces	1 ounce unsweetened chocolate, 4 teaspoons sugar
chocolate, semi-sweet baking	1 square	3 tablespoons unsweetened cocoa powder, 1 tablespoon shortening or oil, and 3 teaspoons sugar
chocolate, semi-sweet chips, melted	6-ounce package	2 squares unsweetened chocolate, 2 tablespoons shortening, and 1/2 cup sugar
chocolate, unsweetened	1-ounce square	3 tablespoons cocoa and 1 tablespoon fat
cocoa	1/4 cup	1-ounce square chocolate
coconut cream	1 cup	1 cup whipping cream
coconut milk	1 cup	1 cup whole or 2 percent milk
corn syrup	1 cup	1 cup honey or 1 cup sugar and 1/4 cup liquid
cornstarch	1 tablespoon	2 tablespoons all-purpose flour; 2 teaspoons arrowroot; or 2 tablespoons granular tapioca
cracker crumbs	3/4 cup	1 cup dry bread crumbs
cream, half-and-half	1 cup	1 cup evaporated milk, undiluted, or 7/8 cup milk and 1/2 tablespoon butter or margarine
cream, heavy	1 cup	3/4 cup whole milk and 1/3 cup melted butter
cream, light	1 cup	3/4 cup milk and 3 tablespoons butter or margarine or 1 cup evaporated milk, undiluted
cream, whipped		evaporated milk (13 ounces) chilled and 1 teaspoon lemon juice, whipped
egg	1 whole	2 tablespoons oil and 1 teaspoon water or 2 yolks and 1 tablespoon water
flour, all-purpose	1 cup sifted	1 cup plus 2 tablespoons cake flour; 1 cup rolled oats; or 1 1/2 cups bread crumbs

continued ...

Ingredient	Amount	Substitution
flour, cake	1 cup sifted	1 cup minus 2 tablespoons sifted all-purpose flour
flour, self-rising	1 cup	1 cup minus 2 teaspoons all-purpose flour, 1 1/2 teaspoons baking powder, and 1/2 teaspoon salt
gelatin, flavored	3-ounce package	1 tablespoon plain gelatin and 2 cups fruit juice
herbs, fresh	1 tablespoon	1 teaspoon dried herbs
honey	1 cup	1 cup sugar and 1 cup water
lemon juice	1 teaspoon	1 teaspoon vinegar
mayonnaise (for salads)	1 cup	1 cup cottage cheese, pureed; 1 cup sour cream; or 1/2 cup yogurt and 1/2 cup mayonnaise
milk, whole	1 cup	1 cup fruit juice; 1 cup potato water; or 1/2 cup evaporated milk and 1/2 cup water
molasses	1 cup	1 cup honey
mustard, dry	1 teaspoon	1 tablespoon prepared mustard
pimento	2 tablespoons	3 tablespoons fresh red bell pepper, chopped
pumpkin pie spice	1 teaspoon	1/2 teaspoon cinnamon, 1/4 teaspoon ginger, 1/8 teaspoon allspice, and 1/8 teaspoon nutmeg
sour cream	1 cup	1 cup plain yogurt or 3/4 cup milk, 3/4 teaspoon lemon juice, and 1/3 cup butter or margarine
sugar, white	1 cup	1 cup brown sugar, packed; 1 cup corn syrup (decrease liquid in recipe by 1/3 cup); 1 cup honey (decrease liquid in recipe by 1/4 cup); or 1 3/4 cups powdered sugar
tomato juice	1 cup	1/2 cup tomato sauce and 1/2 cup water
yogurt, plain	1 cup	1 cup buttermilk; 1 cup sour cream; or 1 cup cottage cheese, pureed

Family fun

See the world daily. If you have a child fascinated with travel or a den that needs a whimsical touch, try wallpapering the room with old maps. This idea is great for covering cracked or damaged walls.

Leave sand at the beach. Take a mesh bag along when you go to the seashore. When it's time to gather your belongings, put small washable items — like suntan lotion, sunglasses, and any shells you've collected — into the bag. Dunk them in the water or under a faucet to remove any sand sticking to them.

Make memories last. Create an artistic memento of your family vacation. Take a lid from a peanut butter or mayonnaise jar. Glue Spanish moss or sea grass inside. Decorate with tiny sea shells or other "finds" from nature. Glue a magnet to the back, and stick it on your refrigerator.

Save your change. If you've lost the plug in your piggy bank, try replacing it with a nipple from a baby bottle. It just might fit.

We "squirrel" away money for a rainy day. So why do we put it in a piggy bank? During the Middle Ages, many household items, including jars where people stashed extra cash, were made of a kind of clay called "pygg." In time they became known as pig jars. Eventually piggy banks were designed to reflect the name.

Pasta to "dye" for. Kids love stringing a macaroni necklace or making a mosaic picture from shells, bows, and other pasta shapes. And the more colorful the better. To dye it, shake a handful of pasta in a plastic zip-top bag with two tablespoons of rubbing alcohol and a few drops of food coloring. Dry it on several layers of newspaper. Now it's ready for the hands of those creative youngsters.

Stay in touch. Use a photo album for a more personal address book. Insert a picture of the family or friend to go with the address.

Inspire a child. Keep an old typewriter out for a child to play with. Even if he can't read or write yet, the letters and keys will spark his imagination and perhaps encourage him to enjoy reading from an early age.

Tag your bags. You can make attractive, low-cost I.D. tags for your luggage from recycled greeting cards. Select brightly colored ones so they'll be easy to spot. Write your name and address clearly on the back of each, and cover them completely with strips of transparent tape. Punch holes, and tie or tape them to the handles of your suitcase.

Brighten schoolbooks. Leftover wallpaper makes attractive and durable book covers.

Dry flowers like a pro. Mix one part borax with two parts cornmeal. Put a layer of this mixture in an airtight container. Place the flower you wish to dry on top of it, and sprinkle more of the mixture over the flower. Be careful not to crush or bend it out of shape. Seal the container, and leave at room temperature for seven to 10 days. Remove the flower, and brush off excess powder with a soft paintbrush or makeup brush.

Light up a jack-o'-lantern. A flashlight is safer than a candle inside your Halloween pumpkin. And it won't blow out with an autumn breeze.

The inspiration for the flashlight actually came from a novelty invention — a lighted flower pot. A Russian immigrant, Conrad Hubert, bought this wacky invention and modified the design into an electric hand torch. Hubert began his life in America penniless. But because of the flashlight, he died a millionaire.

Preserve your newspaper clippings. Newsprint isn't designed to last a long time. But some of life's most special events — like weddings and births — are reported in the newspaper. So naturally you want to keep articles and pictures that are dear to you. To best protect your clippings, put them in polyester film folders with sheets of alkaline buffered paper behind them. Then place them in acid-free boxes, and store them in a cool, dry place away from direct light.

Sew sharp. A dull needle can slow your creative project. But you can sharpen a needle quickly without removing it from the sewing machine. Just stitch a few lines through a piece of sandpaper, and it's sharp as new. And you are back to work in no time.

Create a container for your trinkets. Cut off the bottoms of two two-liter soda bottles. Paint them or cover them with decoupage. Glue ribbon over the sharp edges. To make a hinge so you can open and close the box, punch two holes in the side, near the top of each bottle bottom. Use ribbon or wire to connect them. You might like to line the inside with velvet or another fabric.

Recycled bulbs brighten the holidays. Paint a Santa Claus face and beard on a burned out light bulb. Tie a ribbon around the screw-in cap to make a hanger. Then paint the cap red for the hat, and trim it with decorative fur. Or use artificial snow for the fur trim and beard.

This aquarium is for the birds. If you think you'd enjoy the birds outside more than you do the fish inside, make your fish tank into a bird feeder. Just turn it on its side — after removing water, fish, and whatever else may have been inside, of course. It will provide a protected place for birds to feed. And you can enjoy watching them from all sides.

If you're particularly fond of goldfinches, here's a good way to attract them to your feeder. All finches love thistle seeds, but only goldfinches feed upside down. So put the opening for the seed beneath the perch. They'll be able to eat with no competition from other types of birds.

Keep yarn from getting tangled. Make a holder from a two-liter plastic soda bottle, and you'll have a smooth flow of yarn when knitting or crocheting. Simply cut the bottom off, and insert the ball of yarn. Pull the strand out the mouth of the bottle. Then tape the bottom back on so the yarn won't fall out and roll across the room.

Bank on it. A potato chip can makes a neat coin bank. Just slit a hole in the top, and decorate it with play money.

Extend a doll's life. An old cedar chest is the best place to tuck away that beloved antique doll or teddy bear. It will be safe from moths, and its fabric and paint will be better preserved. Never store these treasures in a hot attic. They need a place that's not too hot, cold, bright, dry, or humid.

Tie a tight knot. Use wet string to tie up a package to mail. When the string dries, it tightens and holds the knots more securely.

Raise money as you raise awareness. Whenever someone in your family leaves lights, stereos, or other appliances on unnecessarily, have them place a quarter in a jar. It takes a while to change habits so you may collect a fair amount of money. You could invest it in energy-saving light bulbs or donate it to a favorite conservation group.

Pop it in the mail. When you have something breakable to mail, if you don't have any of those plastic foam "peanuts" to pack it in, substitute some popped popcorn. It does a nice job of cushioning those fragile items.

> Popcorn may have been part of the first Thanksgiving celebration. According to legend, the Indians provided the Pilgrims with several deerskins filled with popped kernels. Popcorn really caught on with Americans. By the mid-1940s they were munching it at the movies. And the '50s found people popping tons of it to eat while watching television. Today, each person, on average, eats about 47 quarts of popcorn each year.

Reuse lemon-shaped squeeze bottles. When you have used all the lemon or lime juice, refill that handy little squirter with salad dressing to take on a picnic. And refill another with children's shampoo, and toss it in the beach bag for a quick wash-down at an outdoor shower. The possibilities are endless.

Give an old game a face-lift. You picked up a used game at a garage sale. The parts are all there, but the box has seen better days. Cover it with wrapping paper — recycled of course — and it will seem like new.

Bathe baby in a basket. If your toddler's too big to bathe in the sink but not yet ready for the tub, try the wet-crib. Put him in a laundry basket in the tub with a few inches of water. He will have some freedom as you wash him but won't go slipping all over the bathtub. Don't use a basket with broken slats, however, as these can be sharp and dangerous to curious hands and mouths.

Make your own giant chalk. Who would think you could draw on the sidewalk with eggshells? You can by following these simple steps. Save your eggshells until you have 18. Be sure to wash away any of the egg that might be sticking to them. Grind up the dry eggshells with a clean rock on your sidewalk until you have a fine powder. Remove any large chunks and bring the rest inside. You should have three big spoonfuls of powder. Stir together three teaspoons of flour and three teaspoons of hot tap water until it forms a paste. Add the powdered eggshells and mix well. If you want colored chalk, add a few drops of food coloring. Stuff this mixture into an old toilet paper tube, and let it dry for about three days. Peel away the cardboard as you use it.

Fix it up

Sharpen razor blades. When your project requires a lot of cutting, your razor blade can get dull pretty quickly. Get a fine edge back by swiping it across the striker on a matchbook.

Turn a tiny screw. When making repairs to clocks, small musical instruments, and other things with tiny screws, use a sardine can opener as a screwdriver.

Loosen locks. If you have trouble opening a lock, rub the edges of your key with a soft lead pencil. The graphite in the pencil lead will soon have it turning smoothly.

Get to the source of moisture. What do you do about moisture in your basement? First, find out what's causing it. Hang a mirror on the wall overnight. In the morning, if you find it fogged over with moisture, you have a problem with condensation. A dehumidifier should solve your problem. But if the mirror is dry while the wall is damp, moisture is seeping through. You'll probably have to find and patch one or more cracks in the wall.

Attract scattered screws. Keep a magnet on your workbench. It will be handy for a quick pickup if you spill a jar of small items like nails, tacks, or washers.

> You've probably oiled many rusty hinges with the lubricant WD-40. But do you know what the WD stands for? It's Water Displacer.

Cut a clean edge. Making a narrow cut at the end of a thin board is tricky business. So use this trick to make it easier. Take a longer piece of scrap wood, and clamp it to the bottom of the board. It will stay stable while you make a smooth cut through both pieces.

Shave the mystery from finding studs. Here's a quick way to locate a wall stud. Plug in your electric razor, and run it along the wall. You'll hear a different tone when the razor crosses a stud.

Make mahogany scratches disappear. Apply iodine to hide scratches in mahogany and other dark wood. Or rub them with the meat of a walnut or Brazil nut.

Watch out!

Choose your building materials wisely. Pressure-treated lumber is great for decks and fencing, but it can release potentially unhealthy chemicals into the air. Redwood or cedar is a better choice for picnic tables, garden enclosures, or children's play gyms.

Hit the nail on the head. Do you keep hitting your fingers when you try to hammer a nail? Try slipping the nail between the teeth of a comb. It will hold it in place while you hit it, and you'll have no more smashed thumbs.

Drill without splintering. You can stop your drill bits from splintering their exit holes. Just clamp a piece of scrap wood flat against the bottom of the piece you are drilling. The bit will go straight into this "backstop" and won't split the good piece.

Avoid the ups and downs. No need to stop your work to retrieve a tool dropped from the top of a ladder. Make a pocket from a strip of old tire rubber. Nail it to a wooden ladder, or make a strap to hang it from an aluminum one. Insert your tools before you raise the ladder, and one trip up should do the job.

No funnel? No worries. Pour your liquid along a nail, and it will flow right into the container.

Buffer for a better clamp. Never put a clamp directly on the surface of a project. Put a couple of pieces of flat scrap wood on either side of the surface, and clamp onto those. These buffers will not only keep the clamp from scratching the surface but will also help spread the pressure over a greater area than the clamp would by itself.

Spread glue like a pro. Got a large surface to glue? Use a comb to spread out your adhesive for even coverage.

Lead a leak to the drain. A leak in a basement where you've stored boxes of out-of-season clothes or holiday decorations can make quite a mess. Direct the water away from where it will do damage — ideally toward a drain — by creating a channel of caulking compound. The water will move in a stream rather than spreading out in all directions. If you don't have a drain, perhaps you can station yourself with a water vacuum or towels and buckets at the end of the stream.

Slip-proof your climb to the top. Wrap burlap around the bottom rung of your ladder so you can wipe wet or muddy shoes before climbing.

Watch out!

Never stand on the top two steps of a tall ladder. If you do, the ladder is less stable and more likely to topple over. Paint those two rungs red as a reminder.

Loosen those joints. If you want to take wood pieces apart, soften the old glue on the joints with vinegar. For best results, apply it generously from a small oil can.

Saw without splitting. Don't let splintered plywood spoil your project. Before you cut, put a strip of masking tape over the starting point. It won't split when you start to saw.

You need a leg to sit on. A loose chair leg is just waiting to give someone a spill. To tighten it, wrap the loose end with a strip of pantyhose. Coat it with glue and reinsert it.

Get more miles from sandpaper. Dampen the paper backing of a piece of sandpaper, and wrap it around a block of wood. Your sanding will be smoother, and the sandpaper will last longer.

Leave a trail of breadcrumbs. Whenever your fix-it project involves taking something apart, it's also going to involve putting it back together. Make this process easier by lining up each part in order as you remove it. It's also a good idea to jot down the order on a slip of paper, just in case you knock the assembly line out of whack.

Wiper fluid works wonders. Keep windshield wiper fluid in a spray bottle in your car in winter. It comes in handy for de-icing windows and thawing frozen door locks.

Don't be a sore head. You keep bumping your head on a cabinet door that swings open when it should be closed. Glue a piece of magnetic tape to the inside edge of the door. And glue another to the spot where the first one touches the cabinet. It will stay shut until you want it open.

Tacky is better. Repair a spindle that has come loose in a kitchen chair, especially if it's supporting a leg, with a tacky adhesive like yellow carpenter's glue. It's made for wood and is strong and fast drying. Wipe off any excess with a damp cloth. Let it dry overnight — 24 hours is even better — before using it again.

Maybe you have heard the rule about tightening and loosening things like screws or jar lids: "lefty loosey, righty tighty." But do you know the "Right Hand Rule" for tightening nuts and bolts that are sideways, upside down, or at an odd angle? Using your right hand, give a "thumbs up" sign in the direction the bolt is pointing. Then turn the nut in the direction your fingers are curving.

Spools make cool clamps. When you need to hold together a glue job but you're out of clamps, what do you do? You make one. Just take two old thread spools, and run a long bolt through them. Position one spool on each side of the item being glued, and tighten it with a wing nut on the bolt.

Hide that burn. Your kitchen countertop looks great except for that ugly burned spot beside the stove. No need to replace the countertop. Just glue a decorative tile over the damaged area. You'll save yourself some money and add a permanent hot pad.

Repair, don't replace, screens. That hole in your screen is small, but it's still big enough to let in mosquitoes. Take some clear fingernail polish, and dab it over the hole. Apply three or four coats, letting it dry between applications. It will form an invisible barrier that will keep the bugs out.

Stop ceiling leaks in their tracks. If you see a fresh water mark on your ceiling, don't wait to see how bad the leak will get before you take action. If water stands and soaks a large area, that could mean a major — and maybe expensive — repair to the ceiling. As a precaution, drill a hole into the wet spot. Put a container under it to catch any water that might leak out. Find out where the water is coming from and make any necessary repairs. Then simply fill and repaint the hole you drilled.

Remount a non-rickety rack. If your towel rack gets pulled off the wall, don't try to put it back in the same spot. You'll have much better luck if you move it a few inches and start fresh where the wall has never been drilled.

Hush that squeak. Chances are, that squeaky floor is telling you the sub-flooring boards are rubbing against joists that have dried and shrunk. You can easily fix that problem with a drill and a number eight wood screw that's one and a half inches long. First, locate the floor joists near the squeak. They are usually laid in the direction of front to back of the house, 16 inches apart. Next, drill the screw through the carpet and into the joist where the squeak occurs. Now you can make a midnight raid on the refrigerator without a squeaky floor giving you away.

Food preparation

Say goodbye to stale bread. Pop a rib of celery into your bread bag to keep your loaf soft and fresh.

Coffee lovers chill out. When that caffeine urge strikes, make yourself a cup of real coffee in an "instant." Just make a pot of very strong coffee. Pour it into an ice cube tray and freeze. When you want some coffee, toss a couple of cubes in a cup and add boiling water.

Butter up your cheese. Don't waste good semi-hard cheese by letting the cut edge harden or get moldy. Give your cheese a light coating of butter, and it will stay fresh.

Freeze a spare. If you are making a casserole, make an extra one and freeze it for another meal. Just take it out of the oven about 10 minutes before the one you'll eat right away, and let it cool. If using a dish that can handle sudden temperature changes, set it in a pan of ice. If you think you'll need the baking dish before you're ready to eat the casserole, plan ahead. Before filling the dish, line it with aluminum foil. After the casserole is frozen, lift it out and wrap it so it's air tight. When you're ready to reheat it, slip it back into its original container. If there's a crumb topping, leave it off until you're ready to heat it.

Topsy-turvy keeps dairy foods fresh. If you store yogurt, cottage cheese, and sour cream upside down in your refrigerator, they will stay fresh longer. Just make sure the lids are on tight. Transfer these dairy foods to smaller containers when your supply gets low, and they won't go bad as quickly.

Munch on soft marshmallows. Are your mallows hard and stale? Freshen them up by putting them in a plastic bag and dipping the bag in hot water. To keep them from drying out in the first place, store them in an airtight container in the freezer.

Keep cooking oil fresh. Store oil in a cool, dark location, and it won't turn rancid as quickly.

Enjoy summer's harvest all year long. When spring or summer berries are in season — whether growing in your garden or plentiful at the supermarket — freeze some to enjoy in winter. Put them in the freezer on a cookie sheet. When they are frozen, transfer them to freezer containers. They won't stick together, so you can use just the amount you need without defrosting extras.

> If you store your rice in airtight jars, it will keep for a couple of years.

'Berry' firm fruits are better. Always hull strawberries after you've washed them. If you hull them first, they'll absorb too much water and become mushy.

Cold wrap is less clingy. Tired of fighting with your roll of clear plastic wrap? Freeze it. If you store it in the freezer, it will unroll and tear more easily, and it won't stick to itself until it thaws out. Anytime you have trouble getting it to stick to your bowl, try moistening the outer edge of the dish before you wrap it.

Pick a tastier apple. Buy apples that have a bit of green at both ends. They taste better.

Put the snap back in snacks and cereals. If your crackers and cereal have gone a little limp, give them a fresh start. Just spread them on a cookie sheet and heat them in a regular oven at 300 degrees for five minutes.

> Back in the 1930s, Wheaties brand cereal spon-
> sored baseball broadcasts. Radio station WHO in
> Des Moines, Iowa, held a contest looking for a
> Wheaties broadcaster. The winner was a young
> man named Ronald "Dutch" Reagan. His prize was
> an all-expenses-paid vacation to Hollywood. He
> never returned to Iowa — and you know the rest
> of the story.

Store 'egg'stras in the freezer. If you have more eggs on hand than you can use right now, freeze some for later. Just crack one egg into each mold of an ice cube tray and freeze. When the egg cubes are hard, transfer them to a plastic freezer bag. Be sure to wash the trays in hot, soapy water afterward. Raw eggs can harbor harmful bacteria that can make you sick.

Make guacamole tonight. Avocados will ripen faster if you bury them in a bowl of flour.

Stretch summer's abundance. Don't let those extra tomatoes from your garden go to waste. Instead, wash them, cut out the cores, and freeze them whole for soups and stews. When you're ready to use them, hold them under running water, and the skins will slide right off.

Brew fresher coffee with fresher beans. Your coffee beans will stay fresh longer if you store them in the freezer. This is especially helpful if you don't make coffee very often.

Freeze liquids without splashes. When you want to freeze a liquid in a plastic bag, put the bag inside a plastic cup or food container. It will hold its shape while you pour and freeze it. Once it's frozen, if you want the container for other uses, remove the bag. When you are ready to defrost it, slip the frozen liquid out of the bag and return it to the same or a similar container to thaw.

An apple a day keeps sprouts away. Place an apple in the bin with your potatoes. They won't send out buds so quickly.

Make grocery shopping less painful. Keep a couple of laundry baskets and a cooler in the trunk of your car. The baskets will make carrying a load of groceries into the house faster and easier. And the cooler is great for those spur-of-the-moment shopping trips or when you can't go straight home to unload.

Shake salt freely. Few things are more frustrating than a shaker that won't give up its salt. If you add a few grains of rice to your shaker when you fill it, your salt will stay dry and free flowing.

> Over 90 percent of the world's rice is grown in Asia.

Try before you buy. Warehouse clubs can save you money, but they usually require an upfront membership fee. Before you join, ask for a one-day trial to see if you like it well enough to pay for it. Also, investigate discounted rates for your company, civic organization, or other affiliations.

Grease it easy. Save those wrappers from sticks of butter or margarine and store them in a plastic bag in the refrigerator. Use them to grease cookie sheets or baking pans.

Cut costs at the checkout. To save money at the grocery store, think ahead. Plan the week's menu before you go — and make a list. Otherwise, you may end up buying things you don't need and still not have all the ingredients to make dinner every night.

Watch out!

Pay attention at the checkout. Watch the price of items as they are scanned. If a price is different than the price marked, alert the cashier. Stores have various policies about scanner errors. You may get the item free. At the very least, the store should correct the price.

Flatter means a faster thaw. If you buy hamburger in bulk and freeze it in smaller portions, try this tip. Separate it and put it into zip-lock bags. Flatten each one evenly with a rolling pin. Seal and freeze. It takes less space in your freezer, stacks neatly, and thaws out more quickly.

Get the most fruit for your buck. All prepackaged bags of fruits and vegetables are not created equal. Even though they may be labeled five pounds, some will weigh more than others. Test a few on the scale and purchase the one that weighs the most.

Coupons straight from the horse's mouth. Contact manufacturers for coupons. By calling the toll-free number on their products, you may receive several dollars worth of coupons and product samples.

Gifts and entertaining

Make wrapping paper with pizzazz. The colorful Sunday comic pages make great giftwrap, especially for a kid's present. Spray the finished product with hair spray. You'll have a nice glossy shine and no inky fingers.

Keep cookies from sticking together. Few gifts are as appreciated as a freshly baked batch of homemade cookies in an attractive box or tin. To keep cookies from sticking together, separate the layers with paper coffee filters.

Flatten playing cards. Your friends have gathered for a game of canasta. But a rough shuffling has left your plastic-coated playing cards bent. A quick microwave zap should straighten them out.

Hide tiny gifts in tidy packages. Put small gifts inside a toilet paper tube. Stuff in some tissue paper to keep it from sliding around. Then wrap it, twisting the ends and tying with colorful ribbon to look like a piece of candy. This is great for disguising small gifts like rings and necklaces.

Set up extra serving space. You're short on counter space in the kitchen, or you need a little more serving room for a special dinner or party. Consider setting up your ironing board. Protect it with plastic, towels, or newspaper. Throw a tablecloth over it, and an extra table is ready.

Decorate fashionable gift boxes. Cut leftover material into strips — or sew shorter pieces together. Spray starch and iron them. Then tie them around gifts for a pretty designer look.

Something old is new again. Spray an old basket with a fresh coat of paint. Add a bow for a festive touch. You have a decorative gift, as good as new. Give it all by itself, or fill it with fruit or small presents.

Box breakable items for safe shipping. Pack small fragile gifts inside an empty egg carton. Close it up, and tuck it inside a larger box for mailing.

Give greeting cards a new life. Cut out the design from the front of a used greeting card. Paste it on a gift you plan to mail instead of a bow that's likely to get crushed. Your package will look pretty, and you'll save money, too. Cut-up cards make good gift tags as well.

Light up with Life Savers. Use Life Savers candies as birthday candle holders on a child's cake. They're colorful and inexpensive. And the kids can eat them as an extra treat.

> Life Savers drops and mints are available in 12 roll varieties with a total of 25 flavors. The top-selling flavors, in order of preference, are orange, pineapple, cherry, lemon and lime, "wint-o-green," "pep-o-mint" and butter rum.

Serve fun and fruity refreshments. To jazz up drinks for parties, freeze maraschino cherries, grapes, or chunks of other fruits in ice cubes.

Your party is a breeze. For an outdoor party, cover your picnic table with a colorful twin-size fitted sheet. It will look pretty, and the elastic corners will hold it in place even if the wind blows.

Pick a natural place card. Collect foliage from magnolia trees or ivy vines. Select a marker with opaque white, gold, or silver ink, and write names of your guests on the green leaves.

Give a knitter a neat gift. A potato chip can makes a great holder for knitting needles and two or three small balls of yarn. Punch a hole in the top of the can, and pull a strand of yarn through for tangle-free knitting. As a final touch, decorate the can — perhaps with bits of brightly colored yarn.

Flowers stay fresh without a headache. You want your house guests to enjoy the cut flowers throughout their visit. Add an aspirin to the water, and your posies will stay fresh and lovely longer.

Watch out!

Don't put cut flowers near a bowl of fruit. Apples, pears, and bananas give off an ethylene gas that can kill them.

Write like a secret agent. Here's a fun and easy way to entertain kids. Supply them with the juice from a fresh lemon to use as ink. Have them write secret messages using toothpicks, craft sticks, or small paintbrushes. To read the messages, place the paper, once the juice is dry, in the sun. Or hold it near a light bulb. The juice will turn brown, and the words will magically appear.

Find new uses for tissue boxes. They are too pretty to throw away. Once those floral tissue boxes are empty, cut them up for gift tags or bookmarks.

Make an easy decoration. Find a basket and fill it with pine cones. Adorn the basket with ribbon, and you have a pretty centerpiece. You can use it every day, or save it just for the holidays.

Create a giant ice bucket. When you have a party, the tub of your washing machine makes a great cooler. Just fill it with ice, and pack in the cans and bottles. When the party is over, remove any remaining drinks, let the ice melt, and set the machine to spin out the water. You might want to line the inside with a large towel just to keep the cans and bottles from scratching your enamel.

Free coupons make gift giving simple. Make your own coupon book for friends or family. The coupons can be for anything — free baby-sitting, vacuuming, breakfast in bed, dinner for two. The only restriction is your imagination.

Entertain with good 'scents.' Just before your guests arrive, add a drop of perfume to a cool light bulb and turn on the light. As the bulb heats up, the scent will spread through the room.

Wrap it up in a big way. Does wrapping an extra large gift have you stumped? Try using a paper tablecloth. They come in lots of fun colors and designs.

Weave a gift bag. Tie the ends of leftover scraps of yarn together, and wind it in and out of the holes in a mesh vegetable bag. You'll have an attractive sack to hold a gift. Or make a gift basket by doing the same with a plastic berry basket.

Squeeze a special message. You don't have to be a professional baker to decorate like one. Try putting icing in a clean ketchup or mustard squeeze bottle. It will be easy to write a fun message for a special occasion.

A foul ball comes your way — the perfect souvenir for your favorite youngster. As you turn the baseball admiringly in your hands, you might wonder what kind of machine they use to sew those perfect curving seams.

The truth is, although years were spent trying to create such a machine, all "real" — not rubber — baseballs are sewn by hand. It takes an expert 10 to 15 minutes to sew one ball.

Fans love getting baseballs, so teams don't collect foul balls and reuse them like they once did. Today, the average life of a ball is about six minutes. And even when purchased by the thousands, each one costs about $4.

Cut card costs with heart-felt notes. Make your own Valentine's Day cards by writing personal messages on paper hearts. Give them to friends, or leave them around the house for your family members to find.

Health and safety

Protect a sore finger. Slip a small hair curler over an injured finger and it won't get bumped so easily. It can also serve as a splint if you don't want to bend it.

Stabilize your ladder. If you aren't sure your ladder is on a firm foundation, give it some extra support. If it's resting on soft earth, place both feet on a wide, flat piece of wood. If the ground is uneven, position a flat block of lumber beneath the ladder's lower foot.

Relieve motion sickness. Try sucking on a lemon wedge if you get queasy in a car or on a boat. It should quickly ease your discomfort. Ginger is a natural remedy, too. You can buy ginger supplements or take about a tablespoon of powdered gingerroot.

Drive with ears wide open. When driving in fog, roll down a window. You'll hear cars coming before you'll be able to see them.

Make an emergency ice pack. Place unpopped popcorn kernels into a zip-lock freezer bag and keep it in the freezer for emergency injuries. Carry it with you on picnics, camp outs, and to sporting events.

Release an adhesive bandage. You can avoid the "ouch" by soaking the bandage top and edges in baby oil before removing it.

A man who worked for Johnson & Johnson, a company that manufactured gauze and adhesive tape, created little, ready-made bandages for his accident-prone wife. In 1942, the company began mass-producing his invention. They called them Band-Aids.

Get a grip on things. Folks with arthritis may find it difficult to hold and use everyday objects. Here's a way to make it easier. Take the foam tube off a hair curler and stick it on the end of things you handle often — like pens, pencils, toothbrushes, cosmetics, and cooking utensils.

Tea bags soothe burns. You stayed in the sun too long, and now you've got a painful sunburn. Look to your kitchen cabinet for relief. Take two or three tea bags and drop them in your bath. To get the most benefit, hold them under the spout. Enjoy a nice, long soak as the tannic acid in the tea draws heat from the burn. If you prefer, instead of a bath, you can wet the tea bags and place them directly onto your burned skin. Use light gauze to hold them in place.

Practice itch prevention. If you run into poison ivy, head straight to the bathroom. Wash the affected area with lots of warm water and soap. You may be able to prevent a rash if you remove the poison fast enough.

Stop a sting fast. The first thing to do when you've been stung by a bee or wasp is to scrape out the stinger with a knife or credit card. Don't pull it out. That can make it worse. Make a paste of meat tenderizer and water. Apply it to the bite to help break down the venom.

Be prepared for minor disasters. For a cut finger or a splitting headache, fast relief can be close at hand. Always keep some aspirin, bandages, and antiseptic cream in a 35 mm film canister and stow it in your purse, desk, or glove compartment.

Over 70 million pounds of aspirin are produced each year all over the world. People in the United States take more than 15 billion tablets a year, making it America's most widely used drug.

Do a slow shake. Need to cut back on salt? Make it easier on yourself by shaking it from a pepper shaker. With fewer and smaller holes, you'll reduce the chance of overdoing it.

Exercise keeps you in the pink. You'll be safer when biking if you wear pink. The experts say neon pink is the color motorists can see most easily.

Trash the cotton. Remove the cotton from the top of a medicine bottle, especially if it's something like aspirin that the whole family shares. When you touch the cotton, you leave germs the next person can pick up.

A snug rug is safer. Area rugs on tile or wood floors can be a real safety hazard, but you can solve the problem without buying a nonslip underlay. Run a bead of latex or silicone sealant around the backside of the rug, about an inch from the edge. Let it dry thoroughly before turning it over. The sealant will keep the rug firmly in place.

Handle security. Make your sliding glass door doubly safe from break-ins. Cut a section of broom handle just long enough to lie in the bottom track when the door is shut. The lock may fail, but the broomstick won't budge.

Light your way. After dark, you may have trouble finding the front door lock, the curb, or outside steps. Put a dab of fluorescent paint on them and nighttime navigating will be easier and safer.

> If you tend to get carsick or seasick when you travel, tape an aspirin in your navel. Does it relieve the nausea? Some say it does. At least it won't make you drowsy.

Polish off an irritation. If your wristwatch makes your skin break out in a rash, paint the back of the watch with clear nail polish, and you'll be able to wear it again. Repaint it from time to time as the polish wears off.

Make burglars think twice. Leave some kind of gardening tool, like a rake, outside in plain view while you are away on a trip. It will look as though someone just finished yardwork and will be returning shortly.

Store bulbs safely. Daffodil and narcissus bulbs are poisonous. Don't store them in an area, like the root cellar or refrigerator, where they might be mistaken for onions. And it's best not to plant them in the same area as your vegetable garden.

Don't be mistaken for a deer. When you take long walks in the woods, wear something bright orange to avoid being accidentally shot by a hunter. According to the New York State Department of Environmental Conservation, people wearing orange are seven times less likely to be injured than those who don't.

Ease your ears. Flying isn't much fun if changes in air pressure give you an earache. To ease the discomfort, dip two paper or cloth towels in very hot water. Wring them out and put them in two plastic foam cups. Place a cup over each ear. The hot, moist air inside should help equalize the pressure.

Watch out!

When chewing gum became a popular new treat, the medical profession wasn't particularly thrilled about it. One doctor, in 1869, wrote that chewing gum would "exhaust the salivary glands and cause the intestines to stick together." That opinion, of course, has changed, but doctors still don't recommend giving it to small children. At least not until they are old enough to know not to swallow it. There are occasional reports of gum causing sticky problems in the digestive tract.

Soak in oats. If you're suffering from a skin rash, sunburn, poison ivy, or even chickenpox, try easing your discomfort with an oatmeal bath. Cut the foot off a pantyhose leg and fill it with rolled oats. Tie the end and hold it under the faucet as you run a soothing bath. And save the oatmeal bag. You can use it several times.

Tighten the toilet top. The bathroom can be a source of danger for young children. To prevent them from opening the toilet lid, attach Velcro strips to the seat and lid. Just be sure to position them so sitters don't get scratches in tender places.

Tell that itch to take a hike. You had a great time camping — except for all the bug bites you came home with. Douse those itchy spots with a cotton ball soaked in vinegar. It should help relieve the itch.

Relief runs hot or cold. Get relief from sore muscles or a stiff neck. Sew a sock, towel, washcloth, or other piece of material into a pouch. Fill it with dry rice, corn, or birdseed. Add spices, herbs, or essential oils to make it smell good before you sew the open end closed. Store it in the freezer to use as a cool refresher, or toss it in the microwave and use it as a heating pad. To make sure it doesn't dry out too much and catch fire, place a cup of water in the microwave with it.

Holiday fun

Valentine's Day

Show your Valentine how much you care. Scatter rose petals on your dining room table for your favorite Valentine.

Try a little Valentine greenery. Buy a heart-shaped topiary, decorate it, and use it as a centerpiece or give it to your favorite Valentine.

In Victorian times, it was considered bad luck to sign a Valentine's Day card.

In Japan, girls give Valentine's Day chocolates to boys.

Victorians believed if you put a silver coin under your pillow on Valentine's eve, you'd get a proposal by the end of the year.

Valentine's Day didn't become popular in the United States until the 1800s.

Easter

Show the world your Easter eggs. Attach thin ribbons of different lengths to blown and decorated Easter eggs and hang them in your window.

A hot way to color eggs. Drip wax from candles onto your boiled or blown eggs in interesting patterns. When the wax has hardened, dip the egg into the dye. Now you can either peel off the wax or drip on more and dip the egg into a different color. Use the light color dyes first. When you are finished, peel off the wax and enjoy your beautiful tie-dyed eggs. You can get this multi-colored swirl effect by using rubber cement in the same way.

Dye your eggs naturally. Before you could buy fancy Easter egg coloring kits, people used what they had on hand to color their eggs. Here's how you can do it, too. Mix a half cup boiling water, one teaspoon of white vinegar, and 30 to 40 drops of food coloring. Let it cool completely before dipping your eggs.

If you want to go even further back in time, you can dye your eggs using natural food products. First, place your hard-boiled eggs in a pan so they're in a single layer. Cover them with water and add a teaspoon of vinegar. Now comes the fun part. Add a fairly large amount of one of the following items:

strong brewed coffee	*beige to brown*
canned blueberries or red cabbage leaves	*blue*
spinach leaves	*green*
Yellow Delicious apple peels	*green-gold*
fresh beets, cranberries, or frozen raspberries	*light red*
orange or lemon peels, carrot tops, celery seed, or ground cumin	*light yellow*
yellow onion skins	*orange*
ground turmeric	*yellow*

Grow an Easter egghead. Take a clean, empty eggshell with just the top broken off. Fill it with potting soil and sprinkle wheat or rye grass seed on top. Then add a very thin layer of soil over the seeds. Draw a face on the egg and make a ring-stand out of a strip of construction paper. Water your egghead and keep it in a sunny location. When the grass sprouts, your egg will have "hair."

Bring the beauty of spring inside. Cut a branch from a flowering bush or tree, like forsythia, and bring it indoors. Hang decorated eggs or other Easter items from its branches.

July 4th

Salute the 4th. Fill clean, glass bottles with layers of red, white, and blue candies or aquarium rock for a quick and fun July 4th table decoration.

Enjoy the fruits of the season. What would summertime be without watermelon? But this July 4th don't just eat it, use it for a centerpiece that will really wow your friends. You can find lots of patterns and ideas in magazines for carving watermelons into animal and bird shapes that not only look great but hold a fruit salad as well. Or stand it on end, cut it in half, scoop the fruit out, and tuck in fresh flowers. They'll stay positioned nicely if you stick their stems into the rind (you may have to cut a piece off the bottom to make it stable). Or cut one in half lengthwise, scoop it out, add dirt, and plant a pretty assortment of red, white, and blue annuals. What could be more patriotic?

Halloween

Make Halloween costumes in a snap. If you've got little trick-or-treaters to outfit, try starting with a hooded sweatshirt and leotards or sweat pants. These basics can be transformed into hundreds of creatures and characters simply by adding accessories, like tails, wings, ears, horns ... you get the idea.

Try this homemade face paint. Need a safe, easy-to-make face paint for your Halloween costume? Mix one teaspoon cornstarch, a half teaspoon water, a half teaspoon cold cream, and two drops food coloring. It's that easy.

Make cute, edible Halloween decorations. Fill small, clear jars (recycled from pickles, olives, etc.) with inexpensive candy corn. Then buy a half-yard or more of Halloween-theme fabric at your local craft or fabric store. Cover each jar top with a square or circle of fabric, held in place with a rubber band or some coordinating ribbon or yarn. "Scrunch up" the remaining fabric in the center of your table, raw ends folded under, and hold the fabric in place with the jars of candy corn to complete your centerpiece.

Light your way to a safer Halloween. Make Halloween jack-o'-lantern lights for your children by cutting faces out of construction paper and placing them on the lenses of flashlights. It's safe and fun.

Carve a better pumpkin. This year, set tradition on its ear by carving your jack-o'-lantern a bit differently. Instead of cutting a lid on the top of the pumpkin, make a hole in the bottom. Not only will this make old jack more stable, it allows you to position and light your candle more easily.

Be prepared for Halloween. Take a large box or trunk and throughout the year drop in unusual clothes or accessories you'd otherwise toss out, or add pieces you find at garage sales or thrift stores. When Halloween rolls around, you'll have a wonderful assortment of items that only need a bit of imagination to create inexpensive costumes.

Roast your pumpkin seeds for a fall treat. As you hollow out your Halloween pumpkin, don't throw away the seeds. Wash them, pat them dry, and soak them for about an hour in soy sauce, butter, or Worcestershire sauce. Sprinkle the seeds with garlic powder or Italian spices. Roast them on a cookie sheet at low heat — 225 to 250 degrees. After 30 minutes, turn the seeds over and continue roasting for another 30 to 60 minutes. Test by biting into one — they're done when they're crunchy.

> The world's largest pumpkin weighed 1,061 pounds. You could make 550 pies from a pumpkin that big.

Thanksgiving

Set your table with nature's harvest. Hollow out medium to large gourds and set a small water-filled vase or bowl inside. Add fall flowers, leaves, and greenery, and you've got a great centerpiece.

Let the children create fun memories. If you've got a crowd coming this Thanksgiving, set up a separate table for the kids. Cover the table with brightly colored paper or an inexpensive tablecloth. Buy laundry markers so the kids can write what they're thankful for on the cloth or just decorate it during the meal. Each year bring out the old tablecloth to reminisce, then set out a new one.

Small pumpkins make a big hit at Thanksgiving. Use small pumpkins or gourds as place cards for each guest at your dinner table. Or hollow out just enough to be able to insert a candle. Fill in any spaces with pieces of Styrofoam or melted wax. Tie a ribbon around the base of the candle. Light these decorations carefully, and don't leave them unattended.

Feed your feathered friends. This winter, share the holiday spirit with your neighboring birds. Decorate a tree in your yard with homemade peanut butter and birdseed ornaments, strands of berries and popcorn, and baskets of suet.

Set a festive fall table. Hollow out miniature pumpkins and squashes to make serving bowls and containers for cranberry sauces, relishes, dips, soups, or individual desserts. Cut a thin slice off the bottom so the pumpkin or squash will stand firm.

Christmas

Here comes the gingerbread man. Take a gingerbread man cookie cutter and use it to trace shapes from brown paper bags. Decorate with paint, fabric, markers, or sewing notions. Hang them throughout your house or on your tree. Let your imagination run wild.

Give your decorations the look of snow. Use pieces of baby's breath or small branches painted white to fill in gaps in your Christmas tree, wreaths, garlands, or swags — a very inexpensive way to give everything the look of snowflakes.

Bring the outdoors in. For festive decorations from nature, collect sweet gum balls, small pine cones, berry clusters, and leaves. Float a little bit of gold or silver metallic paint on water in a container, like a bowl or wide-mouth glass jar. Dip each item to coat it with a thin covering of paint. Sprinkle with glitter if you want a more glitzy look.

Attach them with clothespins to a coat hanger and hang them over layers of newspaper to dry. Add them to wreaths or table decorations, or use them to fill a colorful basket.

Yule love this holiday idea. Make your own yule log by drilling a few holes in a nicely shaped branch or log; hot-gluing greenery, pine cones, cinnamon sticks, and berries to the top; and finishing it off with tall, red candles. A great addition to any table or mantel.

Let it snow, let it snow. To create a winter landscape for your miniature village, buy quilt batting. Cut it to fit your display area, then arrange your village on this fresh layer of "snow." For even more country charm, nestle a small mirror in the snow to create a pond.

Think ahead. Buy inexpensive Christmas place mats and napkins at an after-Christmas sale and put them away for the next year. Then use them all during the month of December to make meals a little more special for your family each night. Don't save them just for company.

Recycle glass ornaments. Here's a great way to give new life to scratched glass ornaments. Take out the metal neck and hanger, and soak the ornament in bleach for about 10 to 15 minutes. Clean the inside carefully, using a cotton swab. Rinse the ornament and let it dry. Once the ornament is completely dry, use your imagination and fill it with potpourri, dried flowers, tinsel, glitter, colored paper, or lace.

Paint on a little snow. If you want white paint to look like snow for a craft or decorating project, mix very fine sand or sawdust with white acrylic paint, and you've got your snow.

Display your Christmas cards. Place them loosely in a decorative basket, using wadded paper or fabric to support the cards in an upright position. If the basket is shallow, add some bunches of curled ribbons or bows around the base of the cards for a festive touch.

Make a gift tag that really shines. Take an extra large Christmas light bulb and write "To" and "From" on it using a permanent marker. Tie it onto your package's bow for a unique gift tag.

Make your own winter wonderland. Mix together equal parts of white craft paint and liquid dish soap. Paint your window with icicles, snowmen, stars, whatever suits your fancy. Cleanup is as simple as a quick wipe with a wet cloth.

Pine cones aren't just for Christmas. Painted white and decorated, they become Easter trees. With a little imagination and a few craft supplies, they are whimsical turkeys. Glued together, they form a bird's nest that you can fill and decorate for a springtime centerpiece.

And there are hundreds of ways to add them to your fall and winter holiday scheme. Make trees, wreaths, angels, and Santas. Stack them, pile them, dust them with glitter or scented oils, tie them with ribbons, or toss them in the fire. Pine cones are versatile, inexpensive additions to any decorating project.

Before working with pine cones, you should condition them in your oven to melt the sap and add a nice glaze. Use an old cookie sheet or cover a sheet with foil. Place the pine cones on the cookie sheet and bake them at about 200 degrees until the sap is melted and the pine cones are open. You might want to test one pine cone first to get the right temperature. As an added bonus, your house will smell wonderful!

Light your sidewalk with a gift from the East. Contact your local Chinese restaurant and ask where you can buy a supply of take-out containers. Punch designs in the sides, add some sand and a candle, and you've got a new twist on the plain old luminary.

Fireproof your Christmas tree. Into one gallon of water, mix one cup of ammonium sulphate (available from a garden supply store), a half cup of boric acid (available from a drugstore), and two tablespoons borax (available from a grocery or hardware store). Mix well and pour into a spray bottle. Spritz this on your tree and pour the remainder into the tree stand instead of water.

Make your own Christmas tree snow. Gather two-thirds cup liquid starch, two cups soap flakes, two to four tablespoons water, and blue food coloring. Mix together the liquid starch and soap flakes in a bowl. Add the water and beat with a rotary egg beater until the mixture becomes thick and stiff. Add the food coloring a drop at a time, while beating, until the snow becomes an icy-white color. Paint this on your Christmas tree branches. For a sparkling touch, sprinkle some glitter on the "snow" while it's still wet.

Spice up your Christmas tree. Cut netting into 12-inch squares. Place a handful of pine scent or apple cinnamon spice potpourri in the center of each square. Bring the corners together, tie tightly with gold ribbon, and place these "potpourri balls" in your tree.

Get the best of both worlds. If you have an artificial tree but miss the smell of real pine, here's an inexpensive way to have both. Visit your local tree seller and ask to collect greenery off the ground. Or better yet, ask your friends who still get real trees to save the branches and bits they cut off. Place these in baskets around your house, on your mantel, or tie them together for a garland.

Hanukkah/Kwanzaa

Foil sticky candles. Place a bit of aluminum foil around the bottom of each candle to go in your menorah or kinara. You'll be able to remove and replace the burned-down candles more easily.

Decorate for Kwanzaa with tradition. Use the traditional colors of Kwanzaa — black, red and green — in your decorations. Also include traditional African items, such as baskets, cloth patterns, art objects, a seven-candle holder, a Unity Cup, and harvest symbols, like corn and straw mats.

> Auld lang syne is Scottish for "old long since" or simply "days gone by." If you live in Scotland, you stay up to welcome the first person after midnight. This person is called the "first footer." People believe that if the first-footer is a dark-haired man, the family will have good luck in the new year.

Decorating for any special occasion

Try this sweet solution. Use candy as fun, inexpensive decorations for any holiday. Buy colorful, brightly wrapped items to match your theme or decor. Fill glass bowls, baskets, or crockery. They also look great in crystal stemware set on a table. Hot glue them into wreaths, swags, or cover a plastic foam tree, which you can buy at a floral or craft store. You can even use a variety of shapes and sizes as building blocks to make fun candy toys and animals.

Give a personalized wreath. Find out what special hobby or interest the recipient has, like sewing, gardening, dogs, or fishing. Buy small articles representing that interest and hot glue them onto a ready-made wreath. Add coordinating ribbon, fabric, or a bow.

Help your guests find their place. Instead of traditional place cards on your table, personalize individual flower arrangements beside each plate by writing the guest's name in gold ink on a leaf. This can work for any holiday from July 4th to New Year's.

Change your decorations to match the holiday. It's easy to convert your traditional Christmas decorations into beautiful ornaments for other holidays, like Valentine's Day, Easter, July 4th, or Halloween. Simply take your wreaths, candles, and table settings and add ribbons that are more appropriate to your new holiday theme.

Hold onto your memories. Join the scrapbook craze and put together a special holiday album. Include photos and mementos and have family members and friends sign the book and maybe add a special message.

Light up your holiday. Make inexpensive candle holders for any holiday season by decorating clean baby food jars to match your theme and setting a tealight inside.

Decorate every room. When you're planning your holiday decorating, don't forget the two most important rooms in your house, the kitchen and the guest bathroom.

Throw in some holiday pillows. Change the look of your living room or family room by making slipcovers for your throw pillows out of holiday-themed fabric. They're easy to sew, especially if you finish them off with buttons or Velcro.

Heard it through the grapevine? Grapevine wreaths are great for any holiday. Go to your local craft store and buy small ornaments and flower picks, like wooden eggs and bunnies, hearts and roses, pumpkins, witches, four-leaf clovers, flags, snowmen, Santas, packages, dreidels, and gold coins. Hot glue them on, then wrap with coordinating ribbon and add a bow. These are inexpensive enough to have one for every holiday.

Household

See yourself clearly. To prevent your bathroom mirror from fogging up, rub in foamy shaving cream with a paper towel until the cream disappears.

Hot or cold, cleanup's a snap. There are two easy ways to remove the dripped candle wax from your glass candlesticks. Put them in your freezer for a couple of hours, and the frozen wax will pop off easily. Or turn them upside down on a few layers of paper towel in the microwave oven. Heat them on low for three minutes. The paper towel will absorb the wax that drips off. Don't use the microwave method on lead crystal candle holders.

Watch glasses glisten. If you have a display cabinet for your glassware, try lining the bottom and backs of the shelves with mirrors. The reflected light will make your stemware sparkle.

Stand time on its head. Your electric clock has stopped running. But before you take it in for repairs, try one of these tricks. Turn it upside down for a few days. This should redistribute the oil inside and help it run again. Or as an alternative, put your clock in a slightly warm oven for a few hours. If dirt or grime has it jammed up, the heat may loosen it enough to get it going once more.

Make a chipper container for paper cups. Cover a potato chip can with pretty wallpaper to match your bathroom. You'll have an attractive holder for 5-ounce paper cups.

Remove layers of furniture polish. To restore your wood furniture to its original luster, try this homemade wood cleaner. Mix two parts lemon oil with one part vinegar or lemon juice. Use a soft cloth to rub it in and another to wipe it clean.

Turn with the seasons. Use the seasons as reminders to turn your mattress. For example, in spring, switch the ends, putting the head where the foot was. In summer, turn it over, keeping the head at the top. In the fall, swap ends without turning it over. And when winter comes, just turn it over again. Your mattress will last longer and be more comfortable.

Keep out the chill. For extra winter insulation, hang an old shower curtain behind your drapes.

Protect a treasured painting. The idea of sitting by the fire and admiring a favorite painting hanging over the fireplace may seem appealing. But smoke and soot can permanently damage your valuable artwork. So find another spot that's away from air conditioning and heating ducts as well.

Give new life to an old lamp. Cover the base with wood twigs or wrap it with vines. Your old lamp will have a new, rustic look.

Let there be more light. You can get more light from your electric light bulbs by simply dusting them. A clean bulb gives 50 percent more light than a dust-covered one.

> Only about 3 to 7 percent of an incandescent light bulb's electrical energy is turned into useful light. The rest generally goes to waste as heat.

A remote in the hand is worth two under the cushions. Attach a bit of Velcro sticky back tape to the side of your television. And put another piece on the back of the remote control device. When you turn the TV off, just stick the remote control to the side. You'll never have to hunt for it again.

Deodorize your house for pennies. Buy some wintergreen oil, and place a few drops on a cotton ball. Set this in an open glass container, and your house will smell clean and fresh for months.

Lengthen the life of your water heater. Twice a year, drain off a few gallons of water from the bottom of your water heater. You might drain it into a bucket, or you can hook a garden hose to it and run it out a door or window. The "settlings" from the tank can be rusty or murky, so be careful how you dispose of them. Afterwards, your water will heat faster, and your water heater will last longer.

Give books breathing room. You may damage the bindings and scratch the covers of your books if you pack them in too tightly on the shelves. And keep books upright. Leaning puts a strain on the bindings. If books are too tall to store standing up, lay them flat on the shelf.

Defeat moths. You know moths can damage cloth. But did you know they can make small holes in bone and ivory as well? The best prevention is to kill the moth larvae before they hatch. Just put items you think may be infected in the freezer for a few hours.

It's sheer wisdom. Your sheer curtains will resist dust if you give them a light starching. And they'll hang better, too.

Frost your windows any time of year. If you need a bit more privacy in the bathroom or hate looking at a parking lot from your dining room window, try this chic window-decorating technique. Mix four heaping teaspoons of Epsom salts in one cup of beer. Let it foam and sit for at least a half an hour. Apply it to a clean window with a paint brush or soft towel. While it's still wet, you can go back over the window with a tissue dipped in the mixture. Use a dabbing or patting motion. When it dries, you will have beautiful crystals on your window. Although it lasts for some time, you can wash it off easily and reapply as needed.

> Storms and high winds can do a lot of damage to your outside trees, leaving your yard less attractive — and less valuable. If you lose a big tree, you might be entitled to a settlement from your insurance company or even a tax break due to the reduced value of your property. In order to get these benefits, plan ahead. Take pictures of your yard and undamaged trees so you will have a record of the property for your insurer. And when you lose a tree, contact a professional arborist to come out and appraise its value. These two simple steps should help clear away any confusion with the insurance adjustor and tax assessor.

It's not a coin toss. Here's a way to see if a mirror is really an antique. Old mirrors are made with thick glass. So put a coin on the surface of the glass, and check the distance between the coin and its reflection. You might need to compare it to a new mirror to recognize the difference.

Extend the enjoyment of candlelight. Candles will burn longer and drip less if you put them in the freezer for about an hour before lighting them.

Freeze odors away. That book you picked up from an estate sale is beautiful, but the musty odor is straight from someone's basement. And the Tupperware that went on the fishing trip says trout every time you open it. Don't despair. Place these — and other items with odors — in a frost-free freezer. Leave them overnight, and by morning they'll be smelling fresh once more.

Sink one in the bathtub. A golf ball may make the perfect replacement for your worn-out bathtub plug. It's heavy enough to stay put, but if it does get dislodged, it will roll right back into place.

According to the 1998 Guinness Book of World Records, Ted Hoz of Baton Rouge, Louisiana has collected more than 38,000 golf balls with different logos.

Renew an old looking glass. An old mirror can be a treasure. Don't toss it out just because it's begun to lose its silver backing. Put a couple of coats of silver-colored auto spray paint on the back. Seal it with clear shellac, and it's good as new.

A manly alternative to potpourri. If potpourri is a little too feminine for you, how about making some scented rocks? Begin by mixing one-half cup each of plain flour and salt in a bowl. Add one-fourth teaspoon of your favorite essential oil and two-thirds cup boiling water. Mix well. For colored rocks, add one drop of food coloring at a time until the mixture is the shade you want. Form it into balls, let them dry, and display them in a handsome bowl.

Seal your closets. Tape pieces of wax paper on the inside of closet doors that have louvres or slats. You'll keep moths out, and your clothes will be dust free.

Kitchen

Shield walls from grease spatters. Use sheets of clear contact paper over the wallpaper behind your stove. It will protect the pattern from grease and food stains. If the wall is painted, coat it with furniture polish for a no-hassle cleanup.

Sanitize your sponge. Every few days pop your kitchen or bathroom sponge in the microwave oven. Wet it first, then zap it for about a minute and a half. You'll keep it fresh and free of bacteria. Just be sure you let it cool before you take it out.

Set a pretty table. For casual dining, use pretty kitchen towels as place mats. They are durable and will absorb spills — great for kids. And cleanup is a snap. Just throw them in the washer.

Hem a few hot pads. Use the less-worn parts of an old ironing board cover to make hot pads or pot holders. Just cut, double, and hem to use "as is." Or cover with scraps of material and quilt them.

Freshen your kitchen for just a few 'scents.' No need to buy expensive air fresheners. Get rid of bad odors by boiling cinnamon and cloves in water. Or, with the oven door open, "cook" an entire, unpeeled lemon in the oven at 300 degrees for 15 minutes.

Lay a lasting shelf liner. Leftover pieces of vinyl flooring make sturdy liners for your kitchen shelves and drawers. It's easy to cut to fit, you can remove it quickly to clean, and it lasts longer than paper.

Sharpen a dull knife. You can use the base of an unglazed mug the same way you would a whetstone. Just hold your knife at a shallow angle, and draw it across several times in one direction.

Watch out!

Keep kitchen knives sharp. You are more likely to cut yourself with a dull one.

Use paper with confidence. Paper plates are a great convenience. Too bad you can't microwave them, right? Wrong. Contrary to popular belief, paper plates are perfectly safe for microwave use.

Send in the swabs for stubborn hinges. The door to your microwave or toaster oven can stick and get creaky. Clean it with a cotton swab dipped in water and dishwashing detergent. Then use another swab to apply a heat-resistant, silicon lubricant.

Unclog a jammed disposal. Never put your fingers down the garbage disposal. In case it jams, keep a small section of broom handle or a wooden spoon on hand. Use the handle to turn the blades counterclockwise until the clog works itself free.

Get your dishwasher sparkling clean. Fill the detergent dispenser in your dishwasher with powdered orange or lemon drink mix, and run it through a normal wash cycle. This will cut through all the built-up grease and grunge in hidden places.

The first dishwashing machine was invented in 1806 by Josephine Cochrane, a wealthy American socialite. She was tired of having her servants break so many dishes. The invention caught on quickly with the hotel and restaurant trade, but not with homemakers. Surprisingly, women responding to a poll said they found dishwashing relaxing. But by advertising the germ-killing power of the automatic dishwasher, marketers eventually got them to change their minds.

Don't break your glassware. If you pour a hot liquid directly into a glass, it can crack from the sudden change in temperature. This won't happen if you pour the liquid down a spoon into the glass.

Defrost by using your oven. Need to defrost but have a freezer full of food? If you have a self-cleaning oven, you're in luck. Stash everything inside, close the door, and get to work on the freezer. The oven is so well insulated that nothing should thaw for at least a couple of hours.

Pop your cork. You are ready to pour the wine, but that cork just won't budge. Take a hot, wet towel, and wrap it around the neck of the bottle. The heat will make the glass expand a little, and your corkscrew should finish the job nicely.

Dissolve saucepan gunk. It's easy to remove burnt or stuck-on food from your pots and pans. Simply pour in a little fabric softener, and let it sit overnight. Next morning, wash and rinse, and you're ready to get cooking again.

Save your back. When loading the dishwasher, put the silverware holder in the sink. When it's full, replace it with one stoop.

Keep your dishwasher leak-free. If the gasket in the bottom of your dishwasher dries out and cracks, your dishwasher could leak the next time you run it. So if you are going away for a week or two, pour a couple of quarts of water into the dishwasher, and close the door. The gasket will stay moist.

Clean your blender the easy way. Fill the blender half way with warm water. Add a little dish detergent, and blend for 15 seconds. Empty the blender, rinse, and dry.

Dishes are just the beginning. You can clean a lot of things in your dishwasher. It's ideal for figurines, knickknacks, and baby toys. Some shelves and bins from the fridge are dishwasher safe. And do you know the easiest way to clean your stove's burner liners? That's right. Pop them in the dishwasher once a week, and you can put off replacing them a lot longer.

Keep your faucet flowing freely. If you have an aerator on your kitchen faucet, be sure to clean it periodically. Simply unscrew it, and rinse out any particles that could be clogging your water flow.

Watch out!

Paper towels made of recycled materials should not be used in the microwave. They may contain pieces of metal.

Garbage disposals aren't for everything. Onion skins, celery stalks, flower stems, and leaves should not go in the waste disposal unit. They can cause the blades to jam.

Make a tripod for broken stemware. You don't have to throw away a wine glass if the stem gets broken off, especially if it's a clean break. Wash both pieces carefully, and dry with a lint-free cloth. Place the bowl of the glass with the rim down. Roughen the broken surfaces of the bowl and stem with sandpaper. Apply a non-water-soluble adhesive, and put the two ends together. Make columns of modeling clay to support the stem and base. They'll hold everything in place while it dries.

Remove rust from utensils. Place a knife or other rusty utensil inside an onion, and leave for a little while. Then, move it around inside the onion for a bit. You'll remove a rust-free utensil.

Seal with approval. Use rubbing alcohol to clean the gasket that keeps your refrigerator door sealed tight. Then rub it with a little mineral oil to prevent cracking.

Easy-clean the top of the fridge. You finally found time to clean the top of your refrigerator. Now take one more step to make this the last time. Cover the top with overlapping sheets of plastic wrap. Next time, you simply remove them, throw them in the trash, and roll out new layers.

Laundry

Fluff up your down with 'sole.' To perk up a saggy comforter, run it through a low heat cycle in your dryer. Before you start the dryer, toss in a pair of old, but clean, sneakers.

How much is too much? If you cram too many clothes in your washing machine, they won't come out as clean. They can also be damaged. A top-loading washing machine is full when the clothes reach the top row of holes. You can fill the entire tub of a front-loading washing machine, just don't pack the clothes in too tightly.

Squeeze away stains. Keep a plastic mustard or ketchup dispenser filled with liquid detergent in the laundry room. Squirt some directly on soiled collars and other extra-dirty spots to pretreat them before washing.

Don't ruin your pants. The iron won't leave your pants shiny if you use a clean, cloth diaper as a pressing cloth.

Wash two loads in one. To save water and energy, make double use of a tub of water. While your washing machine is filling, add soap and wash items you need to do by hand. You can probably finish before the tub fills up. If not, stop the machine until you're done. Then add your regular load of laundry and turn the washer back on.

Did you ever wonder why Mondays were traditionally chosen as washdays? One story has it that since Sunday was the day when people had the biggest meal, leftovers were available for eating on Monday. Thus, the housewife didn't have to bother with cooking when faced with the burden of washday.

Press a knife-edge crease. If you like sharp creases in your pants, here's how you can get them to last longer. Fold a piece of wax paper over the crease, then iron. A bit of wax heats into the material and holds the crease.

Procrastination pays off. Wait to do the laundry until you have several loads to wash. Then, dry one load right after the other to take advantage of the heat that has already built up in the dryer. This method saves energy, which, in turn, saves money.

Don't skimp at the dry cleaners. Never dry-clean just one piece of a two-piece suit. It may be tempting to save money by cleaning just the pants when the coat still looks okay, but you may wind up with a mismatched suit. That's because color changes can occur in the cleaning process.

Bleach acts faster than you think. Don't leave clothes soaking in bleach overnight. Soaking for 15 minutes is just as effective. Bleach can damage clothing if it soaks too long.

Stop the snags. Keep your clothes looking new by protecting them from snags in the wash. Simply zip the zippers, button the buttons, and fasten the fasteners when sorting your clothes, and they will keep that "like new" look longer.

Dry your clothes efficiently. Don't overload your dryer, always empty the lint filter, and make sure your dryer has proper ventilation. These strategies will help you save money.

The B.J. Johnson Company was one of the first soap makers in the Western United States. Their brand, made of palm and olive oil, became so popular they changed the name of their company to Palmolive. Palmolive soap is still around, but it's not made by the original recipe.

More is not always better. Always follow the directions on laundry products. Using more or less than recommended can damage your clothes or leave them dirty.

Get rid of dry cleaning gases. When you get your clothes back from the dry cleaners, remove the plastic coverings, and let your clothes hang outside or in a large room for several hours. This gets rid of the vapors from the cleaning chemicals.

Spray inside. Spray starch on the inside of clothes, not the outside. This eliminates a slick look on your ironed clothes.

Keep dirty laundry odor free. Leave a box of baking soda in the bottom of your laundry hamper. It will help eliminate odors as it soaks up moisture.

Store your fabrics safely. The pleasant scent of lavender or gardenia may make your lingerie drawer smell great, but avoid floral sachets for storing items you don't rotate regularly. They contain oils that, over time, can damage fabric. You may want to store lavender nearby since it is a moth deterrent. Just be sure it isn't touching stored garments or linens.

Be bold about returns. Don't be afraid to return new clothes after you've worn them. If you followed the label's directions for laundering, but the item was still damaged, the store should give you a refund or an exchange.

Steam away wrinkles. When you hang rumpled items, especially those made from natural fibers, in the bathroom and turn on the hot water, the steam takes the wrinkles out. Here's why. Wrinkles happen because the moisture in the air bonds with the fibers of the fabric. The steam changes the bonds as the weight of the fabric pulls the wrinkles out.

> The sun is the oldest bleach around. For whiter clothes, spread them on a white sheet and leave them on the ground in the sunshine all day. Better still, get up early and place them directly on wet grass. According to legend, dew has the magical ability to whiten.

Always rinse in cold. Save energy and prevent wrinkles by using a cold water rinse regardless of what you are washing.

Tired of losing socks in the washer? Try pinning them together with a safety pin when you put them in the laundry. The socks will stay together through washing, drying, and sorting.

Be gentle on tufts. If your old candlewick bedspread is soiled, take care not to ruin the tufts when you wash it. To clean it gently, place it in a large pillowcase before you put it in the washer.

Don't be shocked. Before you fill your iron with water, make sure you turn the iron off. If you don't, you could get an electrical shock.

Save sorting time. Have separate laundry baskets for every type of load you wash — like light, dark, and delicate. When you take off your clothes, put them in the proper basket. Then, when it's time to wash, the clothes are already sorted.

Do you know what BVD on your underwear label stands for? It's Bradley, Vorhees, and Day, the company's founders.

Spend less time ironing. If you're always at the ironing board, try these tips to cut down on your workload. Shake out each item as you remove it from the washer. Don't overload the dryer. Remove clothes at the end of the drying cycle before wrinkles have a chance to set. Hang them up or smooth and fold them right away. These steps will cut down on wrinkles, but they won't give your clothes a pressed look. For that, you'll have to pull out the trusty iron and ironing board.

Beware blanket fuzz. Soak your blankets in water and detergent for 10 minutes, then wash them on the shortest wash cycle. This will reduce pilling, and they'll last longer, too.

Lawn and garden

Take the pain out of pruning. When trimming roses and other thorny plants, protect your fingers by holding the branch you want to remove with barbecue tongs.

Support healthy vines. Attach six-pack rings to the structure you'd like morning glories, climbing roses, or other vines to grow on. Gently pull the growing ends through the loops. The plastic provides strong but flexible support.

Grow a movable garden. Put an old wagon the kids have outgrown to good use. Drill holes in the bottom for drainage and fill with garden soil. Plant flowers, vegetables, or even a small strawberry bed in it. You can leave it in one spot, or move it during the day to take advantage of morning sun or afternoon shade.

You need to work outside, but there's a breaking news story you want to follow. Use a baby sleep monitor to help you do both. Just put the monitor next to your radio or television. Take the other part outside with you, and you can keep up with the news while you rake leaves or plant the garden.

Baby your hairy dust-catchers. The fastest way to clean most houseplants is to wipe them with a damp cloth. But what do you do with plants like African violets? Their hairy leaves collect a lot of dust, but they don't like to get wet. The solution? Clean them gently with a baby's soft, dry hair brush.

Create a portable leaf pile. Just when you get fall leaves raked into a pile, a gust of wind scatters them again. Contain them in a baby's old mesh playpen. When it's full, drag it to your compost heap. Empty it, and you're ready to fill it up again.

Keep your kitchen clean at harvest time. Use a plastic laundry hamper to gather fresh vegetables from your garden. Then stop by the water hose and wash away the grit. Let it drain completely before taking it into the kitchen. Your housekeeper will thank you.

Take gardening to a new level. Attach a length of guttering to a fence or wall. Fill with soil, and you have a perfect spot for seedlings or container plants like strawberries that have short root systems. These fence boxes are easy to reach and usually stay weed free.

Catch drips from hanging house-plants. Before watering hanging plants, slip a shower cap on the bottom of the pot. Then, if water or dirt washes out of the bottom, the shower cap will catch it.

Plant a sunny bird feeder. Sunflowers are beautiful and very easy to grow. And they can continue to beautify your yard once they've dried up. Simply cut the heads off the stalks, and use twine to hang them, face up, from tree branches. You've got yourself an all-natural bird feeder. When the sunflower seeds are gone, sprinkle more seeds on the surface, and the birds will keep coming to feed.

Did you know the hair on your head contains more nitrogen than the amount in manure? About 30 times more, in fact. So ask your neighborhood barber for a few pounds of this nitrogen gold mine to mix into your compost.

Bury a barrier to aggressive garden plants. If you find that certain plants, especially herbs like mint, tarragon, and marjoram, take over your garden, here's an easy way to keep them in check. Bury a length of stovepipe upright, then plant your herb inside.

Gardening is a picnic with plastic. When the picnic is over, don't throw away those plastic knives, forks, and spoons. They can really come in handy in the garden. The spoons are good for putting just the right amount of soil or fertilizer in the right spot during potting or seeding. And plastic knives and forks make great signposts for finding your way through the garden. Just label the handles with the names of the plants, and stick them into the soil nearby.

Beautify your garden with butterflies. Plant stinging nettles in an out-of-the-way place in your garden. Butterflies will come to it to lay their eggs. And this unusual plant serves another important purpose — it repels garden pests.

Nail down the solution to your cutworm problem. A ten-penny finishing nail may be the way to keep those fat caterpillars from eating your tomatoes and other tender plants. Just drive one into the ground beside each seedling when you plant it. Leave an inch or so of the nail sticking above the ground. The worm won't be able to wrap around the thicker width, so it won't be able to feed on your young plants.

Relieve iron deficiency. When leaves on your houseplants turn yellow, they may need more iron. Give them a steady supply by pushing a rusty nail into the soil.

A match is made in gardening heaven. Get double duty from your limited garden space — plant tomatoes and potatoes together. When your tomato seedlings have grown two sets of leaves, scoop out the center of an Irish potato for each seedling. Fill the holes with potting soil and transplant the tomatoes. Place the tomato-holding potatoes in containers with a couple of inches of soil. When the soil is warm enough, plant them in the garden. The tomatoes will grow and produce fruits during the summer. In the fall, you can harvest the potatoes.

Abracadabra. Make your seedlings grow strong and sturdy by brushing your hand over them several times a day. Commercial growers do this in their greenhouses. And it works!

Make hose handling easy. You'll find it easier to coil your hose on the ground if you leave the water on. An empty hose kinks and twists more.

Prevent drowned plants. If you have trouble telling whether or not your plants need watering, try the pencil test. Push a pencil down in the dirt, and then remove it. Don't water the plant when there is still dirt on the pencil. But do water if the pencil comes out dirt free.

Give plants a nutritious drink. Never waste water you used to cook vegetables. As long as you didn't add salt, you can use it again to water your plants. But first let it cool to room temperature.

Paint your tool handles a bright color. You can find them more easily in the garden. And your neighbors will remember in a glance that they belong to you.

Is it wise to buy the best? Not necessarily, when it comes to garden tools. The cheapest ones tend to break easily while the most expensive tools are usually geared toward the experts. So you may find it most practical to stick with the tools in the middle price range.

This box is for the birds. The next time you replace your mailbox, don't throw out that old battered one. It will make a perfect birdhouse. Just nail it to a tree or pole, or suspend it from branches, and leave it open.

An empty onion bag is ideal for hanging out nesting supplies for your backyard birds. Fill it with straw, bulrush down, cotton, feathers, animal hair, or small pieces of bark and wood. A "builder-friendly" neighborhood will usually attract a good number of settlers.

Plug up hose holes. If your garden hose springs a leak, you can plug it up temporarily with some chewed gum. For a more permanent repair, heat up the tip of an ice pick with a flame. Then gently touch the hot tip to a bit of the rubber around the hole. It will melt and seal it.

Sow quick and cheap. Instead of buying expensive seed tapes, make your own using toilet paper. First, roll out a length of toilet paper. Line your favorite seeds down the center, and fold lengthwise into thirds. Dampen the paper slightly so that it sticks together. Let it dry. When you're ready to plant, lay the tapes in your garden rows, and cover with moist soil.

Wear cleats for a better lawn. Anytime you are fertilizing, watering, or weeding your grass, wear cleats. You'll aerate your lawn without making that a separate chore. With the extra time, you can head for the golf course. After all, you are already wearing the right shoes!

Transplant a shrub. If you need to move a large shrub or a small tree from one side of the yard to the other, a snow shovel makes a good sled.

Painting

Eliminate paint odors. If the odor of oil-based paint really bothers you, make it a little more aromatic by stirring two teaspoons of vanilla extract into the can of paint.

Keep a fresh hairdo. Slip on a shower cap when you're painting to protect your hair from splatters.

Removing old wallpaper is a breeze. Just make a solution of equal parts white vinegar and hot water. Pour it into a pan wide enough for a paint roller. Then simply roll the solution onto the walls. It may take two or three applications, but your wallpaper should peel right off.

Time your paint job. Maybe you need to keep up with how long you spend painting a room. Or perhaps you want to be sure you have time to clean up before an appointment. For whatever reason, you may sometimes need to wear your watch while painting. Cover it with clear tape to keep it clean, and you won't lose sight of the time.

No strain, no gain. You paint a room to make it pretty. But globs in your paint can become unattractive lumps on your wall. To solve this problem, stretch a piece of pantyhose across the mouth of an empty paint can, and pour the paint through it. You will catch all the lumps and guarantee a smooth paint job.

If you won a Nobel Prize, what would you do with the money? Put it into more research? Take a well-earned vacation? Invest it for future generations? Madame Marie Curie, the first person ever to win two Nobel Prizes — for physics in 1903 and for chemistry in 1911 — used some of her prize money for new wallpaper and a modern bathroom for her home in Paris.

Keep paint off glass the cheap and easy way.
When you're ready to paint windows, dampen strips of newspaper, and press them onto the edges of the panes. They'll keep paint off the glass. And they come off much easier than masking tape.

You're on a low roll. Is your back aching from bending over to paint around the base of the walls? Sit on a skateboard, and you can roll along with a straight spine.

Don't glob paint on fences. Painting a wire fence is a special problem. Brushes and rollers just don't do the trick. Try using a sponge instead. You'll be able to put a thin layer of paint right where you need it.

The ancient Egyptians got the pigments for their yellow, orange, and red paints from — of all things — rust. And you thought that's what paint is supposed to prevent!

Bag a paint-free fan. It's time to paint your ceiling. But don't worry about taking down your ceiling fan. Simply slip a plastic grocery or newspaper bag over each fan blade, and secure it with string or a rubber band. No more drips or spills on your fan blades.

Sack your screens. Keep drips off the window screens and glass when painting outside trim. Just remove the screens, slip them into plastic leaf bags, then put them back on the windows. When you finish painting the trim, let it dry before taking the bags off. Cleanup will be easy, and you can still use the bags for leaves.

Punch your paint can. For neater painting, use a nail to make a few holes in the rim of your paint can. When you wipe your brush, the excess paint won't collect in the groove. Instead, it will drain right back into the can.

Clean glass quickly. Rub soap onto the edges of window glass before painting to make cleanup fast and easy.

Beat the paint-mixing blues. Using that wooden stick from the paint store is slow. And it may be hard to tell when the paint is well mixed. Try using an old rotary egg beater. It beats the stick hands down.

Once upon a time, people who wanted their houses painted had to hire professionals who could mix the paint properly. Then two men, Henry Alden Sherwin and Edward Williams, spent 10 years trying to perfect the formula for a quality ready-mix paint. In 1880 they succeeded, and the rest is do-it-yourself history.

Here's a handy little tip. If you have to do some small touchup painting, use a cotton swab instead of a paint brush. There's no waste and no cleanup.

Save yourself some scraping. Before you start painting, rub down doorknobs, hinges, and other non-paint surfaces with petroleum jelly. The paint won't stick to it, so you won't have to scrape away your mistakes later.

Brew up a natural deodorizer. Put a few handfuls of straw in a bucket. Cover it with warm water. Leave it in a freshly painted room overnight, and by morning any unpleasant paint odor should disappear.

Hold it high. You can make a holder to keep your paint can steady when you're painting up high. Slide a broom handle inside the hollow step of an aluminum ladder. Cut a notch in the handle to keep the paint can from sliding off.

Give holes a quick patch. Use equal parts salt and starch with just enough water to make a stiff putty for filling holes in your plaster walls before painting.

Mix a perfect match. Make sure you can re-mix a new batch of paint in just the right shade if you should run short. Put a piece of clear strapping tape over the coded mixing label on the can. That way, if it's accidentally painted over, you can clean it off and read it.

Fade away. If you decide to wallpaper instead of paint, staple the leftover paper to the attic walls. If you need it later for repairs, it will have all faded equally.

Personal care

Cool your cosmetics. You can sharpen your lip, eyeliner, and eyebrow pencils to a finer point if you chill them in the freezer first for about an hour.

Shave time in an emergency. The next time you run out of shaving gel, use hair conditioner. It's a great substitute.

Get the green out. Green hair from the chlorine in a swimming pool can be a real headache. Try some aspirin — but don't swallow them. Dissolve six to eight tablets in a glass of warm water. Pour it through your hair, saturating it completely. Leave it on for 10 minutes, then rinse thoroughly. Shampoo and rinse again, and the green should disappear.

Give your face a golden glow. Puree half a teaspoon of honey and half a cup of sliced cucumber to a fine consistency in your blender. Spread this mixture on your face, and keep it on for about half an hour, then rinse. Your skin will respond with a radiant glow.

Simply shampoo in the sink. The bathroom sink is a good place to wash your hair, but it's hard to bend down and get your hair wet without splashing water all over. You can avoid the mess and make it easier on your back as well. Just borrow the sprinkling can you use to water your houseplants.

> To keep from going gray, some first century Romans covered their hair with a paste of herbs and earthworms and wore it overnight. Others dyed their hair black with a concoction made by boiling walnut shells and leeks.

Cure sweaty palms. Do you avoid shaking hands because your palms always feel damp? Try rubbing them down with a commercial antiperspirant. Your next shake should be a dry one.

Make a milky mask. Deep clean your face with Milk of Magnesia. Just swab on the milky solution until your face is fully covered. Leave it for 10 minutes, then remove with warm water.

Keep hair tucked in place. Do barrettes keep slipping out of your hair? Glue a small piece of foam rubber inside and they'll stick tight.

Condition your skin. Apply hair conditioner all over after a bath or shower. It makes a pleasant body lotion.

> To prevent dryness and wrinkles, Egyptian women in 3000 B.C. made facial masks of milk, incense, wax, olive oil, juniper leaves, and — Are you ready for this? — gazelle or crocodile dung.

Paint some cool nails. Store your nail polish in the refrigerator, and it will last longer and go on more smoothly.

Protect your floor from hair spray. When your hair is all set for the final touch, step inside your shower to spray it. You won't have to clean a sticky film off your bathroom floor or fixtures.

Fruit refreshes your face. For radiant skin, try spreading mashed strawberries or raspberries over your face. The scent is very refreshing, too.

Put your brush where your mouthwash is. To clean your hairbrush, mix a couple of tablespoons of colorless mouthwash with two tablespoons of baking soda and water. Let the bristles soak for about 15 minutes, scrub with an old toothbrush, and rinse.

Buy in bulk but travel light. Skip those expensive travel-size toiletries. You can save money if you pour shampoo, conditioner, and lotions into small bottles. You'll have the advantage of buying in bulk — without the bulk of large containers in your luggage.

> Why does cold cream feel cold? It's made with a lot of water. When you place it on warm skin, the water evaporates, producing the cool sensation.

Look in your clear-view mirror. If you have a medicine cabinet with mirrored sliding doors, open it while you shower. The one underneath won't get steamed up, so you can use it right away. Better yet, keep the whole bathroom free of steam. Run a few inches of cold water in your bathtub, add some hot water, and take a bath instead.

For long-lasting nail polish. Before you paint your nails, clean them with cotton balls soaked in vinegar. Your manicure will last longer.

Mix a honey of a beauty mask. Combine honey, oatmeal, and lemon juice in a bowl. Use enough to make a good paste that will stick to your skin. Leave it on your face for about 10 minutes, then rinse. This mask is particularly good for oily skin.

Practice good toothbrush hygiene. It's a good idea to sterilize your toothbrush occasionally. You can boil it for a few minutes or soak it in a solution of bleach and hot water. Buy a new one about every three months and replace it when you've been sick.

Get rid of unsightly flakes. If you rinse your hair with lemon juice every day, you'll give dandruff flakes the brush off.

Cream away stains. If your skin is stained from dye, food coloring, or paint, wash the color away with shaving cream and water.

A balding firefighter named John Breck helped make the shampoo business a success in America. He developed a number of hair treatments with the hope of stopping his receding hairline. His shampoo became a best seller, but he never was able to stop his hair loss.

Relax your stresses and your tresses. A steam bath or a sauna can do more than make tired, achy muscles feel wonderful. It can give your hair a boost at the same time. Just apply conditioner and wrap your head in a warm, moist towel. Both your hair and your body will feel pampered.

Rx for scratched glasses. If the plastic lenses in your glasses are scratched, here's a clever way to fill in the scratches. Spray Pledge furniture polish on both sides of your lenses, rub it in carefully, and wipe with a soft cloth.

Manicure like the pros. You'll pay big money for a self-cleaning container of nail polish remover, but you'll only spend pennies to make your own. Here's how. Take a foam hair roller and cut it in half. Insert half of the roller into an old film container and fill it with nail polish remover. Dip your finger in the hole and your nail polish will magically disappear.

Frizzes out of control? Make a mixture, one cup each, of water and vinegar. Use this as a rinse after you shampoo and condition. Allow the mixture to set for two minutes before you rinse it out.

Wash away lingering odors. When you've finished peeling onions or garlic, rub a spoon on your hands and fingers under running warm water. You'll get rid of the smell.

Sanitize hair-care tools. Could your brushes and combs stand a good cleaning? Soak them in hot water and one-fourth cup of baking soda.

Stretch your shampoo. Don't throw out a shampoo bottle when it's hard to squeeze out the last bit. Just before it's empty, add water until the bottle is about one-third full. You'll be able to use almost every drop.

Dye by your own hands. You may be thinking about going blonde, but the cost of a beauty salon treatment makes you think again. Consider making your own hair-streaking product. Get some alum, an aluminum compound, from your drugstore and mix it with just enough honey to form a thick paste. With your fingers, paint the mixture onto the strands of hair you want highlighted. Sit in the sun for about 45 minutes, then shampoo.

Pest control

Silverfish take the big chill. Get rid of silverfish and other insects that have infested your books or valuable papers. First seal the items in a plastic bag. Then put them in the freezer for 72 hours.

Spray away spider mites. Combine one-half cup of buttermilk, four cups of wheat flour, and five gallons of water. Spray or pour this onto your affected plants.

Build a better scarecrow. Keep unwelcome birds and other pests from your garden with a different kind of scarecrow. Fill plastic grocery bags with air, tie them shut with a rubber band, then attach them to stakes placed throughout your garden. The wind causes them to sway and rustle enough to scare away crows and such.

Fool the birds. Last year, the birds ate all your strawberries before you had a chance to enjoy them. This year, get a head start and discourage the raids. Paint some stones red, and scatter them among your strawberry plants before the fruits have formed. When birds peck at them, they'll find them hard. They'll give up before the real strawberries are ripe.

> Would a strawberry by any other name taste as sweet? What if it were called a "strawrose" instead? That would be more accurate. Strawberries aren't really berries at all. They are the fruits of a plant that belongs to the same family as the rose.

What 'scent' those moths running? Use cedar chips, lavender flowers, rosemary, mint, or white peppercorns to keep moths from attacking your stored fabrics.

Plant protection in your corn patch. Raccoons love to nibble on corn. So plant squash — which they don't like at all — around your corn patch. Your roasting ears will be safe from these nocturnal corn-nappers.

'Chews' to make bugs retreat. Place pieces of mint-flavored gum — wrapped or unwrapped — where insects enter your cabinets. They'll likely head back out the way they came.

Dustbust those pests. If you have a problem with flying insects in your house, keep your dustbuster handy. When a wasp or bee makes a nuisance of himself, simply suck him up. Just make sure the seals are good and tight.

Save your saplings. Keep rodents from feeding on your young trees. Wrap a few strips of fiberglass insulation around the trunks. The critters won't find them so delicious anymore.

Slug it out. You always knew slugs were attracted to free beer, right? So if these slimy creatures are a problem in your garden, fill some old plastic food containers with the brew. They'll go in for it and drown. Just keep the party going until your slug problem disappears.

> Beer has been a popular beverage since at least 6000 BC. Ancient clay tablets found in Babylon recorded 19 different kinds of brew.

Vanquish red spider mites. You can control these garden pests by spraying leftover coffee around their hangouts.

Do some forest first aid. Don't throw away your leftover interior latex paint. Instead, use it to seal cut branches on trees. You'll keep insects from doing damage.

Lure roaches with red wine. Put saucers of cheap red wine — don't waste the good stuff — under your cabinets. Roaches drink it, get tipsy, and drown.

Send Peter Cottontail hopping on his way. Dust a sprinkling of talcum powder on your plants, and rabbits will steer clear of your garden. Be sure to reapply after rain.

Hit mosquitoes before they hatch. Puddles or other areas of standing water around the outside of your house are an open invitation to mosquitoes. If you can't get rid of the water, pour dish detergent into it. This will kill the eggs and larvae before they develop into biting nuisances.

This mouse trap will bowl you over. To catch mice without harming them, begin with a large stainless steel bowl. Rub butter or oil all over the inside, and put some bait (peanut butter seems to be a favorite) in the bottom. Stack up books or magazines nearby. The mouse will climb up and leap into the bowl to get to the food. Once inside, it won't be able to climb back up the slippery sides. You can then take the bowl outside and let the mouse escape.

Repel insects naturally. If you don't like spraying chemicals on your skin to keep the bugs at bay, try one of these. Mix 1 ounce of oil of spearmint, peppermint, citronella, or pennyroyal with a few drops of baby oil, vegetable oil, or a bit of petroleum jelly. (Never use the herbal oils full-strength.) Rub this onto your skin before you go outside.

In summer, Rudolph, stay away. Borrow from your holiday decorations to keep your garden deer free. Circle your patch with small blinking Christmas lights. Leave them on between dusk and dawn.

Give pests a clean sweep. Add salt to your vacuum cleaner bag to kill insect eggs and larvae that may be trapped inside.

A shocking solution for snails and slugs. Protect the plants in your raised beds by tacking a sheet of copper along the bed's upper edge. When these unwanted visitors crawl across the copper, their slime creates an electrical charge. This will discourage them, to say the least. But make sure no foliage overhangs the edge of the bed. This provides a way into the garden without touching the copper.

Send bushy-tailed intruders slip-sliding away. Keep squirrels out of your bird feeder. Instead of hanging it from a tree or standing it on a wooden post, place it atop a section of PVC pipe. Let 'em try to climb up that.

Apply the acid test to ants. Spray vinegar in the areas where ants enter or gather in your house. They'll stay away.

> No one likes to see a trail of ants marching across their kitchen floor. But if your house is not overrun with the tiny insects — and if they're not carpenter ants — you might consider letting them stay. They eat flea and fly larvae and will attack termites.

Check out this roaring good deer repellent. Need a "strong" solution to your stubborn deer problem? Go to your local zoo and ask for some lion dung. The zoo keeper usually will be happy to give it to you. Dribble a trail of it around your victimized shrubs and garden plants. This exotic manure forms a powerful deer repellent. Smart deer.

Make cheap guardians for young plants. Save some large plastic soda bottles. Cut the tops and bottoms off, forming plastic cylinders. Set them over your tender garden plants, working the bottoms down into the soil. They'll provide protection from hungry pests.

Pets

Pep up a pup's food. Add a little beef jerky to your dog's dry chow. The smell will make it more appealing.

Play a neat trick on your kitty. If you've tried to give your cat liquid medicine and failed, let her need for cleanliness help you along. Just squirt the medicine onto her coat with an eyedropper, and watch her lick it clean.

Milk does a pet no good. Tabby may love lapping up milk, but cats and dogs lack an enzyme needed to digest cow's milk. A steady diet of milk could cause chronic diarrhea. For male cats, it could be worse. They are more likely to develop urinary tract problems from the minerals in milk.

Pass up the plastic. Many animal experts agree that using plastic bowls for feeding and watering your pets is a no-no. Plastic may harbor harmful bacteria. Metal or ceramic is a more sanitary choice.

Make an emergency pet muzzle. Whether it's an injured stray cat or your vet-shy dog, you may need to muzzle an animal to prevent someone from being bitten. A length of pantyhose is a good choice in an emergency. Loop it twice around the animal's jaw, with ends crossed below the chin. Then, bring the ends up behind the ears to the back of the neck. Tie it tightly.

Ditch the itch. If your pet has dry, itchy skin, add a tablespoon of olive oil to his food every day. You should see an improvement within a couple of weeks.

Medicate with care. When pets aren't feeling well, don't be tempted to give them your pain relievers to save money. Acetaminophen, such as Tylenol, is generally harmless to humans, but it's extremely toxic to cats. They don't have enough of an enzyme required to break down the drug. And while vets often prescribe aspirin or ibuprofen for some animals, the doses are much lower than for humans. Always check with your vet before giving your pet any pain reliever.

Rest your pooch before feeding time. Wait for 30 minutes after exercise before feeding Fido. This will prevent a doggie stomachache and bloating.

Give pet hair the brushoff. You've been romping with Rover, and now your clothes are covered with dog hair. If they are clean otherwise, just take them off and toss them in the dryer with a damp cloth. The pet hair should end up in the lint catcher, and your clothes are ready to wear again.

Treat your pet with care. Occasional treats aren't bad for pets and can even be a help in training. But don't give your pet chocolate. It could make him sick or even kill him if he eats a lot of it.

> According to Richard Torregrossa, the author of *Fun Facts About Dogs*, Sigmund Freud's dog once got lost. It jumped into the back of a cab and refused to leave until the driver read its address tag and took it home. That was one smart pooch!

Stop your pup from chewing. Save your furniture and your sanity by rubbing a little oil of clove onto wooden furniture — not fabric — your puppy is chewing. He won't like the smell or the taste.

Make booties for your best buddy. Recycle those old golf club covers to keep your dog's feet warm. If you think he looks silly, just check out some of the outfits humans are wearing next time you hit the links.

Be careful about flea control. Cats and dogs react very differently to some insecticides. A product made for dogs — even in very small amounts — could be deadly for your cat. Always read the product label carefully and follow instructions. If in doubt, ask your vet.

Glow-in-the-dark pets are safer. If you have a cat or dog that runs about at night, make sure passing motorists can spot him. Put a bit of reflective tape on his collar.

Lock up the antifreeze. One of the most common reasons for an emergency trip to the vet's office is antifreeze poisoning. Antifreeze contains ethylene glycol, which is toxic to both humans and animals. Unfortunately, it also tastes sweet, so innocent pets will happily lap up any you spill on your garage floor. It only takes half a teaspoon per pound to poison a dog and even less for a cat. Remember to keep containers tightly closed and clean up spills immediately.

Don't let your gerbil get loose. The bathtub provides a temporary holding place for your gerbil while you clean his cage. He'll be safe since he can't scoot up the steep, slippery sides. Just be sure the drain is tightly closed.

Prevent electrical fires. Keep pets away from the electric wiring in your home. According to the National Safety Council, as many as 5,000 house fires a year are caused by pets chewing electric cords.

Recycle for a lighter Frisbee. If your dog isn't good at catching a Frisbee, try using the lid of a plastic margarine tub instead. Since the lid is lighter, it may be easier for him to handle.

The toy Frisbee came about when flying saucers and tin pie plates, spanning 80 years, collided. Well, not exactly. Actually, back in the 1870s, the owner of a Connecticut bakery decided to sell pies in lightweight pans marked on the bottom with the family name, Frisbee. In the 1940s, about 70 years later, students at Yale University started having fun throwing and catching tin pie plates. A decade after that a representative from the Whamo toy company in California was touring college campuses to promote a toy flying saucer. He saw Frisbee pie plates sailing through the air, and the popular toy soon followed.

Easy way to clean your pet's bed. Simply sprinkle baking soda on the bed, leave it for at least an hour, and then shake it off. Your pet's bed will be as fresh as new.

Make bath time better. Most dogs don't like getting baths. Try to make it as easy on him as possible. If you use your bathtub, put down a rubber mat so he won't slip around and get frightened. And since most dogs hate having water in their ears, if he has upright ears, gently put cotton balls in them before the bath. Only bathe your pup if he's really dirty. Too much bathing washes away protective oils and dries out the skin.

Control fleas and ticks. Add a little vinegar to your four-legged friend's water bowl. Fleas and ticks should stay clear after he drinks this unusual potion.

Avoid expensive pet taxis. Make your own pet carrier with two laundry baskets. Using rope, tie the two baskets together in the back. Once your pet is inside, tie the front of the baskets, too.

According to the American Kennel Club, Labrador retrievers were the most popular breed of dog in the country in 1998. Following Labs in popularity were Rottweilers, German shepherds, golden retrievers, poodles, beagles, dachshunds, cocker spaniels, Yorkshire terriers, and Pomeranians.

Keep countertops cat free. Does Fluffy insist on walking all over your clean countertops? Put down double-sided sticky tape. She won't like the way it feels on her paws. Or, for a noisier solution, assemble a collection of tin cans or aluminum cookware near the edge. Next time she pounces, all that crashing metal will give her a start. She'll think twice about getting up there again.

Need a quick toy? In a pinch, you can entertain a cat with a balled up sheet of aluminum foil.

Clean teeth may mean a longer life. According to some experts, proper dental care can add as many as five years to your pet's life — so brush his teeth. Introduce the practice gradually and gently. Don't use toothpaste made for people. You can buy meat-flavored toothpaste, made just for dogs and cats, at pet stores and some department stores.

Stain removal

Don't make it worse. Always use a white cloth or towel when trying to remove fabric stains. Using a colored cloth may result in additional stains, since the color can bleed from one fabric to the other.

Cover spots on ceilings. Instead of trying to remove a small stain on a white ceiling, just cover it with a dab of white shoe polish. One quick swipe with the handy applicator and you are done.

Get the grease out. You found a grease stain on your suede jacket. Remove it with a clean cloth dipped in glycerin.

Deal quickly with wine stains. You were hoping to impress your date, but then you spilled wine all over your best cotton dress shirt. You don't have time to be embarrassed. As soon as you can, pour salt directly on the stain to absorb the liquid. Soak it in cold water for 30 minutes, then launder as usual. This also works well for removing wine stains from table linens.

Keep off the grass. If you have a grass stain on a colorfast garment — test on a hidden seam to be sure — you can probably get it out with rubbing alcohol. Just dab it on and then rinse.

> One of the main ingredients in many store-bought spot removers is — you guessed it — rubbing alcohol.

Lift carpet stains. To pick up a recent stain in your carpet, mix half a cup each of white vinegar and warm water. Add one tablespoon of dishwashing liquid and stir. Dab this solution onto the stain, then blot it with a clean towel. Repeat this process until all the stain color is transferred to the towel. When you finish, cover the area with a clean white towel to dry.

Counter rust marks. Lemon juice and salt will remove rust stains from a countertop.

It's chop-chop for mildew. The bottom hem of your plastic shower curtain serves little purpose, except to collect mildew and mold. Don't waste time cleaning it. Just cut if off.

Can't remove it? Cover it. If you stain a blouse you can't bear to part with, try adding an applique to cover the stain.

Bleach your bathtub. To get rid of resistant stains in your acrylic bathtub, rub with half a lemon.

Secret to cleaner clothes. To remove grease or food stains from your laundry, mix together 1/2 cup Wisk, 1/2 cup water, 1/2 cup vinegar, and 1/2 cup ammonia. Use this mixture to pretreat the stains, then wash as usual.

Where in the world do people have the most fun in a bathtub? Probably in Nanaimo, British Columbia, Canada. Crowds have been flocking there each summer for more than 30 years for the International World Championship Bathtub Race. In addition to the main event, folks enjoy such festivities as a three-day "Bathtub Street Fair" and the traditional "Sacrifice to the Bathtub gods" boat-burning ceremony, complete with music and fireworks.

Scorch out under the sun. Sunlight may be the best whitener for old linens with scorch marks. Moisten them first, then put them in bright sunshine. You may need to repeat this a few times. For fabrics that aren't so delicate, bleach may reduce the scorch stain. This, too, may require repeating.

Lipstick gets the kiss of death. Rub lipstick stains with petroleum jelly, and launder in hot water.

Rub countertops clean. Those purple pricing ink stains will come right off food containers and onto your countertops. But you can wipe them away with a little rubbing alcohol. It not only removes stains but disinfects as well. And rubbing alcohol will remove grease stains, too.

Polish off floor stains. For alcohol stains on your wood flooring, rub in some silver polish. Follow up with wax over the whole area.

Prevent rust rings. The lids from potato chip cans fit snugly on the bottoms of some shaving cream containers. Snapping them on is simple — especially when compared to removing rust circles from bathtubs and countertops.

For a long time, potato chips were sold only in restaurants. That changed in 1926, when a Mrs. Scudder, the enterprising owner of a potato chip factory, got a bright idea. She began sending her women employees home at night with sheets of wax paper. They would convert the paper into bags, sealing the seams with their pressing irons. The next day, they would fill them with potato chips, and seal the tops with a warm iron. Thus the potato chip became available as a snack food.

Get blood out of a garment. Meat tenderizer breaks down the protein found in blood. That makes it a good stain remover for blood-stained fabric. Make a paste with the tenderizer and cold water. Dab it on the stain, and leave it for about 15 minutes. Wipe it off with a clean cloth or sponge, and launder as usual.

Act fast or tie the knot. Dealing with stains as soon as possible is best, but not always practical. If you can't deal with it immediately, tie a knot in the stained clothing. At least you'll remember to treat it when it comes time to do the wash.

Baby wipes aren't just for babies. Try using a baby wipe on that stubborn spot. Some folks swear by them for stains on everything from carpet to upholstered furniture.

Work from the outside in. When removing a stain, start at the outer edge instead of the center. This method will help prevent rings forming around the stain.

Fight fruit stains on carpet. Wet the stain with water, and gently rub in salt. Let it set for a few minutes, then brush it out and vacuum. Repeat if necessary.

> In colonial America, carpets were made by hand. So generally only the wealthy had floor coverings in their homes. Then in 1839 a power loom for weaving carpets was invented. From that point on, carpets could be mass-produced. Whereas earlier carpets had been rich in colorful designs, these were monotone. But taking out the pattern simplified factory production, making carpets more affordable for ordinary folks.

Don't rub it in. Stains on cloth need to be blotted. Rubbing can damage the fabric.

Arrivederci, tomato. You've made a double batch of spaghetti sauce but hate to store it in your plastic ware. In the past, tomato sauce has left stains that just wouldn't come out. But you can avoid that problem. Just coat the inside of your container with vegetable oil or nonstick cooking spray before pouring in the sauce.

Use white on red. You won't be blue. If you have a red wine spill on your carpet, get it out with white wine.

Remove resistant rust. To get rid of rust stains on tubs and sinks, sponge them with white vinegar, and rinse. If stains remain, rub on some kerosene with a cloth, wash with soapy water, and rinse.

Make mattress stains disappear. Mix together cornstarch and water until they form a thick paste. Pat this on the stain, and let dry for at least four hours. Vacuum off, and your stain should be gone.

Index